1975

MAN'S AGGRESSION

The Defense of the Self

MAN'S AGGRESSION

The Defense of the Self

GREGORY ROCHLIN

Gambit *Boston* 1973

To my wife, Helen

Preface

Man's psychology of preserving himself shows in all his relations, in all his actions, and in all his sentiments. Throughout the course of daily life, no less than in emotional disorders, in adulthood as well as in childhood, self-esteem remains highly vulnerable. What may threaten our accomplishments, imperil our relationships, or deny us rewards risks lowering self-respect—endangers narcissism. In defense against such hazards, and as the instrument of recovery, aggression issues. Aggression may provide the means through which success is assured, by which gratification is obtained, and a sense of worth is gained. Where justification for aggression is lacking, or where it is forbidden by conscience or the superego, the force of aggression is turned inward against the discredited self. In the extreme it threatens one's existence. On the other hand, where vindication is a license for aggression, the violence that is loosened may be without measure.

What I am presenting in this book is the development of narcissism, and I will demonstrate how aggression is inseparably bound to it. Only exceptionally separated, narcissism and aggression together govern human emotional experience with a multiple authority which analysts only dimly perceive.

The term narcissism, in common usage by psychoanalysts, has long been associated more with serious emotional disorders than with the conflicts which characterize everyday life. Its recent somewhat popular use perhaps has taken away some of its clinical cast. But, for our purposes, as no other term seems more suited, the serious objection which remains may be that its meaning is technical. Rather than coin a new term, it seems better to show that a deeper and broader understanding of narcissism extends its role in emotional life from the extremes of clinical pathology into all aspects of ordinary living.

Perhaps it would add to clarification to remark here that I will be distinguishing between "self-preservation" (as of a species) and "preservation of the self" (as involving the human concept of self-awareness). A narrower designation than "narcissism," such as "the self" or "selfhood," fails to grasp and put forward the critical fact that some of our most tightly held egocentric aims are unconscious and/or are supported by hostility.

To show the nature of human aggression more fully, I have brought together various material from different sources. There are two categories of clinical material. The first represents a reexamination of some of Freud's classic and famous case histories. In the interests of showing aspects of them which neither he nor others have studied, I have deliberately set aside the familiar sexual-aggressive conflicts. There is an immense literature on this part of psychoanalysis which needs no recapitulation here. The second is from my own clinical experience with contemporary material presented in the light of its immediate relevance to narcissism and aggression.

An additional store of rich material is drawn upon which supports my argument. Study shows that the relation of injured narcissism to aggression or humiliation to violence is as central to understanding, for example, Medea or Achilles, as it is to Othello or Tom Sawyer.

The necessary references to Freud throughout the book indicate that he still speaks with the greatest, even though, of course, not the final, authority in psychoanalysis. All modern concepts of man's aggression which are not behaviorist stem from his work. Despite extensive literature on the motivation of human aggression, Freud's is the original source of modern enlightenment which more recent efforts have not further illuminated.

The book is about aggression. The question, however, is not what makes people aggressive and hateful, but what makes them so prone to feeling vulnerable and humiliated, and therefore ultimately what causes violence. Much is to be gained from directing our concern to the menace—narcissism—rather than to its consequences. It may improve our relations, affect our actions, and deepen our sentiments.

G. R.
Cambridge, Mass.

Acknowledgments

To my patients who have taught me that the facts of their experience were the medium of proof impervious to polemics I am deeply indebted. The students and colleagues who instructed me far more than they could know also have my gratitude.

I have especially to thank my friend and close associate, Herbert J. Goldings, M.D., Assistant Clinical Professor of Psychiatry, Harvard Medical School. Drawing generously on his encyclopedic knowledge of psychoanalysis, he suggested improvements in the presentation of some of the clinical material.

To a large-hearted friend, Mrs. D. B. Yntema, senior editor of the Atlantic Press, who offered valuable editorial suggestions when the manuscript was merely a rough draft, and to Lovell Thompson who discerned a book buried in my reams of random notes, I am very grateful.

Friends who through their notable areas of competence were freely giving were Robert Grosvenor Gardner, director of the Film Study Center in the Peabody Museum of Archaeology and Ethnology, Harvard University, Dr. Robert Glaser, president of the Kaiser Family Foundation; and Sam Schoenbaum, Franklin Bliss Snyder Professor of English Literature, Northwestern University.

The preparation of the book was made less a chore because Jack Ewalt, M.D., Bullard Professor of Psychiatry, Harvard Medical School, spared me many tasks. He liberally gave me freedom for research and the necessary allowances to work on the material for the manuscript. I am very grateful to him.

For the opportunity to enjoy a scholar's retreat in working on some of the book, I wish to thank the Rockefeller Foundation, Villa Serbelloni, Bellaggio, and especially its director there, William Olsen, and his gracious wife, Betsy.

Pamela Daniels was an invaluable help to me in some of the manuscript and Siiri Woodward and Clair Dunn, for their share in its preparation, also have my thanks. Pauline McLaughlin, my secretary, who knows how grateful I am to her, has also contributed to bringing the book about.

My wife's commitment to this venture is unique. Without her it could not have been accomplished.

Contents

Chapter I

The Defended Self

The compelling imperative for self-preservation is self-love. It expresses itself in an endless lust for a rewarding image of oneself, whether that image is seen in a glass or in another's eye. The further passion for praise, honor and glory makes for an endless marathon. We enter it remarkably early in our existence and leave it only when we expire. Self-love is a process subject to development, responsive to the vagaries of our fantasies as well as to the circumstances of our lives; it is a governing tyrannical principle of human experience, to which aggression responds as a bonded servant.

Neither metaphor nor a mere label, narcissism, this love of self, is the human psychological process through which preserving the self is assured. In infancy, childhood, maturity and old age, the necessity of protecting the self may require all our capabilities. And, when narcissism is threatened, we are humiliated, *our self-esteem is injured,* and *aggression appears.*

As a child grows up, life endlessly taxes him—the necessary attention paid to a younger brother, an admonition expressing a parent's disapproval, an illness which may temporarily impair the control of the sphincters—these are but fragments of everyday childhood experiences where our sense of self is attacked, devalued. The timelessness and the universality of conflicts over self-esteem are reflected everywhere in tales of the human condition, especially where our reach unfailingly exceeds our grasp,[1] and where ungovernable circumstance and chance remain forever out of our control. To redress the balance—to restore our self-esteem, assert our value—in the face of this condition, the defensive functions of aggression are invoked. The aggression generated by the need for restitution may be enormous, but it is not, fortunately, always destructive; it may well be turned into creativity.

From our earliest years narcissism and aggression are found to be linked in an indivisible bond. While the forms this union will take change in childhood, alter with adolescence, maturity and old age, it remains nevertheless a constant part of life. The games, fantasy and play of everyday childhood reveal the rich and elaborate means a child employs, almost from the beginning, to master himself, influence his environment, and affect the relationships important to him—and, above all, the central importance of his narcissism. Whether these means are unconscious, stated only in play or in dreams, or whether they are quite planned, formed into a creative effort or a destructive one, they reflect the child's sense of self—and the associated aggression to support it.

Preserving existence, by definition inherent to all living organisms, unfortunately has been long made synonymous with self-preservation. This failure to distinguish biological necessity from psychological imperative obscures the human need to hold the self inviolate. Preserving existence in man has a unique importance. It sets him apart from all creatures. Remarkably early in life—far sooner than is generally supposed—a child learns that death may occur at some unpredictable moment. It is an understanding which begins to be incorporated very early into his emotional development. Indeed, it is the knowledge of death which gives man his zeal for living. As he contends with the hazards and uncertainties of everyday life, his natural fears for his very existence arise. Together they profoundly govern his conduct. In a child of three years, the fear of death as a real possibility already begins to produce significant psychological effects,[2] and brings a concern with the self into consciousness. It initiates our most essential and elaborate emotional defenses. The call on aggression is strong. And throughout life we ingeniously employ it in unconsciously postponing our end and transcending our fate.

Directed toward the fulfillment of man's aspirations, the mastery of his environment, the acquisition of skills, and the radical deferral of the idea of his end, these efforts serve the self. A threat to an animal's life, when mastered, may leave the creature more cunning, but otherwise unchanged. Whereas man's experience with preserving existence makes him a self-transforming creature. His success or failure in meeting the circumstances of each threat affects his emotional development as a child, alters his character later, and stamps his memory, continually breeding new desires and goals.

Furthermore, man exists within a social system, and his experiences with self-preservation involve, therefore, relationships to and with others. As an infant and a young child, man survives only through the care, help and protection others give him. From his earliest years, the debt owed to others for the security of his existence makes those relationships inseparable from the sense of self. The security of our existence, always precariously held, rests on an ineradicable commitment to others. Parental figures and siblings in whatever degree they may be retained or obscured by newer relations, or indeed repudiated in favor of more rewarding ones, are as tap roots extending into the spring of our unconscious.

Until the turn of the century, psychological study, having failed to reach into these deep-set relationships, explained our behavior as a reaction to circumstance. We have since found that no matter how attenuated early relationships may become in the course of later development, and for whatever reasons they do so, we remain in thralldom to our earliest ties. To lose them would mean to give up our demands for imperishable relationships, and to acknowledge the transience of all things and therefore of ourselves. It would signify, too, a willingness to forego denials of vulnerability and thereby relinquish our religious beliefs, renounce our expectation of altering reality, and thus in consequence abandon wishes for fulfillment. We would also forego a sense of the future toward which we strive and would remain confined to the limits of a present dissociated from a past. There is nothing in the human condition to indicate that we are likely to follow such a course.

Many studies (and personal experiences) verify the conclusion that isolation or separation from those whom we value and the things that represent them is usually tolerated only temporarily, and, when forced, often ushers in profound emotional changes. The essential process of making others important to us—and thus part of ourselves—in large measure is achieved unconsciously through the process of identification. It permanently stamps us. Hence when we suffer the loss of someone valued, the bonds to them are strained and broken but they are not altogether relinquished as though such a relationship had not existed. The altered reality which loss inflicts menaces our existence. It leaves us with a feeling of deprivation, old unconscious conflicts over self-esteem then are aroused, and finally a sense of jeopardy often ensues from which the need for aggression appears. The fact that social isolation is a serious threat to our security is reflected in the psychoses which frequently develop in those who undergo enforced isolation. Deprived of social experience, we are not self-sustaining.

The common supposition that preservation of the self, animal-like, is limited to some innate or predetermined aggregate of biological operations is too narrow a focus. Conversely among psychologists and others the continuing determined inclination to anthropomorphize animal life is no wider.

In contrast to the paucity of psychoanalytic clinical studies of aggression, the efforts by way of animal experiments to explain human aggression are countless. They principally succeed in demonstrating human ingenuity in contriving laboratory conditions for animals. Such experiments may indeed illuminate some facets of frustration and illustrate that it has its part in aggression. But in human experience, frustration as defined and demonstrated through animal behavior represents merely a fragment of our highly complex phenomenon of aggression. And the significant and essential relation of aggression to narcissism is not touched upon—nor can it be. For we have no evidence that anything like narcissism as a dynamic psychological element has a role in animal life.

From earliest childhood, we make critical assessments of our circumstances—those which seem menacing to our relationships as well as dangers involving possible injury or death. At the same time, however, we learn—without instruction—that we shall not wholly succeed in this enterprise, that what is valued may be lost, that what is beautiful may fade, and that what is satisfying may one day displease. Nothing escapes change and little do we fail to notice. To resist, to rail too much against transcience, as some men do, making of their entire lives a vendetta, is to make the "demand for immortality too unmistakably a product of our wishes to lay claim to reality." [3] These experiences are not only the property of the poet and the philosopher; they actively occupy the daily thoughts of every three-year-old child. A child's wish to live is no mere biological expression of self-preservation; man's efforts to survive and his wishes to live are dedicated to dispelling the abhorrent significance of his fate. We do not dismiss ourselves as unimportant, nor do we accept our end or forego our relationships. On the contrary, these values, tenaciously held, give self-preservation its psychological face, narcissism.

The conflict between the realization of death and the repudiation of this knowledge is a lifelong struggle. A rich variety of unconscious defenses are marshaled to overcome our sense of helplessness before a clear but unacceptable fate. Through magic, elaborate and unconscious fantasies of omnipotence, conscious wishes for invulnerability, and the development of religious beliefs, we attempt to triumph over what we will not accept and yet know so well. These powerful forces developed by our need for self-preservation do not, however, rest with spinning skeins of dreams about a secure existence, but rather extend to man's objective achievements, to generating adaptation to and mastery of his environment. This is the course of his self-transformation. And aggression, which is not merely to be seen as a reaction to frustration or deprivation, nor simply as attack or hostile action, is variously and continually employed in the process of self-refinement. It leads to a secured self-esteem. In these essential developments the relationship of narcissism to aggression necessarily is close.

Understanding the bond between narcissism and aggression is central to appreciating the role of each in the dynamic development of character as well as in clinical disorders. This remains, however, one of the least explored areas of psychological research.

In 1914, Freud wrote, "Certain special difficulties seem to me to lie in the way of a direct study of narcissism" [4]—a subject which nonetheless proved to be among the most important in his writing and pivotal in the evolution of his views. The first difficulty is the extreme self-absorption and isolation of those whom aggravated narcissism has turned into patients. The clinical effort to study narcissism even in those who are not pointedly suffering from it tends to increase or intensify their defensiveness and unconsciously to resist its examination. To obtain the necessary access for a direct study of narcissism remains very difficult, especially in the severe disorders, the psychoses, where such psychological processes are clinically studied, and where insight into their pathology is usually gained.

While some psychoanalytic study fruitfully followed the courses Freud suggested, where nacissism is intensified in the study of schizophrenia, ". . . the study of organic disease, of hypochondria and of the erotic life of the sexes . . . ," [5] the results have been meager, and the obstacles remain intact.

Secondly, the theoretical framework which isolated narcissism from aggression left both fields of study relatively fallow. And for reasons which are not clear, the role of narcissism and its relation to aggression has been little studied in organic and hypochondriacal states, and in children with respect to their parents. [6]

Freud, in his paper "On Narcissism," * called the egocentric focus of infants' primary narcissism the epitome of self-containment—a

---

* Freud's editors wrote that one of his motives for writing this paper, the only one he published on narcissism, was to show that his concept offered an alternative to Jung's nonsexual libido theory, as well as to Adler's theory of "masculine protest." [7]

"primary" condition which inevitably alters as an infant becomes aware of the people upon whom he must depend. For obvious reasons, the infant's experiences with these other people are not always satisfying. This has two significant results: first, some basis for disquiet remains; second, the disquiet serves to intensify his needs. The less his demands are satisfied the more the child clings to his egocentricity, and this, while giving his comforts an added value (making the young child even more sybaritic than he naturally is—and quite possibly providing the basis for the excessive importance some adults later come to attach to the love of luxury and pleasure without which they are prone to suffer as from deprivation), also anchors that egocentricity firmly in infancy. When further "failures" occur—the actual loss of someone needed or loved, or not being rewarded with the care and affection, and, later, the praise or distinction we require (or, as children, inordinately wish)—our narcissism, our sense of self is injured. And such injuries to narcissism tend to turn us back toward the self-contained primary state. To consider these experiences as simply specific instances of frustration places the emphasis on the individual's consciousness of being thwarted or checked. That emphasis is misplaced, however, when it is the entire process which invariably generates and includes an unconscious response, which calls for our attention here. Moreover, the notion of frustration applied to injured narcissism tends to offer a reduction of a complex and far-reaching conflict to be conceived of as a mere response to a trick of fortune.

Now, half a century later, we have acquired ample clinical experience to bear out many of Freud's speculations. The failure of important relationships injures self-esteem and lowers it—often unconsciously; on an unconscious level, narcissism is heightened, and one's self-concern corresponds with a diminishing interest in others. This correspondence is manifestly illustrated in the process of aging. It is then that a sense of improverishment associated with the loss of functions and vitality characteristically produces highly egocentric reactions. These often include preoccupations with eating and body care, greediness and hoarding of possessions, and a thrust of activity expressed in aggressiveness as well. This is often dismissed as simply a mark of advancing years; however, it is also the mark of narcissism which poorly tolerates impoverishment and especially the loss of functions once enjoyed. We may make the same observation of young children: they too become highly egocentric when they experience a loss of some functions through illness or accidents and may develop hypochondria like the aged; greed with aggressiveness is also common as they suffer injuries to self-esteem.[8]

We do not need even to look as far as pathology for evidence of the relationship between threatened self-concern and aggression. Instances in everyday life abound. For example, it would seem to be common knowledge that injured self-esteem in a household breeds jealousy or aggravated rivalry for favor. This is the stuff of family life, quite taken for granted; the underlying psychological significance of such conflicts has been obscured by its domestic familiarity and an unwitting reluctance to examine its deeper implications. It has never been systematically studied or clarified theoretically.

We have long known from observation that grief and depression commonly evoke aggression among members of a family. This is usually ascribed to resentment of the threatened or actual loss, or it is attributed to a grievance at being abandoned (often a basis for resentment during mourning). Case material amply supports these interpretations. What is not generally recognized or carefully documented is that ordinary grief has simliar effects. And that the aggression which normally issues and is directed at oneself is often displaced toward one's intimates and others. During grief, it is common for mourners, following a loved one's untimely death, to abuse those who gave first aid or to engage in faultfinding and severe criticism of attending physicians who are alleged to have neglected their patient as though there was the intention of having him die.

Narcissism, threatened or injured in the course of daily family life, is of itself not adequate to the task of recovery. One astute observer described the behavior of a girl whose father suddenly died: "She went about the house wringing her hands like a creature demented, saying, 'It was my fault; I should have never left him; if only I had sat up with him,' etc." He then added, "With such ideas vividly present . . . there would arise through the principle of associated habit, the strongest tendency to energetic action of some kind [which] is notoriously dangerous in the highest degree." [9] These remarks, made by Charles Darwin nearly one hundred years ago about an important aspect of a commonplace event in the psychology of everyday life, frame a query that, to the present, has not been adequately answered: what in our mental life, during grief, should loosen such a stream of self-accusations and find respite in self-destructive acts? Darwin explained such behavior as ". . . rudimental vestiges of the screaming fits, which are so prolonged during infancy." His ideas about biological evolution, freely applied to this observation of puzzling adult behavior, led him to see remnants of infancy carried into later periods of life much the same way that biological analogues of lower forms of life appear in more developed species. Since Darwin's time, however, we have learned from the field work of anthropologists that self-destructive or self-mutilating conduct associated with grief is still common among primitive people. And the Biblical "rending of one's garments" in grief also parallels these observations.

Psychoanalysts who have endeavored in recent years to understand this timeless phenomenon have adopted the view that anger against the loved and lost person is inevitable and probably universal. Historical records, observations of primitive societies, and the modern remnants of these practices support the supposition that we are led to vent our anger on ourselves at being abandoned. The one whom we valued and through whose death we suffer loss lessens us. With his departure, he has, so to speak, taken with him what we gave of ourselves. This sense of feeling depleted is a part of mourning, and not all of it is conscious. We turn away from blaming the dead for our impoverishment and instead take to the sack and smearing ourselves with ashes. We thus forego the pursuit of pleasure and, so to speak, act dead; we are identified with the one who has left us. In grief for the dead we mourn our loss. But the identification carries with it a dangerous element. Inasmuch as we cannot vent our anger on the one who has caused our suffering, not only because it is useless but because to demean one who has been valued would make us guilty, we take another unconscious turn. In our identification with whom we have lost, we often unconsciously and seemingly inadvertently may manifestly attack ourselves.

John Bowlby, with whom most analysts agree as to this tendency to self-attacks, attributes the anger to frustration and separation provoked by the loss. But he assigns the self-destructive wishes and aggressive acts associated with grief to pathology and seems not to recognize that they belong equally to the psychology of everyday life. And that the loss which constitutes a narcissistic injury is not confined to merely serious clinical disorders but is significantly present in all mourning.

A common occurrence that would ordinarily escape clinical notice came to my attention when a young woman, whom I know very well, said to me after a memorial service for a faculty member who had an untimely death, that when the prayers for the dead were being recited she had fleetingly imagined her husband's death. "But," she added, "he wouldn't dare do that to me—leave me by having a heart attack and dying! I wouldn't forgive him for that!" She had no intention of being deprived of her husband. I had commented it would be an infuriating act on his part. She was amazed to note that her speculations gave way to rage. Should he die, especially if it were untimely, she would not want to excuse him.

Such fantasies are transient and commonplace. We note them clinically only when they persist. Nevertheless, even these fragmentary thoughts, and the hostile impulses they occasion, often lead to inadvertent self-destructive acts. Unconscious hostility is frequently associated with slight accidents and injuries or "normal" troubles such as cutting one's finger, reckless driving for some short interval, skiing accidents or simply plain quarrelsomeness. These represent aggressive behavior on the one hand, and, on the other, incidents directed toward self-injury; their "source" may be found in unconscious destructive wishes aimed at others, but with a compelling turn against oneself. This is, of course, not to say that every accident or reckless act has its roots only in self-abnegation, but the reverse is certain—given the self-deprecation, accidents and injuries often are its issue.

Freud's classic work, *Mourning and Melancholia,* which appeared in 1917, forms the basis for our present dynamic understanding of grief. Freud showed that when a loved or needed person is lost, unconscious destructive wishes that are intolerable and may have been once conscious arise, evoking self-reproaches and self-attacks, as in the instance of the girl Darwin described or the case of my young friend. She would be prone, I would expect, to express her remorse over her hostility unconsciously in some self-deprecatory thoughts or acts. We see that in daily occurrence, then, as in pathological states, when self-esteem is lowered by a humiliating experience, by a devaluation of oneself or by sudden and profound loss, narcissism in and of itself cannot enable recovery. Moreover, the degree of aggression it arouses varies significantly, and its intensity may indeed reach such acute proportions that, when directed through the medium of oneself, it may result in suicide.

Another normal and quite usual instance of aggression stemming from injured narcissism has also received little notice. That is our reaction to illness. Yet study shows unmistakably that grave physical disabilities, illness and hypochondriasis have in common an impairment of self-esteem, and have consequent aggressive reactions associated with recovery. In short, all who suffer a loss of function, regardless of whether the basis is in tissue changes or founded on neuroses, suffer a severe blow to their narcissism. For instance: a successful

Air Force pilot, who enjoyed his skill and for it received commendation, lost both feet as a result of an accident on the ground. As he was in excellent physical condition, he made a quick, uneventful recovery. Moreover, he was rapidly rehabilitated with artificial limbs. His adept use of them was remarkable; he played football and danced again, with the feeling that he was no longer handicapped, even to the point of fathering another child to his three previous ones; he once more was ready to fly planes. However, regulation required all pilots to possess their feet. Therefore, he was rejected. The fury unleashed in him alternated with despair. It was not so much that he was denied flying or that he lacked other fulfilling activities. It was that the recovery from the severe blow to his narcissism depended on his flying. His support to his self-regard was being denied him. Regardless of his recovered physical function, in his efforts to regain his self-esteem he became exceedingly aggressive.

Illness of whatever sort, grave or minor, in some measure threatens the integrity of the self. The aggression that illness mobilizes may get recognizably little or no conscious expression in the course of daily life. An eager obedience of the patient to instructions may completely mask the underlying demands for care. For instance, the docility common to the sick during an illness often gives way to a free readiness to voice displeasure during convalescence and, after recovery, to be highly critical of the physician. The commonplace moderate, normal and transient hypochondriacal self-concern associated with even mild illness, which ordinarily escapes scrutiny, expresses the threat to the integrity of the self which any disorder may produce. The proneness to irritability during illness is due more to the unconscious threat to the self than may be properly attributed to the effects of physical discomfort. In other words, it is the disruption in the continuity of well-being which evokes the imagery of an impaired self. The reaction is reflected in aggression.

A recently reported study showed the principal and overwhelming emotional conflict of a dying young woman was not so much over the cancer that was killing her as the loss of self-esteem that was at stake. The grim reality, the certain fatal outcome of her illness, led the attending physicians and her family to abandon all hope for her. But in her view, her plight was not wholly that she was dying, but that she was lost to her family—and that her value was gone. Her aggressive reactions were first directed at them; then she turned her violence against herself. In her grief and despair she became suicidal.

Her illness, she believed, demeaned her as did those who fled from her in their grief. Worthless as she felt herself to be, she wanted only to destroy herself.[10]

Some appear to submit humbly to the deformities of disease and the verdict of death. On closer scrutiny, however, they show their resignation to be founded unconsciously on having struck a bargain with the vagaries of living. It is revealed in the most powerful and universal belief in immortality, which in its organized social form is religion. We are bound, in essence it seems, to the reverse of a Faustian proposition. The compact is that for what we are obliged to forfeit, precious life, we shall afterward be rewarded. The only proviso is that we must in advance prove ourselves worthy; and the final judgment of it will be withheld. The unrepentant sinner, we know, seals his own fate.

It is noteworthy that the most rewarding insights about narcissism and aggression have not come, as Freud thought they would, from a study of schizophrenia, or the "paraphrenias" as they were called at the time, the best known narcissistic states or disorders. Instead, we have learned most about aggression, and even narcissism, from studies of young children. They are the supreme narcissists, and they can be merciless tormentors.

Freud's work on the problem of aggression spans four decades, years of clinical probing and reflection which ultimately were inconclusive regarding the question of the independence of aggression from sexuality and its bond with narcissism. After each foray in this direction, he would return to his initial position. It was a lasting dilemma for him. Only toward the end of his life was Freud able to acknowledge—and, at that only on occasions did he take positions on this issue which he would later reconsider and even retract—that destructiveness was an independent instinct.[11] Although he admitted that its ubiquity alone seemed to be grounds for a theoretical primacy, he himself had too long denied it.

When he published *Anxiety and Instinctual Life* in 1932, he said that he had no great advances to report on the subject: "The theory of the instincts is, so to say, our mythology. Instincts are mythical entities, magnificent in their indefiniteness. In our work we cannot for a moment disregard them, yet we are never sure that we are seeing them clearly." [12] Having spent most of his life clinically defining these instincts, trying to remove precisely that mystery which had previously enveloped them, he seemed to be peering once again into the Pandora's box he himself had originally pried open. And sensing, though not explaining, some of the ambiguity he had left behind him in his previous work, he wrote:

> Why have we ourselves needed such a long time before we decided to recognize an aggressive instinct? Why did we hesitate to make use, on behalf of our theory, of facts which were obvious and familiar to everyone? We should probably have met with little resistance if we wanted to ascribe an instinct with such an aim to animals. But to include it in the human constitution appears sacrilegious; it contradicts too many religious presumptions and social conventions. No, man must be naturally good or at least good natured. If he occasionally shows himself brutal, violent or cruel, these are only passing disturbances of his emotional life, for the most part provoked, or perhaps only the consequences of the expedient social regulations which he has hitherto imposed on himself.[13]

With these comments, Freud, not one to be deterred by social convention or religious conviction when he had a human principle or quality of mental functioning to demonstrate, appeared for once to vacate the field with but a few wry remarks on the human condition. Freud did not answer these questions which he had raised, nor did he attempt to explain his failure to make use of what he plainly knew. This seems to be the only instance in his extensive writings in which he suggests that presumptions, conventions or even expediency might have influenced his work.

For reasons we may never know, Freud on one occasion revealed he was not content with his repeated insistence that aggression was always bonded to sexuality. Virtually at the end of his life, in 1937, replying to an inquiry from Princess Marie Bonaparte (his former student and a psychoanalyst herself) with respect to a lecture he had recently given about aggression, he reaffirmed a position he had had a few years before. It was to the effect that aggression could be independent of sexuality. She had expressed her enthusiasm for this view. *But,* a few weeks later, he sent her a note to not overestimate his remarks about the destructive instincts having independence from sexual life—to disregard them, as "they were tossed off." [14] Had Freud clearly held to the idea that aggression may have independence from sexuality, not only would the nature of aggression itself have been probably better understood, but also his views of narcissism might have been quite different.

We have only slight indications from Freud of the influence or thought of other psychoanalysts on his own work. Others were engaged in the same research on problems of aggression. It is curious that those whose efforts enhanced the validity of his own work should have received so little notice from him in this area—such as Karl Abraham,[15] who was among the first to write on the psychoanalysis of aggression beginning in 1912, and who, up until his death in 1925, had contributed clinical studies which have continued to be regarded as basic and valuable. Helene Deutsch[16] described important and original findings on the same subject which she began publishing in 1932, and which have remained classics in clinical studies of aggression.

As early as 1909, Freud showed he knew he was in a dilemma when he said, "I cannot bring myself to assume the existence of a special aggressive instinct alongside of the familiar instincts of self-preservation and of sex, and on an equal footing with them." It was not until fourteen years later, however, in a footnote to one of his most famous cases, that he was prompted to write that he was "obliged to assert the existence of an 'aggressive instinct', but it is different from Adler's. I prefer to call it the 'destructive' or 'death instinct'." [17]

Among the many surveys of Freud's theory of instincts, one of the best was an early one by Edward Bibring.[18] Bibring called attention to the important point that, as a matter of clinical fact, aggressiveness at those times when it is turned on oneself seems to contradict self-preservation. It was this observation by Freud which led to his supposition that there was something inherent in life itself which produced self-destructiveness, or made it possible. Bibring followed Freud. It was this theoretical paradox, rather than a directed clinical study, which might have resolved it, which inspired lengthy debates and even polemics by various students of human behavior over the so-called death instincts. For the clinically sophisticated, the matter was of no lasting interest. But the idea of a death instinct has held an enduring attraction for academic psychologists as well as some of psychoanalysis' severest critics.

That the concept of the death instincts was, at best, an abstraction, a wholly theoretical hypothesis and entirely without any clinical verification, which Freud himself called attention to, seems as regularly to be ignored as it is confused with an unconscious death wish or suicidal acts.

In the fascination with these notions, an idea lost sight of, behind Freud's theory, was one of his enduring convictions. It was that aggression, like other psychological phenomena, one day would be explained by its origins in some as yet undiscovered chemistry or biological structures. The theory represents Freud's unsuccessful attempt to account for aggressiveness. Perhaps in this respect it was the more notable as the effort in which he considered aggression separate from sexuality: it takes a "silent" direction, not in the service of survival but in opposition to it. He wrote:

> On the basis of theoretical considerations, supported by biology, we put forward the hypothesis of a death instinct, the task of which is to lead organic life back into the inanimate state.[19]

To explain the puzzling patent fact that he had found a self-destructive aim in human life opposing all efforts to live, he postulated the death instinct: ". . . we are driven to conclude that the death instincts are by their nature mute and that the clamor of life proceeds for the most part from Eros." [20] Freud thus proposed that the sexual instincts propagated, supported and sustained life against a continuous descent relentlessly drawn by the death instincts toward destruction. This struggle constantly introduced fresh tensions which were not resolved but were terminated finally with our end.[21]

Since so much in human existence, which Freud called to attention, was aimed at perpetuating ourselves and extended even to the wish for immortality, he was obliged to reconcile the conflicting issues. The resolution of these two competing forces was explained by him by the supposition that the dangerous death instincts were perhaps rendered harmless by the powerful pursuit of pleasure through "striving for the satisfaction of the directly sexual trends." [22] To support his view, he showed that the aim to be gratified was so forceful that our knowledge or expectation of extinction in effect served to prepare the way for a belief in an elaborate fulfillment after death. To Freud, the dogged strength of our wishes for gratification formed the basis of a belief that we may escape our fate. And thus in the satisfaction of erotic life was the triumph over the self-destructive elements. It was as if the human pursuit of satisfaction and thus to live won over the presumed biological ones of self-destruction. Those who engage in polemics over the death instincts, whether they claim them as a real phenomenon of emotional experience or hold the idea up for ridicule, struggle with a straw man. The basis of self-destruction was a riddle Freud did not wholly solve.

Whether self-destruction is deliberate, or founded on some unconscious or even presumably on an instinctual basis, it captures the fancy of many who ponder man's fate. In recent years, one of the most popular and widely read protagonists of the death instincts has been

Norman O. Brown.[23] His so-called psychoanalytic interpretation of history shows that he conceives of the death instincts as an actual phenomenon, somehow transformed in the unconscious into aggression. Brown shares in the common confusion and promotes it by labeling demonstrably unconscious aggression, when turned against the self, death instincts. Had Freud not held so firmly to his notions about the death instincts, both mute and unobservable, misconceptions would be less persistent. Moreover, he and others after him might have further developed a systematic theory of aggression founded more on evidence than on supposition.

Any theory of human aggression should attempt to explain the common and often imperative wish to give up one's life. Whether it is to be for a high purpose or to put miserable agony to an end, the recognized desire to forfeit one's existence needs still to be illuminated beyond the assertion that some sort of compelling force draws us toward death or that intolerable circumstances may be overwhelming. Citing heroes in the countless instances in history, in the timeless myths and legends, provides us with examples of giving up life, which cases of suicide also demonstrate. But they furnish us with no concept to explain the readiness or the wish to forfeit existence.

The common denominator in suicide which the hero shares with the villain is in the wish to quit life. The aim in either case is the sacrifice of oneself. And it is dictated by feeling less worthy than if the self were preserved. What may appear to be a resignation to death, either through suicide or a heroic death, is in actuality a dread of the degradation of the self from which there is no expectation of recovery. The need to redeem oneself from ignominy is the compelling and governing wish. To give up one's life to satisfy one's narcissism on the surface may appear to be a contradiction. But, of the two, it seems narcissism is the more important. The self is best served through maintaining self-regard. If in order to do so, life must be forfeited, the risk to our existence comes from whatever menaces our narcissism.

Our defenses against self-destructive impulses will not spring into action only when we begin to contemplate suicide. They are perfected long in advance of such inner dangers. Aggression intended toward others which precedes attacking oneself is as typical of a child as it is of an adult. However, the sense of feeling limited, perhaps even helpless at times, hence victimized by fears of being attacked or persecuted, are common experiences of young children. And while there may well be ample justification in reality for a child to assess the world as hostile, in the course of doing so it serves to deny his own aggressive intentions. A young child's aggressiveness is as notorious as his unwillingness to acknowledge it (as we shall observe in the next chapter).

How correctly a young child perceives his milieu must remain a matter of conjecture. But his response to his own inner aims leaves less to the imagination. As we have mentioned, a child does not view himself as aggressive even though he may be in the throes of it. Perhaps this is due to the fact that the earliest unconscious form of emotional defense is denial. Not as some would suppose of the external world but of those wishes and impulses deemed subject to evoking censure or discipline from others. Beginning to deny one's own inclinations does not require that they must first be precisely defined. How great a gap there is between repudiating one's aggressive impulses and attributing them to others, and in the course of it to develop fears of being attacked or menaced, may not be handily stated. But it is characteristically displayed by a child of three years. This mental process, "projection," as it is called, is one of the child's earliest and most effective defenses to lighten the burden one's aggressive wishes may create. And it is not readily relinquished in adult life.

Beginning in the early thirties, as child analysis commenced to develop, children were studied in the expectation of discovering in the early years of life those episodes which were carried forward virtually intact into the adult years. And, it was expected that later, as before, they would make their mischief. It was thought that the acute sense of helplessness experienced by adults in a period of clinical depression was but a return to childhood experiences of total dependence on others, of fears that wishes would not be met, and of an overwhelming sense of one's limitations. These ideas and the feelings of worthlessness, cardinal features of clinical depression, were thought to reflect a specific history of identical feelings experienced in childhood.

The discovery of the child's emotional life encouraged analysts to take retrospective excursions into the psychology of children. And as a result, the critical distinctions between adult fears (and even memories of childhood fears) and a child's actual condition tended to be obscured. The view that in moments of distress in which adults may revert emotionally—which occasionally occurred, and under certain clinical conditions, as in psychoses, was both common and often lasting—to the infantilism that was once a child's reality gained currency. It followed from such ideas that the delineation of adult disorders from a child's normal condition became increasingly difficult to discern.

The search for a prototype of the emotional life of adults believed to be buried in one's childhood continues to be conducted by many analysts. There appears to be an unwillingness to abandon a determinist orthodoxy shaped from the discovery by Freud that the basis of our emotional disorders rests only in unresolved childhood sexual conflicts. Every adult neurotic condition which promotes flight from distress toward some pleasurable experience or which may evoke associations to childhood is assumed to be directed unconsciously to some actual encounter. As there are satisfactions to be retrieved and as gratification may be reexperienced, the tendency to unconsciously return to them occurs. These occurrences are so predominantly erotic that the aggressive ones by comparison seem exceptional. Studies focus on sexuality, its development and conflicts.

Freud's clinical attention to the unconscious conflicts he discovered to be associated with aggression did reveal that even if we are engaged in aggression only in our wishes, fantasies or unconscious—rather than in fact—we are also nonetheless deeply concerned with curbing it. Generally, the result is a sense of guilt; conscience becomes more severe and more sensitive, and we refrain from aggression against others especially when they are personally important to us. The morality we develop is the very evidence of our unconscious aggressive wishes. In our inclination to ward off self-punishment and at the same time to inflict pain on ourselves, Freud saw an apparent flat contradiction of that unmistakable and powerful urge to the pursuit of pleasure which he himself had shown to be so fundamental to human existence. It was a dilemma he saw as a great danger menacing our mental life.

"The suffering itself is what matters; whether it is decreed by someone who is loved or by someone who is indifferent is of no importance. It may even be caused by impersonal powers or by circumstances." [24] The need to take suffering menaces self-preservation; the wish to turn the cheek and to take the blow invites the danger to oneself. The temptation, Freud thought, is to explain this attitude as solely a case of the destructive instinct "now raging against the self," [25] and leave out that some gratification exists in it. His examples include those cases in which "neurotic" suffering vanishes when there is occasion for "real" suffering, such as the misery of an unhappy marriage or the development of a serious organic disease.

There are many other examples to be cited of real suffering which dispels the misery of neurotic anguish. For instance: family life is replete with episodes of accidents and hurts to oneself which follow angry outbursts. Such injuries become the real occasions for agony. Nor is it uncommon to find a successful criminal who becomes careless and thus ensures his apprehension and punishment. Malefactors who repeatedly leave half-purposeful tracks by which they will be traced and discovered fill the dockets. In addition to those who actually court punishment, innocents may respond to real penalties. It was common to find that prisoners confronted with the "objective" hardship in concentration camps enjoyed the freedom, often for the first time, from a variety of psychosomatic disorders. Subjected to real hurt taken over by their jailers, they seemed no longer to hurt themselves. On being liberated, most of them once again suffered from their former illnesses (see Chapter IX).

To account for and cover adequately the development of self-discipline, which from an early age begins to exact its demands by the "need for punishment," is too simple an explanation for a process that embraces conflicts in all aspects of everyday life no less often than it does those in serious psychological disorders. Freud's proposition here that we are reckoning with some aspect of the superego, first installed by others (parents and the whole social mold) to create an ethical predisposition or sense, which is furthered by oneself,[26] continues to be valid. But as a "need for punishment" appears in a young child far in advance of a developed conscience or a punative superego, we must therefore conclude that required restraint of aggression impresses a child. He solicits it. And within a short time, he begins to adopt governing himself.

Given a license, by way of permissiveness, to be aggressive, a young child will soon feel in jeopardy. With his characteristic tendency to self-reference coupled with naturally projecting his wishes or impulses and acts on others, he will regard them as taking those liberties he enjoys but disallows himself. Unwittingly, he fashions his own caution. An unconscious imperative to curtail his aggression forms. It mitigates the fears he may be attacked. Therefore, to test the limits of one's expectations, which all children notoriously are compelled to try, represents the unconscious and as often the deliberate wish to provoke pains and penalties. The suffering is needed as it defines the state of one's condition.

For instance, some of Freud's cases, such as Little Hans, the Wolf Man, and clinical examples of my own cited elsewhere here, show that the formation of fears, phobias and nightmares and similar but less terrifying reactions unconsciously place self-restraint on aggression in the service of feeling safe and secure.

Granting oneself a license to be destructive inevitably creates conflicts. It brings into emotional development not only a "need for punishment," but additional safeguards appear unconsciously as aggression persists, in the form of anxiety over what might happen, anticipation, and expectations of disaster. The exercise of aggression invokes deterrents to being violent and is often unwittingly expressed in the neurotic dread of losing those we love. It may be displaced, too, turning into a tenacious hold on what we possess. Each of these conflicts, which involve self-concern, is unavoidably rooted in our narcissism.

Then there are the countless occasions throughout life which, rather than restraining aggression, call it forth and reward it—in the acquisition of skills of the many technological, productive and artistic achievements which make for social adaptation. Even as we point out that civilization must be defended against individual license, and that limits to our aggression must be set and enforced, we can neither forget nor ignore that it was in part the force of aggression—however sublimated—which created the civilization to be preserved. It therefore appears that whether our aggression places us in jeopardy or makes us secure may depend more upon the service in which it is employed than upon its inherent characteristics.

One of Freud's most enduring notions on aggression he expressed in what often has been referred to as his "hydraulic metaphor." He said that we are subject to a flow of psychic energy issuing from a reservoir fed by urgent springs of impulses and needs within the unconscious and in our biological structures, a reservoir which supplies the power for all mental activities.* If this flow is impeded or dammed up, it will create severe conflicts; the excess energy will be turned to

---

* With respect to aggression, what may be our biological endowment from which mental functions develop and then continue to draw upon, is a question which invites a misleading answer. The question is leading in that it suggests that our instinctual legacy exists as a platform or base, separate and perhaps even distinct from the necessary social influences without which we do not properly exist. Hence, whatever our physical constitution and its genetic complement may be, they are not separable for assessment from social experience. We are obliged to accept, therefore, that our inherited proclivities may not be defined simply as some foundation in us with which our social experiences become engaged. Rather, it is that our emotional development is expressive of the phenomenon of an amalgam which begins to be fused with our birth. The course of this development shows best in the vicissitudes of narcissism and aggression.

aggressive or self-destructive ends, erupting in cruelty and violence against others or against oneself. This force is credited with biological reality. While excesses of energy flow are thought to turn correspondingly into excessive activities, and are not necessarily desirable, a so-called normal flow, Freud thought, may go into ordinary or normal activities of a constructive nature, or be taken up by efforts exerted in pursuits representing sublimation, i.e. socially acceptable as well as personally gratifying ends. There are parallel popular beliefs about aggression which argue that without a proper discharge, aggression accumulates and will burst its dam at some unpredictable point into violent if not dangerous acts. To the present, psychoanalytic theory and popular belief have little that distinguishes them here, as each explains the dynamics of aggression along the lines of Freud's turn-of-the-century physics model of hydraulics.

The reasoning behind it, both scientific and popular, is that aggression will accumulate if not allowed to flow out. Darwin declared that man would not be such a brute "unless he has the brute nature within him";[27] and a half-century later, Freud used the same argument as the basis of his instinct theory (when he showed that aggressive conduct derives from our aggressive aims, conscious or unconscious). During the first decades of this century, Cannon's basic work in physiology gave added support to the conception that aggression was a discharge phenomenon, by showing that certain stimuli directed to an animal's brain tissue provoked a reaction of rage.[28] The display of brutishness, the demonstration of unconscious destructive aims, and these new studies of brain physiology seemed to converge and to establish that man harbored an elemental reservoir of hate from which his violence flowed.

Other fields of psychology have engaged in experimental studies with animals over the past century and an extensive literature has accumulated showing that, under certain laboratory conditions, animals respond with aggression to certain stimuli. A parallel to man is often drawn from these experiments, and the general conclusion has been that men, like animals, harbor aggression which circumstances will elicit or release. Aggression is thus generally conceived to be a spontaneously erupting, hostile or destructive force, or a "natural" response to threatening or menacing circumstances or conditions. This view, however, tends to obscure the distinction between self-preservation in animals, and what it means emotionally in man to be ever mindful of himself. The resistance of a century ago to the revolutionary idea of man's descent from animals seems largely to have disappeared. It has given way to an all-embracing notion. Often carried well beyond the limits of scientific evidence, the notion is that man and animals are more alike emotionally than not, especially with regard to aggression. Hypotheses based on this idea frequently suggest that the direction of man's aggression throughout the course of civilization has somehow taken a bad turn. And that were man more animal and less human, he might then be able to enjoy an existence more in harmony with nature and with his fellow men.[29] Such ideas suggest that aggression functions only to consolidate security or to ensure survival.

It is surprising that in the social sciences in general we take such pains to avoid the concept of instinct in all areas. But in the elusive search for the role of aggression in the unconscious, uninhibited speculation exists.

An extreme position, but one that nonetheless is very influential among psychoanalysts (chiefly in London and in Latin American countries), is that held by the late Melanie Klein, her associates and followers. Their notions of the aggressive aims of young infants include the supposition that they unconsciously entertain cannibalistic fantasies, unconscious anxieties of death which are attributed to the passage to birth, and a variety of other ideas thought to stem from a child's hostility toward a world he regards as malevolent. These assumptions continue unaccountably to have a viability among many psychologists despite the clinical facts which would dispute them.

Even though it at times appears as if we are indeed mere children in adult form, the analysis of the fantasies and acts of such moments reveals that while childlike aggressiveness and destructiveness may be satisfying, such aggressive reactions affect self-regard. The endless stream of circumstance, caprice and accident which is the condition of everyday existence leaves neither narcissism intact nor the feeling of self-esteem stable. Narcissism, at best in precarious balance, calls on aggression to maintain its equilibrium. Hence, what may bring down the level of self-esteem leads to the commonest form of neurotic conflict we fall heir to and the form of emotional experience which most frequently becomes pathological, depression. And central to this conflict is aggression.

Far in advance of conflicts arising from sensuous experience, those associated with narcissism and aggression in relation to those emotionally most important to us begin to have a profound effect on our entire early development. This follows from the self-transforming quality which characterizes human life; self-awareness, self-criticism, self-estimation and self-esteem are all actively developing in our youngest years. These activities engage the small child to a degree that fully substantiates the proposition that whatever else he may be he is also a little Narcissus. Furthermore, no other characteristic is more vigorously defended than his narcissism—or is more in need of defense. Aggression is necessarily brought into its employ and never leaves its service. If we take these facts into account, and give to narcissism its ascendant emphasis, then the role of aggression becomes much more clear. We are then able to understand that the vicissitudes of everyday life, just as emotional disorders, invariably engage our narcissism. And the recovery from injuries to it demands the services of aggression.

Some of our worst failures more often than our successes may compel exertions to change, much as the lack of fulfillment in a relationship or a valued enterprise may initiate in us the process of making restitution for what we lost. Hence, it is in the regenerating of ourselves that we find ample confirmation of the powerful incentives to recover from the countless disappointments, frustrations and displeasures we never really wholly accept. What affects self-regard affects narcissism, compels us to act, to venture, to risk. In the course of such pursuits, we may exceed a previous resolve, transcend an earlier (often outworn) sense of ourselves, and thus elevate our self-esteem with which we are enabled to further make our narcissism secure. Often our development gains.

Paradoxically, we seem more compelled to act from what injures narcissism or menaces self-esteem than what comforts it. The incentives which stem from these sources often carry us to our highest achievements. They also, however, give legitimacy to the greatest violence. This is our relentless pursuit, above all to preserve the self. Freud thought it to be a biological summons to which we are inexorably obedient. It is however a psychological phenomenon. St. Augustine called it the *libido dominandi* that he sought to exorcise—man's narcissism. It governs our existence, calls on aggression, violence and hate. It menaces all creatures, even those we come to love. Against our narcissism, none are secure. Neither are we.

Chapter II

Aggression: Modus Vivendi

Aggression in man has been explained biologically as the eruption of instinctual forces, emotionally as some compelling need to engage in violence, and philosophically as a component in man's nature expressive of an imperative to master his universe if not his future. Most writers on human violence, whether theologians, scientists or philosophers, both before Darwin and since, continue to draw heavily on analogies with animal behavior. Since it is thought to parallel human aggression, it is assumed to explain it. Indeed, it is often suggested that the two are identical. *If true, that fact is merely coincidental.*

There is an overriding distinction between man and all other creatures which tends to get lost in such conjectures. In man, aggression is his way of life. In animals, it is usually the result of a specific circumstance or particular event which provokes it.

The greatest single influence on modern understanding of the psychology of human conduct is, of course, Freud; however, as we have seen, his conceptualization of aggression (and, indeed, all the theories which derive from his work) was incomplete and misleading so long as aggression was considered to be bound up inextricably and solely with sexuality.

Freud's most original and fateful contribution to human knowledge came with the discovery of unconscious motivation and the findings, through his analysis of adults, that a child's existence embodies a sexual life, and that the conflicts associated with this "infantile sexuality," as he called it, affect the formation of character and conduct throughout life. What part aggression takes in the process of emotional development, in everyday existence, in our common psychological disorders, or in the frequent madnesses we fall heir to, Freud acknowledged years later he had unaccountably set aside.

A review of even his earliest cases shows that aggression in man, however it may become differentiated by circumstances or elaborated by events, is no mere expression of an inchoate instinct—nor is it simply a "reaction." Into whatever instinctual (or biological) roots in physiology aggression may be traced (a question to which the answers remain locked in the minds of infants) in man, it is a lifelong, *developmental* function which profoundly affects emotional growth and learning, promotes important defenses against the conflicts it gives rise to, and exerts a constant influence on the shape and stature of our self-image throughout our existence.

Freud published the first psychoanalytic study of a child, "The Analysis of a Phobia in a Five-Year-Old Boy," in 1909. This, the case of Little Hans, familiar to every student of psychoanalysis—which offered confirming, conclusive evidence of Freud's startling discoveries about the unconscious role in psychic life of infantile sexuality, the Oedipus complex, and the fear of castration—demonstrated the fact that these phenomena were more than conjectures; they were palpable realities.*

In addition to its importance as the first account of child analysis, Little Hans has an added significance, although Freud himself did not develop it. The case materially contributes to our understanding of aggression. He showed that Hans unconsciously feared mutilation or "castration" as a direct result of his "romantic" attachment to his mother, a "complex" Freud had previously discovered from his analysis of adults; but this does not explain the unusual aspect of the case, the severity of the phobia of being attacked and mutilated. Hans ventured on a sexual errand and became fearful of an attack and injury: he began as an aggressor and ended as a victim, and this is the key to the full understanding of the case.

Freud's objectivity in this case was extraordinarily served by the unique circumstance that the material for it was not derived from his own observations. It came from the parent's reports of their experiences with their child. Hans' parents knew Freud and were, in fact, among his first adherents. They lived some distance from Vienna, and how the remarkable plan for the unprecedented psychoanalytic treatment of the child was arrived at is not clear. The venture commenced with the reports Hans' father sent to Freud in 1906, when the child was about three and a half years old, and continued until 1908, when

---

* Interestingly enough, however, aside from this, the case of Little Hans offered Freud no new insights. "Strictly speaking," he concluded, "I learnt nothing new from his analysis, nothing that I had not already been able to discover (though often less distinctly and more indirectly) from other patients analyzed at a more advanced age." [1]

Hans was about five. On one occasion, Freud had a conversation with the boy, but he did not then see him again until many years later. While Freud laid down the general lines of treatment and continued to give it some direction—the boy was to be "neither laughed at nor bullied"—the analysis itself was to be carried out by the child's father who wrote Freud regular reports. "The extraordinary pains taken by Hans' father were rewarded by success," Freud wrote later, "and his reports will give us an opportunity of penetrating into the fabric of this type of phobia and of following the course of its analysis." [2]

Hans was described by his parents as a direct, straightforward child. Freud wrote that he was "well formed physically, and was a cheerful, amiable, active-minded young fellow who might give pleasure to more people than to his own father." [3] The phobia was first described in a letter addressed to Freud in 1906:

My dear Professor,

I am sending you a little more about Hans—but this time I am sorry to say, material for a case history. As you will see, during the last few days he has developed a nervous disorder which has made my wife and me most uneasy, because we have not been able to find any means of dissipating it. . . .

No doubt the ground was prepared by sexual over-excitation due to his mother's tenderness; but I am unable to specify the actual exciting cause. He is afraid a horse will bite him on the street, and this fear seems somehow connected with his having been frightened by a large penis. As you know from a former report, he had noticed at a very early age what large penises horses have, and at that time he inferred that, as his mother was so large, she must have a widdler like a horse.

I cannot see what to make of it. Has he seen an exhibitionist somewhere? Or is the whole thing simply connected with his mother? It is not very pleasant for us that he should begin setting problems for us so early. Apart from his being afraid of going into the street and from his being in low spirits in the evening, he is in other respects the same Hans, as bright and cheerful as ever. [4]

Some months after this communication, the boy's father wrote Freud that Hans had been ill with influenza which kept him in bed for two weeks during which the phobia markedly increased. We do not know whether Hans may not have taken many opportunities to masturbate during this period in bed. But his mother had cautioned him against it, and although we cannot know what mixture of motives led her specifically to warn the child, the fact that she spoke to him

about it would certainly have had the effect of increasing his fears. And indeed, according to his father, Hans' fears of being hurt were intensified. In addition, a week after the illness, Hans had a tonsillectomy, and the phobia grew even worse.

At Hans' age of four, children commonly, because of their naturally heightened sexual interests, are attentive to their genitals and they may masturbate, especially when confined to bed, as in illness or convalescence. Under such physical restrictions the active sexual fantasies, normally incorporated into play, find expression more directly in masturbatory behavior. We also know that the sexual wishes of a child this age are cast into imagery of violence and thus give rise to heightened fears associated with them. And, furthermore, studies show that while a child may accept, for instance, the rational explanation of the need for a tonsillectomy, he also regards it with apprehension and suspicion, as a mutilation[5] reminiscent of his fears of it in connection with sexual ideas. Thus, Hans' phobia worsened as a reflection of the significance to him of his actual experiences—experiences which coincided precisely with the Oedipal age, the time of childhood characterized by intensified sexual wishes which evoke defenses associated with them.

The effects of an illness, a period in bed, and then the experience of surgery—even the simple removal of tonsils—were events which Freud knew were important to a young child, even though in 1906 he was not yet able to appreciate their full emotional significance. That could only be demonstrated decades later. At the time, however, all signs seemed to Freud to confirm the fact that the boy's fears derived from his sense of having set himself up as his father's rival for the affection of his mother. It was not until Hans' breakdown in a neurosis that "it became evident to what a pitch of intensity his love for his mother had developed, and through what vicissitudes it had passed." [6] But it was precisely this deeply emotional gratifying attachment which also brought in its train, reactions of anxiety which evoked the formation of the symptoms. Hans' father was more correct than he could have known when he wrote at the outset that the mother's tender love for the boy was the prepared ground in which the symptoms flourished, and Hans' expectations of being attacked by a horse were indeed a direct outcome of wishes associated with his love for his mother.

Since 1909, countless similar instances have amply verified that Hans' case was not, in most respects, unique. But while a child's Oedipal wishes and their consequences are now recognized to be commonplace, the development of a severe phobia in connection with them is *not* usual, and an explanation of Hans' phobia is long overdue. We just assume from experience in other and similar instances (for there is only the one hint of it in the letters from Hans' father) that Hans' mother's deep attachment to her son was taken by him to be seductive. From his own close relation with her, the intensity of his wishes was almost inevitable, and corresponded with the intensity of his desire to be rid of his rivals.*

The father's letters show that Hans was normally but deeply troubled by sexual matters. The anatomical differences between men and women caused him to draw a normal but nonetheless "alarming and misleading conclusion" that women were castrated men, and the effect of this was profound. Children often put themselves in the place of others, especially their parents; and in this instance for Hans to put himself in the place of his mother was, as Freud wrote, "bound to have a shattering effect on his self-confidence." [7] But Hans also identified himself with his father, whom he took to be big and possibly as dangerous as a horse; he wished not only to be like his father, but also, as his rival for the mother, to displace him. This took the form of wishing, as Freud showed, that the father should be "permanently away—that he should be dead." [8]

But he loved his father also. "Hans was not by any means a bad character. He was not even one of those children who at his age still give free play to a propensity towards cruelty and violence. . . . On the contrary, he had an unusually kind-hearted and affectionate disposition; his father reported that the transformation of aggressive tendencies into feelings of pity took place in him at a very early age." [9] The father's remarks on the transformation of his son's aggression is indicative of an unconscious need on the boy's part to modify his aggressive aims that had begun to take place earlier than the present outbreak of fears. Now Hans' more active sexual wishes, associated as they normally would be with aggressive ones, were certain to heighten his fears even more. As an unconscious measure to mitigate his apprehensions, the development of affection in place of aggression serves that function. The father was in no way able to scrutinize his son's condition more closely than to observe and enjoy the fact that

---

* A little boy in corresponding circumstances who had a poor relationship with his mother would be spared Hans' fate but he would not escape the effects of his "failure" any more than Hans could avoid the results of his "success." The outcome of these experiences varies, but not the problems attendant on their essential nature.

the boy's aggression was transformed somehow to compassion. The fact that there is no basis to doubt Hans' love for each parent should not obscure the fact that he expects this love to have a serious and hence threatening outcome for himself. His wish that his father might die was so intense that it was translated into a belief that it might, in fact, happen; and that possibility made Hans afraid, because part of him at least wanted his father nearby. He told his father, "When you are away, I'm afraid you're not coming back home." [10] Thus, the wish, expressed as a fear, emerged as anxiety, first for his father and then for himself. In addition to the defenses which develop and form against fear and anxiety is the expectation of violence—of harm to oneself proportionate to the harm wished against others.

Hans' anxiety was expressed in a fear that he would be hurt by a horse. The focus of this fear on the large size of the animal convinced his father that these fears and fantasies applied to him. Freud agreed. Anxiety can be dealt with at the price of installing inhibitions and prohibitions, an unconscious process which may result in the development of phobias, and this is what happened with Hans. He manifestly gave up being aggressive toward his father in favor of showing his tender love. His persistent fears and phobias betray that, notwithstanding his affection, there remained the unconscious expectation of some kind of severe harm to himself. Consciously, the boy was aware only of his frightened reluctance to leave the house, for fear that a horse might hurt him. This phobia sprang not only from his unconscious fears of castration but also from something which has received scant notice in Freud's report: the fact that Hans had not, with the development of his new tenderness, altogether abandoned his hostility. The boy's aggression "aimed" to victimize his father, and the issue went beyond the anxiety generated by an infantile sexual wish. His intentions were destructive; for example, despite their mutual trust and carefully cultivated and remarkably intimate dialogue, Hans was reluctant to divulge to his father a dream which concerned his wish to kill him. He had to get rid of his father—a fancied undertaking certain to arouse substantial anxiety in a five-year-old boy.

Hans' father on the other hand, was taken up with the child's forbidden *incestuous* wish. And Freud was intent on demonstrating the boy's infantile sexuality and that in his play he revealed he was in conflict over primal themes of sexuality and birth. The boy was shown that "his fears and phobias were the result of expectations and fears of punishment from his father against whom he held evil wishes." [11] In Freud's view at the time, however, the "evil wishes" for which little Hans could well expect retaliation were sexual in nature, not aggressive.

"Hans really was a little Oedipus who wanted to have his father 'out of the way,' " wrote Freud.[12] Years later in 1924, he came to believe, "To an ever-increasing extent the Oedipus complex reveals its importance as the central phenomenon of the sexual period of early childhood." [13] He regarded the Oedipal phase of a child's experience as the culminating one of infantile sexuality. The whole "complex" takes in the characteristics of the child's earlier erotic life brought to the Oedipal age:

> Although the majority of human beings go through the Oedipus complex as an individual experience, it is nevertheless a phenomenon which is determined and laid down by heredity and which is bound to pass away according to programme when the next preordained phase of development sets in.[14]

It is doubtful that many analysts would today couch the emergence of the Oedipus complex in such genetic terms as Freud did a half-century ago, or refer to its collapse as he did as being the time for its disintegration, "just as milk-teeth fall out when permanent ones begin to grow." [15]

The whole "complex" is now recognized as more complicated. The Oedipal phase comes to an end and is normally abandoned by the child as a profitless, dangerous venture in which his entire erotic capital was invested. As the child develops fears about his wishes, he anticipates attacks upon himself as a consequence of them and increasingly dreads a colossal failure—one which, moreover, comes true. In one way or another, the denouement of the Oedipus complex is the child's humiliation. All these elements were present in the case of Little Hans. Freud summed up his experience with the declaration, "I never got a finer insight into a child's soul." [16] Focused on his discovery of confirming evidence for his theory of infantile sexuality, however, he left to one side the fact that the Oedipus complex is both introduced by (fantasied) violence and finally abandoned because of (fantasied) violent retaliation.

Freud was amply rewarded in the case of Little Hans with evidence that his reconstruction of early childhood sexuality based on adult cases was correct. Furthermore, the little boy's sexual experience, while active, seems to be quite an ordinary one. Had Hans' parents been less sophisticated, the phobias probably would have been laughed at, and the child perhaps bullied. Had the fears been indulged with kindness, they would have probably given way to other symptoms. The parents would then likely suppose that, with the disappearance of the original symptoms, the basis for them had also disappeared; actually, however, in such cases, the erstwhile phobias are generally replaced with new fears, equally elusive. Hans' phobia is indeed still frequently observed in children in its contemporary manifestations such as the fear of dogs or monsters, recurrent periods of nightmares, or exaggerated reactions to slight injuries which seem to represent to the troubled child a world of grave risks.

The reports which Hans' father submitted to Freud were careful and detailed; they contained more about Hans' conflict than Freud, in 1906, could have used. For instance, not only did Hans fear that he would be attacked in the street, but as evening came on he became increasingly nervous and wary: he sometimes expected to be the object of some injury. His nightmares show that he saw himself as a helpless victim. He confessed that large animals frightened him because he expected them to be violent toward him. As we have seen, Hans unconsciously associated them with his parents, especially with his father. Freud pointed out that this was bound to remind Hans of his own smallness and limitations, and thus make him more apprehensive. The father thought Hans must be affected specifically by how large his mother must appear, much as his son might regard him, too, as no less big than a horse. While Hans might well have imagined a penis as large as a horse's hidden somewhere in his mother (a child's common fantasy), would not his father's penis in fact by comparison with his own appear immense to the little boy? In the comparison Hans was bound to make, he could only be a loser.

Hans resorted to a game which Freud came to see many years later, in 1920, as a child's unconscious defensive device to overcome the fear of being attacked.* In play, Hans took the part of the creature who scared him. He played horse, bit his father, and pretended to threaten him. He also played horse master, whipping and teasing horses. In that role he had nothing to fear.

When Hans came into his parent's bedroom at night, this same process was at work. When he was questioned about his unannounced appearance and asked what he had in mind, he admitted he was thinking of shooting people dead with a gun. And he had his father, not his mother, in his sights. When he was ordered back to his own bed by his father with the threat, "Your fear of horses won't get better,"

* Anna Freud, in 1946, elaborated on her father's discovery, in her famous work, *The Ego and the Mechanisms of Defence* (New York: International Universities Press).

he countered with the bold reply, "I shall come in all the same, even if I am afraid."

Hans had a baby sister, Hanna, whom he also wished dead. He said, "I'd rather she weren't alive . . . I can't bear her screaming." One day when his father said Hanna had to be held when she was bathed or she would fall in the water, Hans added, "and die!" But as we have seen, Hans was troubled by these wishes and did not want his father to think him wicked. Burdened with anxiety as the boy clearly was, his suffering was nevertheless also as much a product of his aggressive aims, wishes, impulses and conduct.

The case of Little Hans was critical in Freud's amendment of his theory of the origins of anxiety; whereas he first thought that anxiety emerged as the surfeit of undischarged or rather accumulated excitation, he came to view it rather as a reaction *to a situation of danger.* In this case he showed that it was the boy's unconscious fear of castration which imposed severe, indeed crippling, restrictions on him. Anxiety became "a fear of danger actually impending or [one which] was judged to be a real one." [17] But Freud did not here include Hans' aggression, both in its conscious and unconscious aspects, as an intransigent source generating anxiety and thus constituting an inner wellspring of danger. Instead Freud considered the boy's "aggressive propensities to have found no outlet";[18] his sexual excitement had caused them to be restricted. "It was then the battle which we call his 'phobia' burst out." [19]

Freud asked what led to the transformation of Hans' childish longings and ambivalent wishes about his parents and infant sister into anxieties of clinical proportions. He was not able to say then whether it was the child's intellectual development or his emotional development which was not equal to the task of mastering his wishes, or if the aggressive impulses associated with the child's sexuality reaching a peak of excitement, made the boy become fearful and phobic. He concluded, "This question must be left open until fresh experience can come to our assistance." [20]

A possible clue to some of Freud's reluctance to entertain the idea of the independent role of aggression may be found in his remarks in 1908 on Adler's theory of the aggressive instincts. Referring to the Little Hans case, he wrote, "we seem to have produced a most striking piece of confirmation of Adler's view." [21] Nonetheless, he refused to give equal footing to a discrete and independent instinct of aggression "alongside of the familiar instincts of self-preservation and of sex." [22] Freud did not credit the defense of the self as giving rise to aggression independent from sexuality or that aggression had independence as an instinct. Perhaps Freud resisted altering his position to give aggression the independence he later came to consider because it may have meant coming to grips once again with Adler. He was loathe to do that. And in view of his acknowledged uncertainty and the obscurity of his theory of the instincts at that time, Freud may have thought the controversy would be an exercise in polemics with Adler, or it would mean that he would have to bring out new clinical evidence which Freud admitted he did not have. Freud was in no doubt about the validity of the evidence he had gathered. He held to what he had. But he refused to engage in suppositions on what future evidence there might be.

In the case of Hans, in certain respects, we often have only inference to draw upon. However, analogous clinical material suggests that phobic reactions which express a patient's sense of himself as a helpless victim of attack and injury, reveal the intensity of a wish-turned-threat. The wishes to be aggressive are disquieting intentions. This is to say that such wishes may be felt unconsciously to be of sufficient intensity to create a fearfulness of acting on them. The symptoms which follow are the phobias or dread of carrying out one's intentions. They arrest action to narrow limits. And to that extent the scope of aggressive actions is reduced. It spares those who otherwise might be attacked. Furthermore, by the unconscious process of attributing one's own wishes to others, the wish to be aggressive turns into a threat of being attacked. Both Hans' phobia by day and his nightmares during sleep, in which he viewed himself as victim, are to the point here. The aggression felt toward someone whom we value or who represents a value to us turns unconsciously against ourselves. We may become phobic, thus victimizing ourselves and effectively prohibiting aggression toward others. Moreover, such complex psychic responses do not originally develop with regard to strangers or those with whom we have an indifferent relationship, but instead to those we most love or value. For example, Hans' fears of horses originated with his conflicts in relation to his parents. His fears were displaced to form a phobia about certain animals. He dreaded the sight of horses and developed phobias about leaving his house fearing the confrontation. He was at first, of course, unaware that his intense fears and phobias derived from his unconscious conflicts in regard to his parents.

Hans became particularly aggressive when his self-esteem was in jeopardy. His play, more often than his direct conversation with his father, showed that aggression was as central to his inner life as his sexual conflicts. His fantasies emphasized the importance he gave to his father's position in the family, and the satisfaction he gained from the games in which he triumphed over him.[23] Hans enjoyed acts of violence which he would commit, such as biting his father playfully, then kissing him to undo his aggression toward him. He played he was a horse, bit his father much as he feared he himself might be bitten.[24] When he played that he was in his father's place, he often became aggressive, and when fears arose in conjunction with his being in such a role, he abandoned it and felt humiliated. When Hans' Oedipal wishes collapsed in failure, his self-esteem too was deeply compromised, giving way to violent destructive wishes. Some were aimed at his father, others extended to include his sister Hanna. But in the final analysis, he, and no one else, is the victim. He is obliged to remove himself from the dangerous scene. He turns his violence on himself, and phobic fear and immobilization are the direct result. Very fearful of attacks, that is of being a victim, he radically restricts himself. It spares him injury. The more he "heeds" his phobia the more restricted he is, and the less exposed. As he begins to give up his great ambition and with it his rivalry, the threat subsides and he is prepared to emerge from the family triangle to the safety of the next phase of a child's development, latency.*

---

* Actually, Hans was not a severely emotionally beset child. The circumstances which brought his parents and Freud together on his conflicts gave Hans a unique place in the annals of psychoanalysis. By clinical standards, the boy showed a common phobia. Its dynamics are usually not illuminated and it does not come to clinical notice until it persists, as often happens, by continuing into later periods. The child is either then treated or as probably more often occurs, he is laughed at or bullied. The symptoms are frequently driven into other forms, usually of an aggressive nature. The clinically well-known "counterphobias" are examples of such reactions. The neurotic reactions accommodate themselves to a degree and the individual may become fearless rather than fearful, bold rather than timid, and aggressive instead of fearing attacks. The counterphobias represent the powerful effort to deny the fears and dreads and at the same time effect an inflated self-assurance. The children who are often admired as fearless, performing feats of daring and driven to accomplishment, on closer scrutiny show that their fears and phobias were driven into their unconscious. Many acts of bravery and heroism as well as foolhardiness, on analysis, have revealed that they were manifest expressions of and reactions to fears. The war hero who at great risk to himself has saved a comrade, unconsciously rescued himself. Such acts are no less deserving of our admiration because the unconscious motivation for them has roots in the narcissistic need to save ourselves. The tendency to identify ourselves with our fellows does not stop when we see them suffer or in jeopardy, and if our altruism carries us to be charitable, are we not the better for it? "Use every man after his desert, and who should 'scape whipping?" [*Hamlet.* act II, scene 2.]

From the time that Freud described the severe loss in self-esteem a child suffers as the inevitable outcome of the Oedipal rivalry, the specific nature of the emotional conflicts which issue from what can only be termed a debacle, from the child's point of view, have not received the systematic attention and delineation they deserve. Psychoanalysts have paid notice only in passing to the fact that the child's most serious ambition is doomed from the outset, and that this thwarted ambition becomes associated with an aggressive reaction.

As a child moves into the next period of his emotional development, which Freud designated the latency period, he takes with him his diminished self-esteem and wounded pride, but he also carries along his aggressiveness to be put to the service of reparation. And in Hans' case, for example, instead of finding this aggression turned in on himself as before, we would expect that in the new circumstances of school and in new friendships with *boys his own age* he would successfully deploy his ambition and aggression in more "realistic" rivalries and competitions. Freed from the perilously dependent ties of family intimacy and from the charged singularity it promotes in a child, the latency period allows a broader experience in which the mastery of the environment, the development of skills, and the formation of new relationships are called on to enhance the capacity for being a part of a group. Sexuality, at least in its more manifest forms, is somewhat in abeyance until the onset of puberty.

The thrust of aggression, which arises as a reaction to the special conflicts of one phase of a child's life and conveys him into the next, usually appears as merely a burst of activity. He seems to be propelled by his changing physical development, and while this may in part be true, this activity also shows a powerful "responsive" effort—to restore self-esteem.[25] The sense of limitation and narcissistic injury join to compel efforts at recovery. The need is great. Like a phoenix, from the ashes of the Oedipal misadventure, the child in latency emerges.

Nevertheless, when the narcissistic blow strikes too severely at a child's sense of worth, the aggression "released" often is not successfully employed in the new, sublimated goals of, say, technical competence, intellectual achievement or competitive sports. Rather than furnishing relief, aggression can also become entrenched in hostility. Under such conditions, many of the same achievements may appear to be acquired but they fail to raise self-esteem. Instead rage and violence are perpetuated. The child's accomplishments are notably egocentric and their social value to the child is sacrificed to the disquieting demands of an unremitting concern with self-esteem. I would like to demonstrate this by presenting, in some detail, the cases of two little girls, both of whom had to give up their childish self-concern too early, a process which generated an amount of hostility which could not be satisfactorily sublimated, only repressed.

A child's social experience calls constantly on his powers of accommodation. To make social adaptation possible, his natural egocentric aims must yield. Thus, Hans' father, with whom the boy wanted a good relationship, was a strong socializing force before which Hans' narcissism was modified. Sometimes, however, children younger than Hans are prematurely compelled to give up much of their quite natural egocentricity or to transcend the standards of infantile existence. As a result, they seem socially very mature and exceptionally poised. When the process of narcissistic gratification has been arrested, however, in favor of a relationship in which the child panders to the egocentric wishes of another—usually an adult the child needs desperately to please—such a child must early acquire an inner governance over his aggression. Social experience demands it.

Peggy, a three-and-a-half-year-old child, was enrolled by her mother in a kindergarten, under the falsified age of five years. The mother wanted a place to deposit her daughter each day in order to free herself, not for regular employment, but to work for political action. The child did not appear to be her alleged age, but the mother gave the plausible explanation that Peggy was somewhat immature.

Peggy had been left by her mother before. From the time she was two, she was often deposited with a variety of friends for long periods while her mother was engaged in her political activities, which, at times, took her away from the city. Both parents, in fact, went their separate ways, having divergent but not conflicting interests. They had no serious doubt Peggy would be well cared for, and thus they had little anxiety about leaving her. Furthermore, she did not seem troubled by their absences. Wherever she was left, she adapted herself quickly and well, often to the astonishment of others as well as her parents.

The child came to my attention when she was about four. At school she developed, or rather persisted in, tantrums whenever her performance of a task was other than excellent. No one had demanded perfection of her; it had become her own need. She had poor relations with other children, for she was as critical of them as she was of herself. It was on the teacher's insistence that the mother brought Peggy for treatment.

Peggy was a clever child who rapidly learned adult ways and adult games. She preferred the company of adults and only suffered other children with contempt. She spoke to me as though she were not a child. Often she was dressed like her mother whose miniskirts and long hair gave her the appearance of an overgrown child and Peggy, with similar hairdo and clothes, looked very much like a dwarfed adult.

At first she held herself aloof, with controlled, adultlike behavior. After many visits which invariably began with our playing adult card games she knew very well, she permitted herself to play with dolls. She was fearful of acting (in her word) "babyish" should she ever acknowledge the presence of toys in the room. Finally, when she occasionally allowed herself to play with a baby doll, she too became a "baby": a screaming, hungry, enraged child. The baby would not speak, nor would Peggy permit pretending that it could speak. Peggy, who ordinarily spoke with disarming sophistication, had no language that she would allow the baby, only screams. Nor was it possible to persuade her to have the baby give up its anger. There were episodes of going back to adult games such as gin rummy, Monopoly, poker, etc., but the return to play with dolls brought on the infant who over and over again behaved with the same rage. Once she threw herself into the spirit of it, Peggy played out with a passion a personal drama with the dolls, and she would stuff herself with candy and smear herself with it angrily. In her role as adult she rarely ate candy and was always fastidious.

In treatment she continued to insist on a clear distinction between what was make-believe or pretend—in other words fantasy—and what was real. She was eager to establish and to affirm that fantasy was of no account, not admissible, and that only what was "real" mattered. Only with great reluctance would she allow herself to develop fantasies, and she readily abandoned them with evident relief for a concern with what was merely factual. To her, fantasy meant giving way to impulses, losing control.

Katie, at the age of three, was brought for treatment by her mother, who reported that her child was very aggressive, had rages and nightmares. After a brief acquaintance, the father had disappeared; his whereabouts were unknown, and his daughter had never seen him. The mother and the child lived alone. From the time Katie began to walk, she was an independent child. Indeed her mother relied on her self-assurance, on her gregarious readiness to be friendly, and on her companionship. The mother confessed that for years she had had many fears and phobias, and that her child, as her steady companion, was able to give her the reassurance she required.

Katie often had nightmares and ran to her mother's bedside in fright—only to be turned aside angrily and ordered back to her own bed, whereupon she would then obediently leave. It was Katie who did the comforting on many occasions, and her mother depended upon it.

At nursery school, Katie became a problem because of her aggressiveness and her inability to play or have much of a relationship with other children, although adults found her very winning.

The first impression Katie created was a disconcerting one. She behaved so like an adult and yet she was so young, only three. Her voice was clear, she spoke with an easy command of a large vocabulary, and this in crisp, sophisticated sentences. In her play she had a singular interest and no other fantasy than to mock infants and very young children. On those occasions only, would she abandon herself to the stature and role of an infant. Her aim was single-minded: to expose babies as demeaned creatures. She would creep about on her hands and knees, giggle, throw articles about, and refer to the destructiveness of the small children she condemned. At those times, she would also lapse into fragments of infantile speech which she would then disparage.

Katie had one prevailing preoccupation: a story with many variations that she played out on several of her visits. The theme of the story was that a mother and a child were each afraid of the other; each feared the other would poison her. The story went on and on about the attempts of each to escape her fate. In the course of the play, Katie insisted that when a doll was killed, which often occurred, it was an absolute and irrevocable event—an insistence quite contrary to a child's usual play of casually undoing such an outcome.

Children when engaged in play about death, as a rule, are eager to revoke its finality.[26] Therefore, we find that much as a child may be playing at dealing out death, playing a return from it is no less common. Katie permitted no fantasy about real experiences and, like Peggy, she resisted any extension of one into the other. To undo the underlying intent or motives associated with killing or death, the girls resorted to insisting the reference to death or killing was "just play."

In the beginning, Katie denied that the fears repeatedly recounted in the story had any relation to her every day apprehensions or her nightmares. She held firmly to her notion that children were of little value, but that to be like an adult was ideal. What further separated a child from its mother was demonstrated when Katie demeaned and mocked babies, depicting them as demanding, furious at not having what they wanted, and helpless to fulfill their wishes, in contrast with the powerful, self-disciplined adults who seemed to get whatever they wanted.

Peggy and Katie are remarkably similar children. Each has a mother who demands precocity in social development. Despite the fact that Peggy's mother is often away and leaves her with virtual strangers whereas Katie's mother cannot separate herself from her child, a close tie binds mother and daughter in each case. The degree of intimacy which develops in both cases depends chiefly on the child; the mother makes no significant accommodation or contribution to it. The relationship is accomplished at the *cost* of the child's infantile wishes which are not eventually and largely abandoned—as normally happens when they are even moderately gratified. Instead, the chief result is that they are strongly repressed, that is, they are dealt with as prohibitions. Childishness emerged in these two little girls only when their rages seemingly were displaced onto young children or, for example, when Peggy showed she could not tolerate a less-than-perfect performance at school. The façade of precocity exhibited by both children (which in some respects was a real achievement of adaptation to the extraordinary conditions in which they lived) satisfied the infantile needs their mothers had ignored. Only with strangers or with other children who were, quite naturally, a threat to their costly accommodation, was the underlying vehemence vented: the contempt for infants and young children that Katie and Peggy both expressed was a confession that amounted to a self-attack. Childhood, in their manifest opinion, deserved abuse. But clearly these loud protests were a self-condemnation.

The cases of these two little girls illustrate the dynamic nature of a child's narcissism. When their value simply as children was ignored, the girls were thus demeaned. Each played out the childish needs which had been denied her; and even at that young age, self-attacks and self-hatred issued as reactions which represented the child's notions of the mother's judgment. At such an early period of emotional development, self-censure is a prematurely acquired characteristic. It appears as social precocity and is achieved at the cost of impairment or injury to self-esteem, with the consequent mobilization of aggression in the child who feels "devalued." The intensity of rages, uncontrollable violence and nightmares such as these children experienced neither promotes nor serves recovery from the narcissistic injury. The aggression which thus materializes when taking oneself as the object of contempt fosters further self-restraint. The children, as a result of the intense and particular relationship these mothers have demanded of them, are in no family triangle from which to break out. On the contrary, because of the intimate dependence each of these children has had on her mother, the aggression released here makes relationships even more precarious. Thus, the probability of criticism for aggression from oneself and hence the expectation of it from others is great. And, as we have seen here, self-esteem is in greater jeopardy as the need for it intensifies.

After many months of often tediously repetitious treatment sessions with each child, changes occurred. The mock adult games were replaced by more periods of doll play in which the contemptible baby was often on stage, a creature of excessive egocentric demands. Whether the baby was portrayed to be stupid or hungry, to soil, or to be pitifully inept and, therefore, abused, its exclusive concern was with its appetites and their gratification. In this doll play the differences between Peggy and Katie were negligible. The little girls' persistnt condemnation of babies ruled out any legitimate needs; and the degree of control required of an infant reflected the stringent demands of their own mothers. Their compliance was the main line of defense against the prevalent fear of being abandoned and the risk of being destroyed. My pleas on behalf of the baby, and my arguments that caring for a baby's needs gives it a sense of goodness and worth and reduces its fears, were finally heard—although not without many disclaimers on each little girl's part and immeasurable rulings against the baby's case. As the underlying value of a child gradually became established, however, first Peggy and later Katie outwardly diminished their aggression. The clinical results were good.

Neither of these two children gave up their precocity nor their adultlike conduct. They could not be expected to. The enormous narcissistic value invested in maintaining such conduct, supported as it was by their mothers, would remain. Nevertheless, their developing tolerance of infantile and childish wishes assured me that there would be for them less need for aggression and therefore less self-censure. Time and development are on the side of precocity and adult conduct. Children like Peggy and Katie, as they actually become adult, will be more divided from early childhood wishes than is usually the case.

We all carry our childhood with us. In the face of anxiety, we are inclined to return to its falsely remembered security and with it attempt to bridge the distance that separates us from our earliest years.

We long for the self-oriented gratifications of young childhood with its denials of conflicts, and an assumed freedom from fear or supposed inhibition. Normally, recovery from such brief excursions into infantilism is easy. In the case of Peggy and Katie, however, such regressive gaps are precariously bridged. Their precocious early development rests on strong prohibitions formed against indulgence in anxiety-laden childlike behavior. Tangible accomplishments, through industry and activity, inordinately prized, are achievements by which self-esteem is won. Paradoxically, the self is valued only for what one can accomplish. It is the only measure of worth when relationships cannot furnish it.

The examples of Peggy and Katie show that the course of childhood narcissism, when not significantly modified, advances from one period of emotional development to become increasingly resistant to influence. In studies of adult life, we find similar cases in which narcissism has continued unaltered from the earliest years. Conveyed thus from childhood, narcissism gives to adult character a childlike egocentric quality which serves in times of stress more than any other element to bolster self-esteem. Peggy and Katie were helped considerably by it in their need to maintain the strictness with which they held in check their deeply seated infantile aims. As they demonstrated, only by achievements and not through relationships was their worth established. Infants, pathetically lacking in achievement or accomplishment, in the little girls' view, were correspondingly worthless. Infancy was thus a dangerous condition. Ostensibly, they removed themselves from it.

The two girls are in an earlier phase of development than Hans. Like them, he was obliged to give up some of his egocentric wishes for the sake of a continuing dependent and important relationship with his parents. But unlike him, they gained no real independence as a result. Their fate was to remain caught in an exclusive relationship with their mothers which dictated that only performance gave value. Their relationship with others, as in the case of Peggy, whose father was fond of her, must remain at a superficial level. The girls enjoyed the admiration their maturity earned them. But it was mere veneer; the underlying infantile aims and demands were not relinquished. They were repressed. They represent, as each child shows, a devalued, demeaned self, bound to infantilism which must be denied and from which rage generates and gives vent to destructiveness and violence. In their view, the ideal of being like an adult meant extending their egocentricity simply to a larger scale. It obliged them to behave and perform as though they were adults. In a sense, the girls succeeded: Peggy and Katie were pseudo-adults.

Helene Deutsch in a classic psychoanalytic work, published originally in 1942 and revised in 1965, demonstrated the existence of a form of emotional disorder to which she gave a name that every student of psychoanalysis is now acquainted with—the "as if" personality. She explained that her only reason for "using a label so unoriginal" was "that every attempt to understand the way of feeling and manner of life of this type forces on the observer the inescapable impression that the individual's whole relationship to life has something about it which is lacking in genuineness and yet outwardly runs along 'as if' it were complete." [27] The "as if" personality is the matured form of the emotional disorder with which Peggy and Katie were threatened. It is too soon to know how effective the treatment was of the two little girls in preventing the development of the "as if" characteristics described by Helene Deutsch.

The first impression these people make is of their being completely normal. They are often intellectually gifted and may bring great understanding to intellectual and emotional problems. And while they frequently pursue creative kinds of work, the result is likely to be a skillful imitation lacking the slightest trace of originality. Their relationships are often intense and may even give the clear signs of friendship, love, sympathy and understanding; "but even the layman soon perceives something strange and raises questions he cannot answer." [28] It is soon evident to the analyst that the relationships lack warmth, that the expressions of emotions are formal, and that inner experiences are shallow. The differences between these empty forms and what others may experience under similar conditions escape such people. The apparently normal relationship to the world, while not similar, corresponds to a child's early years of imitative behavior or mimicry. And the readiness to mold oneself in accordance with what others may think or feel appears to suggest an accommodation or adaptation to others. It is in fact, however, a superficial plasticity which characteristically lacks discrimination. One person may be readily exchanged for a new one and no deep sense of loss is experienced. There is also a constant search for guidelines of behavior which is not confined to the close scrutiny of the conduct of others. The search may extend to an overliteral interpretation and uncritical devotion to manuals on how to entertain properly, control anger, influence people, or raise children. Dependence on fashion magazines for ideas on how to dress is extreme; and in one instance, a patient followed a stranger in the street and purchased often inappropriate garments in a mood of identification with the unknown model. Often articles from newspapers on the conduct of marital relations are saved for use as instruction in the conduct of married life. Men in their daily occupations follow similar imitative patterns: perhaps in their choice of language or even the conscientious use of abilities, and a strict adherence to conventional thinking which abhors critical judgment and which at bottom utterly lacks individual distinction.

The need of the "as if" character is not to find ways to adapt to the behavior of others but rather to discover what conduct to follow. The importance of relationships is for the guidance others furnish; their value is otherwise limited. A subordination to the wishes and needs of others in the "as if" personality does not take place as normally occurs. Ordinarily, accommodations to our friends challenges one's individual narcissism to yield and even to recognize another's need and to wish to satisfy it. The resistance of the "as if" person to the demands of intimacy, by a manifest compliance and a passive conformity with often a slavish imitation of devotion and identification, masks a deep unconscious hostility. It is associated with the threat to the "narcissist" to quit some egocentricity that a real relationship poses. The unconscious resistance to make such sacrifices generates hostility. It is as hidden from oneself as it is from others. These "abnormal" distorted personalities do not belong among the commonly accepted forms of neurosis, and they are too well adjusted to reality to be called psychotic.[29] The same may be said for children like Peggy and Katie. As pseudo-adults, they are often rewarded for remarkable achievement in adaptation to their circumstances. As a result the deeper implications of their precocity usually go unrecognized.

To give up infantile aims for mature ones does not rest so much on graduation from childish to sophisticated tastes as is commonly supposed. Instead, it depends upon developing a value invested in satisfying someone else. As we acquire a recognition of the narcissistic need in others, our wish to meet it will not evoke childish fears of being ourselves deprived. The gratification of others sustains and often enhances self-esteem—but it is a process the infantile character does not engage in and from which the "as if" person is excluded.

Infantile wishes endlessly press hard to be satisfied. Their resistance to being either relinquished or suppressed brings out aggression. To govern it, inhibitions and harsh controls unconsciously form. And, as we have learned from little Hans and the two girls, bringing aggression under the rule of defenses finds its reward in self-esteem.

This principle emerges very early. In their brief existence, the two girls clearly show that their prematurely advanced ego development is aimed, among other functions, at the strict rule of their aggression. These children are not simply frustrated infants. Their needs as well as their "natural" infantile reactions to frustration (including rage and violence), having no currency, earn them rejection and thus further increase their fury. Their pseudo-adult behavior is the result of a precocious ego development, reflecting the effort to govern outbreaks of aggression and to promote the restoration of a good self-opinion.

One mother abandons her child in order to pursue her own personal aims; the child "complies" with her by repressing her rage and her fears of being utterly abandoned. Just the opposite, the second mother needs her child as a constant companion whose presence mitigates the intensity of her fears; her child must repress her own fears in order to comfort the mother. Each mother serves herself and, as a model, reinforces the child's egocentricity. As the mother's demands force the daughter to yield to the mother's narcissism, the child's emotional development is deeply affected. The modification of childish narcissism, which is normally achieved as its demands are shaped through complementary or mutual relationships, is no longer possible. In each of our cases, the mother's influence was so demanding that it produced, in the child, a denial of what she was.

The endless conflicts generated by narcissism are by no means confined to childhood. They give shape to a paradox which persists throughout life, pressing us to reach beyond our grasp and to conceal from ourselves the truth of our lot. Our lifelong intention is no mere pursuit of pleasure or even simply survival. As slaves to the imperishable fantasies of narcissism, we endlessly seek to close the distance between our wishes and our deserts. Even a highly successful and publicly recognized life does not release the victim.

For instance, in the mature individual we find: a scientist in his mid-forties holding a virtually unbroken record of academic achievement, one beginning in childhood. He would be hard-pressed to recall his many rewards and the numerous occasions of public recognition of his accomplishments. Furthermore, in school and college he had won distinction as an athlete, and as a writer. His life work was acknowledged to be important. In short, he was a man who had cultivated his generous endowments and reaped rich rewards. He was, however, unable to free himself of what he knew to be an irrational conviction of worthlessness and a sense of an uncertain, hazardous future. He would say of himself that he was a transient and that he had not much time in which to prove his value.

As a child, this man's outstanding abilities had gained early attention. He was rapidly singled out as exceptional and his precocity was encouraged. However, this remarkable endowment of intelligence and competence was exploited by his extremely egocentric mother. She remorselessly goaded her son to perform and excel. His childish wishes to please each of his parents seemed inexhaustible. His father's favor was easily gained; he was a prominent and successful man who was committed to his wife's service from the moment he left his desk. And his son's aims, too, were regularly sacrificed to the mother's ambition and caprice. While the boy took great pleasure in the prizes and medals he won, like his father he laid what he gained at his mother's feet. Her demands were exorbitant. Dissatisfied, often over a trifling disappointment, her rages went on until everyone in the house capitulated. She was a narcissistic despot.

"It was a climate of giving in for the sake of mother. I did a slow burn. I was angry, rebellious, and still had to constantly sacrifice for her. The rages I'd have made me guilty and bad. When my anger and resentment came out, I would think of myself as unloving, ungenerous and undesirable—worthless. I just felt I didn't belong. I knew I was a source of pain and trouble, renegade and no good. I had to give things up for her sake. What I did for her reduced me. I can give and be loving but only if the other person values my sacrifice. I get angry when I think of it. I got no compensation for my sacrifice.

"There are two sources of feeling worthless. One is the way you are treated. The other is the way you feel. Serving without reward, I just get furious. I see myself as angry and I see myself as hurtful. If I don't serve my mother, I am doing evil. That way I can generate my own lack of worth. And so long as I serve her, I get deeper and deeper in debt. It got so that my only sense of worth to myself was when I served her wishes. I recall her reminiscences about me as a child. What a good mother she thought herself—by *my* achievements! If sometimes the results were not so good, I was letting her down. It was my fault and I was bad. Even now, if I serve others, as I do, I devalue myself. Then the whole thing about being angry begins and I feel worthless. But if I don't do this, and serve myself, I am too much like my mother, who does as she pleases, and I don't like myself for that either. Now with my own life, far from my parents, I am still the same way.

"I must work to prove my worth. I have an obligation to leave behind no trail of time wasted. I must feel worthwhile. I recall a vague but definite memory that I wanted to run away from home. I wanted to go where I could do a great work—it was not any more than a wish to enjoy pride in myself. It would relieve feeling very hurt. I remember my mother saying to me, 'I really don't need you.' She said it so many times and in so many ways. And I still feel the hurt. I think to myself, why should anyone have any interest in me? I'm not a very interesting person. What I have done others could do. I focus on what critics would say, not on the praise I get. The feelings about myself are flat. When I get a medal, I say to myself, 'Who, me?' I thought making myself valued would get me out of this. It was the emphasis on what I could do that I hoped would be it—but it's really being worthwhile to others that works. And somehow I can't believe or be convinced that this is possible.

"A recent experience was when I just recovered from almost losing my temper. It was as near as I ever got to openly being angry. I went to a meeting and I was placed inadvertently off somewhere. It showed, I felt, disregard or disrepect for me. I knew the actual circumstances were not important, and that it was because of some accident in the arrangements. But I began to feel very upset. I thought, I don't want to know who treated me with such ignominy. It's a fantasy about myself that I don't want confirmed. I want to think it was just an accident, a mistake, and that it was not purposeful. I don't want to entertain the idea it was anything but an accident. When I am not acknowledged, certified as worthy, I feel I am nothing. When I am treated as no good, isn't it confirmation that I am inferior? I can't stand that. It causes me to rage.

"It's a sad state when someone so gifted gets abused by a cruel world. It's my due to be rewarded. But actually the most private thought I have is that I really deserve nothing. I am miserable at that. I hate myself. I then do to myself what others do to me or what they should do. I demean myself. It's safer somehow, and gratifying, and compelling. As such a person, no demands are placed on me. But I can't like myself. How to get self-esteem without being aggressive—that's the dilemma!"

This scientist's conflicts are easily identifiable clinically. His underlying incestuous childhood wishes are plain in his need to win his mother and in his unconscious defense of detesting domineering women (whom he succeeded in avoiding since he left home as a youth). He is not married. He remains aloof from very intimate relations. But as he is socially attractive, he is sought after and enjoys a circle of friends. Since his work absorbs his interests and brings its rewards, the need for intimacy is not pressing; his longings for a family recur from time to time and he then becomes saddened at the limitations on his life that such wishes bring out. But if we confine ourselves to this narrow, conventional psychoanalytic explanation of his difficulties, we restrict our understanding of him. In some respects he is like the two little girls. He too was a precocious child, and like them, his fury lay buried under real accomplishments.

The essential development in young children of close and loving relationships, if they are to grow up to be convinced of their own worth, will not be realized so long as prizes are awarded for performance, rather than to the person himself. In family circumstances such as these, the child must establish his self-esteem almost entirely through his accomplishments. When, in turn, this condition coincides with the natural desire of any child to master his ever larger social and physical world and with the burgeoning of his maturing narcissism, he will surely find himself handicapped in later life by an unquenchable thirst for great and conspicuous achievement. The ordinary contentment that men derive from the conviction of simply being liked will be denied him.

When a child attaches importance to others, his natural egotism yields, as it must; and his narcissism does not remain exclusively focused on himself. In the cases of Peggy and Katie, and the scientist, this failed to happen. Furthermore, the scientist's suffering shows that despite his formidable achievements and his earnest engagement in the service of others, the struggle to establish for himself his own worth eludes him. This highly talented, articulate and eminently successful man remains a victim of his mother's tyranny; he also was goaded by it to achievement. Her failure to support his development for its own sake formed in him the conviction that he was himself of little consequence, and an abiding deep resentment of this—and of her. Only performance and excellence mattered. This view of himself is among his earliest and latest reflections; without doubt, it propelled him to exert his gifts so as to find relief from the oppressive burden he perpetually tried to dislodge by winning honor. Yet his most successful projects, as well as his most intimate relationships, are blighted by the obsessive intrusion of this concern with his worth—and a disbelief in it. The vain but unaltered expectation, dating from early childhood, is that perhaps achievements will accomplish what an impoverished relationship failed to do—the nourishment of self-esteem.

He could not see, until after many hours of analysis, that his feelings of worthlessness were outside the context of his intellectual and professional merit and that they referred rather to his relationships in which his worth did not rest on performance. They alone could have convinced him of his value had he not been certain that only by his achievements could his worth be permanently established.

His analysis revealed how deeply resentful this sense of valuelessness made him feel. Because his work often failed to relieve him of his bitterness, that, too, became a focus of his anger. His memory of anger was one of his earliest recollections. In his thoughts, obsessively, *he* was the victim of his attacks. As a child when he fought with other boys, he was often winning and would stop the fighting and be self-critical. His claim to feeling unworthy was unshakable. There is a parallel in the two little girls who play at assaulting and mocking infants and infantile conduct. They were unwittingly depicting themselves as objects of abuse and hate. They had become, as all small children, identified with their mothers—in this instance women who did not tolerate childishness because it conflicted with their own narcissism. Peggy and Katie naturally followed suit.

The process of identification with one's mother is normal enough. But when she is herself too childishly self-serving, a serious conflict arises in the child. The child's own natural narcissism is opposed by the mother's; the child adopts (through identification) the mother's attitude. It means to become as narcissistic as she. And also as intolerant of it in others as she. The internal or unconscious struggle in the child is the conflict between self-concern coupled with aggression to assert it and a strong self-condemnation of it.

The scientist had that experience. His feeling worthless, while turning him to constant, even at times to feverish, production, also generated great hostility. Much as he held his mother accountable for this (and it should be pointed out that he was only somewhat less angry with his father for failing to rescue him from her), his aggression, like the girls', was not directed chiefly at his parents but at himself. Similarly, little Hans, when threatened with the risk of being "put down" or demeaned, defended his egoistic aims by becoming aggressive, even though in his case the cause was his own extravagant narcissistic wish to replace his father. He then became fearful and phobic. These manifestations of dreading an attack, from the one toward whom he himself held destructive aims, in effect made him his own victim. His self-begotten ambitions which entailed his being aggressive and destructive were intolerable. He unconsciously dissociated himself from them. It occurs by way of attributing the violent intentions to his father or the symbolic representation of him, the horses who would bite the boy. With this development the child feared being hurt, became anxious over what unforeseen might happen and from which the inhibitions issued.

We thus find in little Hans, as in the others, that the development of fears, phobias, anxieties and inhibitions are functional. They effect both a powerful curb on aggression and on the other hand a strong incentive to employ it.

Freud thought that the transformation from, and the surrender of, an existence devoted to serving oneself, to one directed to include the needs of others came by way of the only erotic relationships which inevitably develop. The powerful effect of gratification that the child derives held Freud's attention. But the child's dependence on others and the satisfaction they furnish him does not signify relinquishing some of his narcissism for them, as we might suppose and as psychoanalysts have long thought occurs. Though it is plain that from the beginning a child is committed to others, the enormous value accorded them is for their service and its significance to his egocentric aims. From this nucleus of value, the formation of a relationship takes shape in which others gain their early importance. Their value to him, when he is less dependent on his egocentric aims, comes as a later development. However, despite its often unrecognizable subsequent modification, the deep narcissistic attachment to parents remains. In the unconscious fantasy of orphans and foundlings, another facet of this is revealed. Regardless of the circumstances, they carry a deep resentment at having been left or abandoned. It puts their own worth in question. The conflicts over it extend to include the surrogates or adoptive parents and often may affect the nature of all relationships throughout life. In another chapter, the case of a young man suffering amnesia is illustrative.

From serving oneself to acquiring altruistic aims directed toward the needs of others represents an important development in narcissism since aggressiveness seems then to be relinquished. This observation led Freud and others to suppose it meant also that some modification in the so-called aggressive instincts had been achieved. However, when we withdraw the value we may have placed in another, as well as when we feel ourselves humbled, study shows that aggression in all its violence may erupt.[30] The changes observed, we may conclude therefore, are only apparent. Of central importance is the demonstrably plain fact that while the modification in narcissism is achieved, its proneness to injuries remains and tends to give it a highly unstable character. The result is that a readiness to be aggressive quickly mobilizes. Humbled by others, we are likely to attack them when we ourselves fail.

The turn from egoism to altruism, as Freud called the development from instinctual life to a social existence, is only in part induced by the social and cultural environment, i.e. by "external compulsion." [31] The influences, which come to modify the primary condition in human experience, are quickly and decisively operative. But in addition to these external influences there exists an inner self-transforming process. It is no less forceful. The compelling need for social and altruistic transformation is indeed rapidly shaped in each individual. The human need for a social life—to form relationships with others, and to be valued by them to whom, in turn, one gives importance—is probably the strongest civilizing influence of all.

It is the company of others which civilizes us. From infancy the lifelong need of a relationship compels us constantly to forego some of our aggression. The human child is given some measure of relief by those caring adults upon whom he depends for his often extravagant needs, wishes and impulses pressing for gratification, and the route of his "adaptation" is thus laid out. As a child's natural demands begin to be satisfied, his enjoyment is the incentive which promotes the needed relationship. A child's aspirations, like his appetites, are neither moderate nor modest. He plainly shows, moreover, how little he either aims, has the initiative, or is in fact able, to govern his wishes when they are not fulfilled or to restrain the aggression which often issues from dissatisfaction. His resistance to learning to limit himself or to accept the disciplining of his aggression is as notorious as his incapacity to curb his appetites. Thus, the child must begin the long process of acknowledging his limitations and accommodating himself to them, modifying his aggression into the development of skills which will extend his grasp, and transforming the aggression issuing from unfulfilled wishes into achievements which have at least some social utility. The rewards of this chastening experience commence only with his relationship (at first dependent) to and with others through whom satisfaction may be realized. A child's capacity for self-fulfillment is small indeed—and in irksome contrast with the magnitude of his needs and demands. The excessive gratification or easy indulgence of a child's wishes, however rewarding to him momentarily, serves to appease his narcissistic needs; but in doing so, paradoxically it intensifies them. A child's narcissism—in a broader sense, his egocentricity—is not merely to be satisfied. It is something to be changed. The more narcissism is fulfilled and remains unmodified, the more absolutely its demands become an entrenched resistance to social adaptation.

Too little attention has been paid to the fact that as a child's satisfaction is assured his narcissism is supported. More notice is given to the child's negative reactions to frustration, to the fury at being deprived and the aggression thus loosened, than to the positive significance to him when he is indulged or pandered to. This is no argument for Spartan austerity and deprivation in child rearing. I do not wish to make a virtue of hardship, for it is generally known that the unremitting experience of emotional privation directly imparts a quality of hardened aggression. What has not been fully appreciated, however, is that the rapaciousness stemming from circumstances of deprivation or denial extends beyond mere physical need into the psychological realm of self-esteem. Early associations of deprivation combined with a lowered self-esteem are the stuff from which a child's aggression emanates.

In human experience, deprivation—regardless of its source or cause—is not sheer frustration. Whether it evokes an elaborate or simple reaction, that reaction includes feelings of damaged worth. It is a narcissistic injury. In the years of early childhood, when a sense of self-esteem is newly unfolding, deprivation of whatever sort, even in a dream or a fantasy unfulfilled, may be consciously experienced as a loss or lowering of self-esteem, and aggression inevitably issues in some form.

The paradox is that the indulged child tolerates any deprivation poorly and is affected by it even more severely than one who has been less generously cared for. The more narcissism is indiscriminately satisfied, the less strain it bears. As the egocentric character of early childhood is extended through excessive gratification, it shows as an unconscious resistance to change with less and less effort at accommodation to others. The ordinary search for satisfaction or pleasure is not necessarily toward a fuller indulgence, although that may be present, as it is a hardening lack of compromise. And, since the company of others requires narcissism to yield to a social commitment—

that is, to be less self-oriented—it simply brings on conflicts and re-sistance to the sacrifice of having to abandon any narcissistic aims.

Narcissism, like its defense, aggression, depends upon others for its early discipline. A child left to his own devices may precociously acquire some seeming governance over his own impulses. But, as we have seen in the illustrative cases of Peggy and Katie above, these two children unconsciously repressed and retained—virtually unmodified —their underlying narcissistic infantilism. Openly, they complied with their mothers' immediate demands and expectations, while within themselves they did not relinquish either their egocentric aims or the readiness to implement them with force. Children who, for whatever reasons, are unable to alter their child's narcissism at the same time fail to develop the corresponding defenses against the variety of forms their aggression may take. Their social relationships founder, some-times disastrously. Although in other respects they may succeed in turning egoism unconsciously to some constructive, albeit self-serving, purpose and work industriously to accomplish such purposes, it is the *modification of the egocentric aims themselves,* together with curb-ing their implementation, which is an essential process in the social experience of growing children, not to mention grown men and women. In short, both narcissism and the aggression which is found in us to be intimately associated with it have a role in human affairs, with no analogy in animal life.

Chapter III

The Darwinian Legacy

Extending one's self-esteem to others, by valuing them in some measure as oneself, allows men to live together in a compatible social order. It also creates some of our deepest conflicts. Efforts to reconcile hedonistic self-interest and "sociability" have a history as long as the history of philosophy itself. But, it took Darwin's discoveries in the nineteenth century to put this conflict into a new "scientific" framework, and, for many, this resolved the issue once and for all. The question of the legitimacy of man's individual pursuit of pleasure—as a doctrine of human conduct—is central to moral theory and moral precepts, thus to both philosophy and ethics. The developing scientific scrutiny of this problem over the last two hundred years, however, has tended to remove the subject of hedonism from its traditional position in moral philosophy and bring it into the sphere of psychological inquiry.

The hedonistic elements in everyday life gained formal recognition in the vigorous doctrinal debates on humanitarian ethics which engaged eighteenth- and especially nineteenth-century theology—and took on an importance they were not henceforth to lose. In psychological conceptualization, hedonism developed into an important motivation theory. It held that human action is motivated by the "pursuit of happiness"—or, in other words, self-interest, guided by the aim of seeking pleasure and avoiding pain. And the theory found support among a powerful array of eminent moral philosophers—Hobbes, Hume, the Mills and Spencer.[1] The enormous impact of Darwin's theory of evolution was here, as elsewhere, to enliven the old polemics with the introduction of a radically deepened scientific perspective.

In the light of Darwin's ideas, it seemed that *all* behavior might now be reduced to a single simple formula: that pleasure attracts and pain repels. The discovery that the pain/pleasure concept was not exclusively applicable to human behavior but extended "downward" to include the lowest order of living creatures was as astounding as it was novel. It exposed an alleged higher order of emotional complexity in man as a myth. A conclusive link between man and all other forms of life seemed forged. The philosophical question of man's relationship to his fellow creatures had heretofore reached an impasse unsurmounted by the best conceptual reasoning. But, once the issue became a scientific one, the impasse seemed to vanish overnight.

The Origin of Species was published in 1859, and with it the empirical foundation of the stunning concept of the elementary continuity in all animal life was firmly established. The significant psychological implication of this was the expectation that as biological investigation revealed the course of man's evolutionary descent from animals, similarly studies of animal *behavior* would reflect the evolution of human *conduct.* This notion was a powerful impetus in launching the new research in behavior in the final decades of the nineteenth century. Under the radical and powerful influence of Darwin's discoveries, the dynamic psychologists dissociated themselves from what had become (in moral philosophy and pragmatic psychology) the tyranny of hedonism as an explanation of human motivation. In addition, then, to man's biological inheritance from animal ancestors, the further and far-reaching possibility that this evolutionary continuity might apply equally to the mind was inescapable. Darwin himself believed this to be the case and furnished his evidence in *The Expression of the Emotions in Man and Animals* (1872).[2] It was in this work, together with the work of others, notably Spencer (whom Darwin credited with having a similar interest in the emotional life), that the evolutionary doctrine was extended to the mind.

Beginning nearly a century ago and continuing into the present, laboratory and field studies have appeared in profusion, seeking to prove unequivocally that the behavior of certain insects, birds and fish, not to mention mammals, is parallel to and, in some instances, even identical with, human conduct. By the early decades of the twentieth century the distinction between animal and human motivation had been transformed into a continuity of the mind on an evolutionary scale in which there is, presumably, no missing link. American psychology, still very much in its infancy, enthusiastically embraced the Darwinian point of view. As Edwin Boring puts it, "American psychology . . . inherited its physical body from German exerimentalism, but it had got its mind from Darwin."[3]

In recent decades, the employment of ever more complex technological innovations, coupled in some instances with cybernetic theory and the sophisticated use of electronics, has further invigorated experimental psychology. A persistent discrepancy between method (or rather "technology") and theory, however, has resulted in an all too often overweening emphasis on research design and a serious neglect in the area of careful conceptual reformulation. For example, experiments designed to measure behavioral responses to punishment or deprivation, to observe and test "extinction-induced" aggression, to locate and measure self-esteem[4] are models of research in psychology; but as neither new nor original concepts of human motivation have issued from such work, they remain merely the ingenious application of new technological mastery to theories of behaviorism conceived nearly a century ago. And, at present, there are few indications that experimental psychology is likely to change its direction.

The main course of psychology has flowed from the all-embracing proposition that motivation is circumscribed by the search for reward and the avoidance of pain, and that all organisms follow the paths of least resistance and learned responses in the direction of the greatest advantage. Behavior then appears to be primarily reaction to circumstances, governed by the ruling principle of reward versus deprivation. The behavioral scientist in the laboratory saw that his task was to learn what conditions affect our perceptions and what responses are conditioned by our experiences. Thus, he was free to rule out the direct study of man's motives—a subject, it was claimed, still the more appropriate concern of those whose province was ethics or philosophy. And furthermore, with this view—and only with this view—could psychology dispense with the nettlesome question of the unconscious and its stubborn, protean contents, and maintain its claim to be a "true" science of the mind.

Psychology, launched on this scientific course, continued to gather momentum in the last decades of the nineteenth century. Its legitimacy as an intellectual discipline was substantiated by the popularity of animal experiments and laboratory studies of perception, sensation and artificially isolated partial aspects of behavior. A psychology no longer bound to philosophy and theology, nor to the so-called introspective method of investigation which was unsuited to quantification and conventional measurements, seemed to constitute a new and potentially enlightening discipline safely beyond the reach of controversy. It no longer depended, as it once had, on the intellectual authority of such famous researchers as Spencer, Helmholz, Weber and Fechner. Psychology was in a sense depersonalized; self-scrutiny and the examination, study and analysis of others' motivation were discredited as the methodological core of the discipline. A new freedom and independence from insoluble subjective dilemmas and ideological or moral argument seemed possible, and the experience of it was exhilarating.

The milieu and the mood of experimental psychology—the measurement of intelligence with elaborate *a priori* tests; the focus on psycho-physiology by means of observing sensation, perception and, in the last decade, cognition; and the use of statistical methods of correlation*—were remote indeed from the psychology of everyday life. The psychological phenomena reproducible and observable in the laboratory were a far cry from the "human condition." In Boring's words, "Empiricism had become experimentalism." [5] Indeed, in the latter nineteenth and well into the twentieth century, illuminating insight into both the conflict at the core of human nature and the nature of human conflict issued more from the evocative pen of the artist than from the laboratory psychologist's experimental precision. Ibsen's *Hedda Gabler* and *A Doll's House,* Flaubert's *Madame Bovary* and Jane Austen's *Emma* were profound expositions of the psychology of women. Dostoevsky's *Crime and Punishment* and the philosophy of Nietzsche, together with Freud's monumental *Interpretation of Dreams*—the "royal road" to the unconscious—conclusively challenged the utilitarian pain/pleasure calculus and exposed it for the oversimplification that it was.

Such works clearly revealed a grasp of the universal complexity of human experience which went well beyond the simplistic tenets of contemporary religious doctrine and indeed rivaled the classic dramatic literature of Sophocles, Shakespeare or Molière. Ibsen showed a more profound understanding of the tension between individual and society than his contemporary, Professor Emil Kraeplin, a renowned teacher of clinical psychiatry who influenced an entire generation of medical students. Zola and Proust were as frank as Krafft-Ebing about man's sexual longings—and more enlightening. A psychology of human motivation was coming into view, but not on the experimentalists' horizon. There was no hint that a revolution was about to break in either the crude animal research of the time or the ever more rigorously refined laboratory work of the behaviorists.

Since the turn of the century, animal research has reflected an in-

---

* First introduced in 1886 by the genius of Sir Francis Galton, a pioneer in the new psychology.

creasing ingenuity, but, it is based on technological rather than conceptual advances. And behaviorists have come to regard animal behavior as merely a simplified version of human conduct, the complexity of which they do not deny. On the other hand, they have assumed that as animal research became more carefully differentiated, the task of understanding the psychology of man would at the same time be simplified; that is, through the application of technically more sophisticated methodology borrowed from animal study, the intricacies of human psychology might finally be clarified. This concept, which Boring dubbed "one of the newer faiths of behaviorism," [6] still has great currency among experimental psychologists who cling to the belief that the range and power of man's abilities can be measured by his adaptive or discriminatory performances in a laboratory setting.

Consequently, behavioral psychologists, operating with this "faith," designed research in which some item of human behavior is isolated for study. In recent years the conduct of the young child has been selected. It was all too easily assumed that a child's behavior would somehow be of a more "elementary" form than an adult's—corresponding to his developmental immaturity. And further, this lower order of complexity, it was assumed, would more closely approximate that of a young animal. Hence, the findings in the study of the young creature's behavior, it was anticipated, would be analogous, and indeed even "applicable," to the human infant.

Harry Harlow, in his presidential address to the American Psychological Association Congress in 1958,[7] elaborated on these assumptions in describing the great difficulties he encountered in the use of human beings, especially young children, as research subjects:

By the time the human infant's motor responses can be precisely measured, the antecedent determining conditions cannot be defined, having been lost in a jumble and jungle of confounded variables.

Many of these difficulties can be resolved by the use of the neonatal and infant macaque monkeys as the subject for the analysis of basic affectional variables. . . . The macaque infant differs from the human in that the monkey is more mature at birth and grows more rapidly; but the basic responses relating to affection, including nursing, contact, clinging, and even visual and auditory exploration, exhibit no fundamental differences between the two species. Even the development of perception, fear, frustration and learning capability follows very similar sequences in rhesus monkeys and human children.[8]

In the past half-century the instances in which significant findings from animal experiments have been translated into workable hypotheses or fruitful new insights with respect to human relationships or motivation are conspicuously few and widely separated. Among the most distinguished efforts to bridge the gap between animal experiments and human experience is, of course, Harlow's work with monkeys.

Through an ingeniously contrived series of carefully conducted experiments—now regarded as classic examples of psychological research—Harlow has shown how quickly his infant monkeys "attached" themselves to their "surrogate" mothers, and how enduring this "affection" is. Assuming these results to be directly applicable to human infant experience, he supposes to have demonstrated an elementary process at work in the foundation of human relationships. He concludes that human experience merely represents a higher order of complexity than that of other primates and even, in some instances, of other lower species.[9]

Allowing such a supposition is to forego, first of all, the critical distinctions between infant monkeys and human babies. Harlow himself especially emphasized it as necessary for its experimental convenience—namely, that in monkeys motor development is more rapidly advanced from the outset. This difference in a critical developmental variable could hardly be noteworthy for purposes of "experimental convenience" only, and at the same time have no significance for the outcome of the study when the very success of the study depends upon it. Indeed, Harlow's experiments have given us a definitive picture of the variables of monkey development; however, the gap between the monkey and the human experience of infancy remains.

The behaviorist hypothesis that we can learn something about human motivation by isolating a fragment of human behavior and studying it vicariously, through experimental research with primates, has no more distinguished or respected exponent than Harlow. His classic work in which he used primates rather than humans as research subjects depended, among other things, upon the fact that their nervous systems are homologous. He further assumed that measurements of significant variables in one species were just as applicable to the other. However, the research preference for a macaque monkey, because his developmental "map" is simpler and the behavioral variables fewer, avoids—it does not resolve—the problem of the experimental "inaccessibility" of the human infant.

The very fact that the human infant experiences his first critical attachment while his nervous system is still relatively immature and undifferentiated is in itself one of the most suggestive factors in the development of early human relationships. The essential characteristics of the human infant's dependence on his mother, the oceanic quality of this relationship, must indeed be bound up with the very "confounded jumble and jungle of variables" which Harlow considered an insurmountable obstacle, and from which he turned away to the primates.

Harlow's investigation of the nature of love, by way of primate experiments, produced undeniably interesting and curious phenomena; it did not, however, illuminate the essence of love. His conception of the nature of love, as it may be expressed in an infant's attachment to its mother, seems evident from his conviction that the macaque is a more felicitous research subject than a human baby, and just as good a demonstration model. He plainly implies that the nature of love is like the nature of their nervous systems—homologous.

This and other laboratory studies of animal life, attractive to the experimenter by virtue of the "accessibility" of the subject, are doomed almost by definition to disappoint the hopes of those seeking enlightenment on the more intractable human predicament. The obstacle here has to do with the central role of the unconscious in human motivation and behavior. The vast, diverse and rich store of studies and experiments with animals over the past century has yielded us a magnificent body of data on the *behavior* of most species known to us. From it, however, we have no evidence that a dynamic unconscious exists in animals. It is entirely justified, therefore, that these laboratory studies are restricted to the assessment of reactions to external stimuli and "environmental" conditions, with no deeper consideration given to the problem of motivation. Indeed, the psychology of such phenomena finds its appropriate designation in the term, behaviorism.

To acknowledge our ignorance of whatever "motives" animals harbor or employ is one thing; however, to assume (even temporarily for experimental purposes) that we, too, therefore, lack them, or that our motives are just too difficult to measure and hence whatever yields a simple measurement is a proper substitute, leads to a reductionist oversimplification. The flaw is, as we have suggested, that experimental attempts to discern from animal behavior the nature of human motivation suspend everything we know about the dynamic power of unconscious processes in human experience. The study of human motivation can ill afford to bypass Freud's radical discoveries, for regardless of the undeniable influence of external circumstances on our conduct and achievements, the lifelong central role of our inner conflicts (of which, by definition, we may be entirely unaware) is inescapable.

The unique feature of man's mental life is his unconscious. The deeper problems of relationships with others, concepts of the self, the growth of self-esteem and the ego ideal, and ultimately the formation of the superego and the workings of conscience are no mere "reactions" to the problems and opportunities of our everyday existence; rather, they reflect the accrued evidence of an unconscious past and the tides of inner life. Whether the critical experiences of childhood are interpreted as the development of the cognitive functions, stage by well-defined stage, "along an underlying continuity," as Piaget has originally and elaborately outlined,[10] or are subsumed under a plethora of learning theories which focus on our exploratory behavior to test and somehow "know" the environment, the clear implication of human development is that the sense we make of it all derives from the meaning to us of our experiences. And a critical part of that "meaning" is its continuing presence as a dynamic power of past experiences in our unconscious.

Countless experiments, elaborately conceived and technically complex, have been devised in profusion to test other human mental functions. For example, many recent studies in experimental psychology have been devoted to an explanation of some facets of memory function. In the past decade we have seen the increased application of the so-called "signal detection theory" in such experiments. Thus, memory is regarded as a system of signals which may be weakly or strongly emitted, received or blocked at certain "thresholds," deposited as "traces" in some "retention cell" to be retrieved later under certain given conditions. It is measured through ingenious tests, the results of which are computed according to elegant mathematic criteria.

The conceptual definition which inspires such studies describes the task of human memory as follows: ". . . to detect information regarding some aspect of the environment, process the information in some manner, and transmit it in whole or part to some response agency which effects appropriate adjustments in the environment. The ultimate performance of the system is related intimately to the ability to detect and process relevant input information." [11] Such definitions and the methodology from which they derive, however, underestimate or ignore many profoundly influential aspects of memory function, some of which extend beyond conscious awareness. One of these, for example, is the process of association and its substantive images which may, on the one hand, produce inhibitions to a point of amnesia, or release a flood of responses in a completely untoward and contrary direction.

The more our emotional life proves to be of unanticipated complexity, the stronger seems the conviction in some academic quarters that full understanding of this complexity depends upon ever more complicated methodology and "advanced" research techniques. Current research trends in academic psychology, as suggested in the examples cited here, seem to bear this out. Furthermore, the emphasis on technological sophistication has gained an enormous impetus from the invention and proliferation of advanced systems of data collection. The manipulation of large quantities of data under simulated experimental conditions can produce an apparent relationship of variables with a claim of statistical validity. What often goes unmentioned —or denied—is that statistical computations, regardless of mathematical accuracy, inescapably reflect the "experimenter's bias"— namely, all the values and concepts that determine the nature of the data to be fed into the machines. Isaiah Berlin sums it up in a recent essay:

> What scientific method can achieve, it must, of course, be used to achieve. Anything that statistical methods or computers or any other instrument or method fruitful in the natural sciences can do to classify, analyze, predict, or "retrodict" human behavior should, of course, be welcomed. . . . It is a far cry from this to the dogmatic assurance that the more the subject matter of an inquiry can be assimilated to that of a natural science the nearer the truth we shall come.[12]

The historical course of psychology as an experimental science was mapped, for the most part, in the latter half of the nineteenth century by pioneer investigators of sensation such as Weber and Fechner, or Helmholz in the particular areas of vision and hearing, and Wundt on perception. These men were the forerunners in the study of what has come to be known as man's cognitive behavior. They also marked the end of an era, for in the 1870s psychology moved out of the period of discovery and gradually took on the attributes of a "movement": as one aspect or another in experimental work won adherents, controversy had less and less to do with the nature and substance of the human psyche and was more and more taken up with methodological and doctrinal competition. Further, whereas behavior received increasing attention and study, consciousness was denied importance as a central subject for investigation.[13] This exclusion of Freud's discoveries beginning at the turn of the century seemed to seal psychology once and for all within its narrow limits, and indeed probably indirectly encouraged psychoanalysis along its independent path as a method of psychological inquiry. Psychoanalysis also quickly came to be associated with, and defined by, its own movement. The chief effect of this division was that psychology refined its professional emphasis on behavior as it relates to the quantifiable circumstances of external reality, while psychoanalysis went on to uncover the unconscious mental processes governing human action from within. Rarely did the two perspectives intersect or overlap. The experimental science steadily grew remote from the empirical one.

Thirty-seven years ago, Henry Murray issued a call to caution in academic and experimental research psychology. Heavily engaged in psychological research himself and drawing his conclusions from the wide perspective of many years' experience, he felt obliged to speak out:

> The truth which the informed are hesitant to reveal and the uninformed are amazed to discover is that academic psychology has contributed practically nothing to the knowledge of human nature. It has not only failed to bring to light the great, hauntingly recurrent problems, but it has no intention, one is shocked to realize, of attempting to investigate them. Indeed—this is the cream of the jest —an unconcerned detachment from the natural history of ordinary mortals has become a source of pride of many psychologists.[14]

Since Murray wrote these words in 1935, only very slow and partial advances have been made in academic psychology. For one, the problems of everyday life only gradually came to be considered an appropriate subject for serious scientific research. Thus, academic psychologists, influenced by the work of other social scientists, began to design quantitative "survey research" from which indices could be derived to estimate the probability, say, that "first-born children are more often maladjusted than intermediate and last-born children," or that "union members in closed shops are less militant than union members in open shops." Although there is, of course, no shortcut or easy path to the source or "cause" of either maladjustment or militancy, nevertheless this kind of exploration of social research possibilities in the field of psychology, based on data gathered from "real life" behavior rather than "constructed experimental situations," was a welcome step in the direction of research realism.[15] On the other hand, experimental psychology, despite this apparent willingness to incorporate other social scientific perspectives, has remained aloof when it comes to those two areas of motivation which are especially salient in Freudian inquiry—namely, aggression and sexuality.

Raymond Cattell, an authority on personality and psychological testing, states categorically that research strategy can ill afford not to enlist the help of the mathematical statistician in solving problems in psychology. But we are obliged to consider the nature of the "problems" to which he refers. He regards clinical notions of personality as rough-hewn and approximate—no substitute for experimental evidence. His bias is that of most academic psychologists: the laboratory, not the therapeutic setting, is the appropriate milieu for the study of personality. Thus, experimenters would apply themselves to "manipulative" experiments in order to derive genetic, physiological and learning laws which govern personality. As the more stressful emotional situations—moments of crisis—are ill-suited for controlled experiments (their timing is often unpredictable, for one thing), Cattell proposed that factor analysis simply be applied to describe and interpret neurotic states, personality types, motivation patterns, behavior disorders and a host of other widely diversified emotional responses.[16] Such methodological proposals of course reflect a conception of personality as structure rather than process.

Talcott Parsons, whose theoretical work in social science and in the field of social relations is outstanding, defines human conduct as a "property of behavior in terms of feedback relations between stimulation (expectancy) and motive force as outputs of these two units of the system to each other. The phases of an action process may be treated as coordinated but differentiated phases in the input-output relations between these different parts of the system." [17] Such a conception of conduct is a simplistic model developed from a behavioristic design. It seems complex only insofar as the variety of reactions reflects a wide spectrum of so-called different systems of response. But what is overlooked in such a scheme is that our daily life does not consist merely of a range of reactions (however rich or extensive) to the stimuli of external reality, nor is the substance or "meaning" of our inner experience, as it finds outward expression, in any way conveyed by the mechanistic caricature, "output."

To sum up, where academic or experimental psychology and psychoanalytic psychology part company—indeed, they seem never to have been more than acquaintances—is over the question of the "accessibility" of human nature. So long as experimenters restrict their attention to manifest variables—to the observable, the testable, the measurable—thereby suspending the knowledge that we are never free from the dynamic laws of unconscious motivation governing emotional development any more than we are free from engagement with a social environment, their formulations, however correct, will fall short of complete discovery.

David Rapaport, reflecting on why this process of discovery has stalled, wrote, "If logic, methodology and mathematics were the pacemakers of development in sciences, this development could be fast enough in psychology. But the pacemaker is not methodology—it is human invention." [18] To date, no science has adapted methods more assiduously from a greater variety of fields, or developed fewer of them uniquely its own and produced such modest "invention" as academic psychology.

Today, as in the past, we cannot afford to neglect looking to our novelists, poets and dramatists for the "deeper truths" of human nature in everyday life which conventional psychology fails to yield. For example, William Faulkner's *Intruder in the Dust* conveys to us with an immediacy and clarity unmatched by any work in laboratory or experimental psychology, an understanding of the human capacity for enormous rage and its consequences in self-destruction. In this novel, Faulkner portrays the life cycle of the Southern white, gripped in a vise with his black neighbors—of a lifelong tragedy of violation, guilt and humiliation, fury and ultimate degradation. William Styron's *The Confessions of Nat Turner* takes us into the everyday life of a Negro slave who revolts to find an escape from the tyranny in which he is caught, only to become himself murderous and tyrannical, and to ensure his end. As for the psychology of degradation, so for the insight into feelings of well-being and personal worth. All the statistical measurement, analysis and correlation of quantifiable indices of high and low self-esteem,[19] no matter how careful the research design and valid the results, yield no hint of the enormous importance we attach—at every level of consciousness—to self-esteem. For a sense of this, we turn again to prototypal figures such as of Ulysses or Anna Karenina.

The highly sophisticated discoveries in recent decades of the structure of nervous tissue has fired the hope that these new findings will bring human motivation into a closer tie with specific neurological fabric. The reasoning held to is that human emotional conflict has some seat in a tissue and that the task simply is to find it.[20] However, the expectation that studies in the physiology of sleep and dreaming, for example, will unravel the unconscious psychology in dreams promises disappointment.

Freud's empirical discoveries, particularly the evidence of the overwhelming significance of that "other" dimension of human motivation —the unconscious—dealt conventional psychological theory an unanticipated blow. It has yet, despite its attempts, failed to recover. Interestingly enough, its efforts have been by way of an all the more zealous and unswerving search for parallels between man and animals. Indeed, within the last decade a whole new and extensive literature has sprung up, attempting to demonstrate motivational contiguity between animal and human aggression.[21]

Both psychoanalysis and academic psychology were struck hard by the Darwinian force. Since the final decades of the nineteenth century, it continues to exercise a dominant influence on virtually all psychological formulations. We see this in the view that of all the creatures who more or less successfully encounter their environment, man, the most versatile, is no less psychologically than biologically also the "fittest." Adverse and intractable as his environment may be, his mastery of it is seen as his most distinguishing feature. And persevering efforts to extend the idea of biological evolution to man's social experience seem never to flag.

Since Darwin's time, developmental psychology and, to a degree, comparative psychology have assumed an inborn biological organization which serves as the structural basis of all development. And, man's complex emotional organization is considered the result of the impact of his experience on that organic structure.

The principal original psychological theories of modern times— Freud's and Piaget's as well as Darwin's—are founded on the same premise. Moreover, there is no missing link between animals and men; rather, men are simply more highly differentiated. Indeed, as Peter Wolff has shown, psychoanalysis and Piaget's developmental theory, in all their respective complexities, differ mainly in *method*. Their common objective for study lies in the constant interaction between man and his environment, and to ascertain the critical variables in this process of human adaptation.[22] Their basic views, however extended and developed, are firmly rooted in the mid-nineteenth century and reflect a substantial intellectual debt to Darwin.

In Freud's countless references to man's biological origins affecting his psychological destiny, we see how extensive Darwin's legacy was. In fact, Freud went so far as to state that one day man's psychology would be conclusively traced to its biological, and perhaps, finally, even to its elemental chemical sources. Even though he was to accept that our social experience serves essential functions in our emotional development, to describe some of these functions systematically (as in his concept of the superego), Freud's ties to the Darwinian world view were demonstrably firm. About the process of man's evolution Freud wrote, "The acquisitions he has substantially made have not succeeded in effacing the evidences, both in his physical structure and in his mental dispositions of his parity with animals." [23]

In Freud's view—and that of most analysts—the Darwinian hypothesis that man's biological continuity with animal life extended to include mental experience seemed as entirely legitimate as it appeared to be logical. Freud's own towering conception of unconscious mental processes was inseparable from his belief that the human mind works from "our instincts which cannot be wholly tamed." [24]

Translating his concepts of unconscious functions, which he had himself discovered, into the language most familiar to him of neurological processes, he said, "Man's mind is not a simple thing. On the contrary, it is a hierarchy of superordinated and subordinated agencies, a labyrinth of impulses striving independently of one another towards action, corresponding with the multiplicity of instincts and of relations with the external world, many of which are antagonistic to one another and incompatible." [25] Freud was stating in effect that it was not simply that man's unconscious was beyond his own grasp, as it was that its tap roots, imbedded in structures as unknown as they were beyond his control, left man at the mercy of his instincts. Moreover, the psychoanalytic discovery that the human "ego is not master in its own house," [26] led Freud to reason that in the final analysis when our chemical nature would be discovered, we would then rule our menage.

However, the unique human process of socialization, which the Darwinian theories do not take into account, is that while it binds us together, it also promotes in us a self-governing command. Within a short time of our birth, and long before we are emotionally fully formed, we are required by those who care for us to suspend and even to abstain from certain elementary sources of gratification. Toward those whose interference delays satisfying our earliest needs and so easily invokes our fury, we are obliged to curb our aggressive conduct. These injunctions, in abundant variety, constitute a large part of every child's encounter with those who must look after him. And this experience of relentless admonitions, suppression of impulses, and thwarting of expectations, at the behest of parents and then of other representatives of society, begins to effect a self-transformation in the young child who unwittingly incorporates, *as part of himself,* the very injunctions he so reluctantly accepts.

The beginning of a powerful agency of inner surveillance is thus launched. It dictates the compromises a child commences to make with his wishes and needs, a process of self-regulation which often does not, as we shall see further on, directly or even accurately reflect the demands of others on him. Indeed, an excessively indulged child may impose stricter curbs on himself than a firmly disciplined one. To this self-modifying process of conscience, which goes beyond awareness into the deeper reaches of the unconscious, Freud gave the term superego.

Thus, the central formula of utilitarian psychology—that we strive for reward and avoid pain—insufficiently comprehends the human condition. It neglects the critical and unique role of self-reference in the mental processes. A child's natural egocentricity is expressed not simply in conscious imitation of those around him; self-reference becomes a much more ample matter as the child incorporates the characteristics and qualities of those who are intimately engaged in his care and whom he thus values. Another equally essential aspect of our emotional development in early childhood is the self-transformation that issues from our engagement with daily life. And these two processes, self-reference and self-transformation, neither depend upon nor necessarily reflect circumstance alone, but also derive from our experiences—what those experiences have meant to us, how they have become a part of us, and how we are unwittingly altered by them.

These experiences are a unique and determinant part of each individual's personal history. It is in dreams and fantasies that our unconscious past is to be found. There our earliest wishes still press to be satisfied. They express themes of childhood carried over in infinite repetition into adult life. Our unconscious past is no mere storehouse of dated, forgotten or hidden chronicles; it is a dynamic experience with which we live.

The self-assessments and transformations we derive from the unconscious are part of the psychology of everyday experience and govern the course of that experience as surely and as fully as every conscious moment of reflection, deliberation or choice. Even in our fantasy life, though partly removed from the immediate demands of everyday reality, our conscience surveys us still, and we are unfailingly affected by the claims of those we value and love. Our responses to such claims unconsciously evoke defenses in support of our wishes, regardless of whether we satisfy others or ourselves, and the conflict of interest is joined.

It is part of our nature and a lifelong imperative of our existence to be engaged in social relationships, and thus also in the conflicts associated with them. In another context,[27] discussed in a later chapter, I suggest that even under conditions of the most acute or severe isolation, as in serious psychoses, some relationship with others is apparently psychologically mandatory, and is indeed maintained even in hallucinatory experience. Our need of relationships persists under the most adverse physical conditions as well as in such serious pathological states. It is the unique quality of man's social existence which seems to elude those who would apply the simple pleasure/pain formula indiscriminately to all living creatures. Social relationships require that from the beginning we continually modify our egocentric aims and yield up some of our narcissism. We transfer the high esteem in which we hold our own well-being and interests to the needs, wishes and well-being of another. The bonds which form between us derive from the reciprocal or mutual value we accord each other, and are to be distinguished from the bonds which hold animals together.[28]

Freud's view, expressed a half-century ago, was that the pleasure/pain principle is applicable to animals and men both. The chief difference between them in this respect, he declared, is that we recognize what animals do not—namely, that the real world may not provide immediate gratification of our needs—and we learn (albeit painfully) that by deferring to circumstances or conditions which thwart our aims, we may later assure ourselves a more certain satisfaction. He attributed this unique "learning" to the operation of our higher faculties, to our power of reason. This analysis still holds as far as our material pursuits and efforts to master the environment are concerned; however, our problem-solving efforts are never outside the context of close association with others—an exceptional circumstance in the animal world.

In applying the pleasure/pain principle to human relations, Freud noted that when someone we love or care for (thus someone to whom we have extended our self-esteem) disappoints us or deprives us of the pleasure we expect, not only do we feel mistrust and discontent, but our narcissism, like the pseudopodia of the amoeba in a noxious environment, is withdrawn. The relationship is endangered and may cease to exist, and, in compensation, our self-regard increases. Self-esteem thus impaired in a relationship which fails, he argued, may thus find a self-induced recovery.[29] Recent studies show that this is only partially the case, however, for increased egocentricity, self-regard and self-serving are never completely adequate to the task. The empirical fact is that by ourselves, stripped of relationships, we cannot effectively nourish or sustain our narcissism.

If the survival of bees or fish or birds or beasts depends upon their conforming to swarms or schools or flocks or herds, there may be a certain analogy with human social organization, but this is insufficient grounds for arguing causal connection or social descent. Groupings or colonies of insects, for example, are "social" only in a metaphorical sense. For instance, when D. I. Wallis refers to colonies of insects he explicitly means those which live together in biological inter-dependence; individual insects perform as component parts and only metaphorically as organs support the whole organism.[30] The industry and "cooperation" of insect colonies are fascinating, no doubt, so much so that the subject has entered into our folklore and inspired our anthropomorphizing.

But to extend the analogy beyond its metaphorical usefulness is to conceal the critical disparity between human and animal "social" organization and obscure the unique features of human psychosocial development. In man, to acquire, develop and sustain a relationship we need and value is to divert some of our fundamental self-centered-ness. As suggested above, this takes the form of serving another's interests, of social accommodation. We transfer some of our narcis-sism, the psychological facet of self-preservation, to another whom we thus come to favor at least as much as, and perhaps at times even more than, ourselves. This transforms us. Our effective survival depends upon the success with which we make this our way of life. So long as we value the relationship with another, our self-esteem—the con-sciousness of narcissism—is supported. Should we lose what we prize, however, we forfeit self-esteem at the same time, and this lets loose our aggression. Thus, when we no longer feel loved or valued by another, or when we withdraw our love and regard, narcissism is by definition impaired and self-esteem lost; and only then is aggression or destructiveness (either toward others or toward ourselves) re-leased. When narcissism is threatened, lowered or hurt, aggression issues to redress the balance.

The attempt to make inferences about human aggression from observations, experiments and studies of animals now represents nearly a century of effort. The body of evidence which convincingly suggests the limited applicability of these studies has been grossly neglected. The critical weakness in the hypothesis which would extend the principle of our biological continuity with animals into the psychological and behavioral spheres is that it fails to recognize that our unique social requirement *alters our functions,* especially those related to narcissism. Human aggression would not alter us, any more than animal aggression modifies a creature who engages in it, were it not for the fact that very early in our development it becomes inseparable from our narcissism, and its unstable fortunes in our social relationships.

The extent to which human experience—the unspectacular, everyday garden variety—is bound up with the fluctuating vulnerability of human narcissism and the role of this, in turn, in the daily drama of our invariably fitful "social relations" is amply suggested in psychoanalytic data, evidence quite neglected by analysts themselves. Take an example. Four-year-old Nancy, with a newly acquired sense of purpose and achievement, began to take pride in choosing each morning the clothes she would wear to school that day, and with some help from her mother she dressed herself. One day the little girl chose things which did not suit her mother's taste and aesthetic sense. "Orange socks don't go with a red skirt." Her mother demanded Nancy's compliance, and when she failed to get it promptly the two argued. The child's stubborn defense simply brought on her punishment. Nancy had been encouraged in her efforts to be independent. She had learned to dress herself and perform other small tasks for which she was freely praised. The disagreement with her mother which brought criticism and punishment implied a loss of favor. Nancy's fury that her own taste and wishes were discredited by her mother plus her tears and feelings of humiliation are the most obvious facets of the child's experience. The injury to Nancy's narcissism probably was not especially severe, and the recovery from it was prompt; however, such an event represents countless similar everyday experiences in a child's life. The importance of such apparently minor crises lies in the fact that they temper narcissism and prove to us how prone to injury our self-esteem is, and how quick to surface is our aggressive response. The narcissism of the young child, injured in the conflicts of ordinary family life, finds routes of recovery built into each phase of emotional development. Whether in the foregoing of erotic wishes toward a parent during the Oedipal years, or in the mastery of skills and the forming of friendships independent of family ties during latency and adolescent development, these are the steps which prepare for an adult relationship in which the fate of narcissism, i.e. our readiness to commit some of it to another, is central to vitality.

Nowhere are we linked more surely to animals than in our need to be satisfied, a need forged from the very strength of our appetites. Yet, whatever biological relationship there may be between us and other creatures in the press to find contentment, the satisfaction that we find, or fail to find, is never without that particular meaning to us which derives from our narcissism. Satisfaction supports narcissism and is felt as self-esteem, while the lack of gratification has the opposite effect. And perhaps nothing separates us from our animal ancestry more sharply than this.

The connection between gratification and self-esteem is a human one—neither an animal nor a biological "reaction." What significance the satisfaction of appetites may hold for animals we can only conjecture; however, the ample and convincing experience of everyday life shows that our gratification cannot be defined merely as the arrest and cessation of inner impulses and "irritating" external stimuli. To whatever gives us pleasure we invariably assign a value which immediately compromises our willingness ever to give it up. Yet, required as we are to yield some of our self-satisfaction if our social needs are to be met, we are obliged to begin very early in life to renounce some of our impulses, wishes and egocentric aims—in short, to blunt the edge of our narcissism. Without the guiding authority of others who are loved and valued, and unless as children we gradually learn to grant the demands of those all-important "others" a certain priority—often at the expense of our own wishes—we fail to develop as social creatures. As we shall see later, when this necessary modification in narcissism does not take place, or when such transformations in the service of growth are reversed, some of the most serious emotional disorders appear. The intense and exclusive narcissism of infancy must indeed be brief, given the compelling importance attached to the central authority figures of early childhood. The necessary society of others is the civilizing power.

As we have noted, direct observation and study of both animals and children have achieved widespread methodological currency in recent decades, and the published results of such work are extensive. Indeed, child development was yet another field influenced by the scientific search for similarities between animals and men. Darwin himself apparently undertook some "field work" in child development. In 1877, he wrote that he had kept a diary "with respect to one of my own infants. I had excellent opportunities for close observations and wrote down at once whatever was observed." [31] In the words of one critic, he then and there set a precedent for a "riot of parallel drawing between animal and child, between primitive man and child, between early human history and child" [32]—a trend, if not a riot, which has extended into widening circles of speculation about such parallels and continuities.

Within the psychoanalytic profession itself, some clinicians have earned a growing popular and professional following, especially among ethologists, anthropologists, and psychologists, through their efforts to close the gap between animal research and the study of human childhood without at the same time forfeiting the theoretical or methodological premises of psychoanalysis. The subject of aggression, especially and persistently, seems to provoke analysts to compare and identify man's earliest intimate social experience—his family relationships—with animal social orders. Here the eminent British psychoanalyst John Bowlby, for example, emphasizes the analogy between animal family life and the human family. He writes, "Man has no monopoly either of conflict or of behavior pathology . . . a goose can court a dog kennel and mourn it when it is overturned. Ethological data and concepts are therefore concerned with phenomena at least comparable to those which we as analysts try to understand in man." [33] It would be odd, he continued, not to recognize the similarity and evolutionary continuity in infant feeding, juvenile play, reproduction and other behavior, when we share with the lower species' anatomical and physiological characteristics. A decade later, Bowlby declared that his clinical findings in studying the relationship of very young children with their mothers led him to share Harlow's[34] conviction of the critical similarities between the earliest attachments of monkey infants and those of human children.[35] He went on to supplement his essentially psychoanalytic discussion with a restatement of the Darwinian assumptions in the light of new knowledge of brain physiology derived from the field of cybernetics.[36] Based on the concept of electrical circuitry, or "feedback," experiments in electrical stimulation of the brain have consistently evoked similar behavior patterns in animals and man, he reported. Thus, man and his fellows seemed "closer kin" than ever before, and theories of behavioral as well as biological continuity between them received heady confirmation.

Bowlby is perhaps the foremost Freudian to move to infuse orthodox psychoanalytic theory with contemporary ideas in biology and behaviorism. To explain emotional life as the expression of components of brain function, however, is—once again—to rule out the dynamic role and determining influence of the unconscious. While seeming to fulfill Freud's prophesy of a half-century ago that one day human conduct would be discovered to issue from sources in our metabolism, the current "applied" use of theories of electrical circuitry and chemical balance to explain man's conduct and deeds is, rather, part of the longstanding grand search founded on the assumption that there are direct links between animal biology and human behavior.

As the focus of theoretical psychoanalysis has shifted, relatively, within the last thirty years, from adult neurosis to the emotional development of children themselves, this attention to the development crises and the critical relationships of infancy and early childhood has provided the occasion for a renewed round of analogies with young animals. The popular tendency to regard young children as more animal-like than adults has always been widespread. It is a well-known common practice of young children to compare and identify themselves with animals—in itself a fascinating subject for students of child psychology. The professional indulgence (deliberate or unwitting) in such comparisons, however, by psychoanalysts and others who should know better, confuses rather than clarifies matters unless the limits of metaphorical analogy are made unambiguous. Bruno Bettelheim, the child psychologist, for example, in his authoritative description of the periodsof "special sensitivity" in a child's very early development,[37] makes comparative reference to the many studies of mammals and birds which show that imprinting takes place at a "certain well-defined stage of development specific to the species." In any highly social species, the characteristics of its later social relations are "set" at some precise and critical moment in early development; this process is the same in a young infant as it is in a puppy. The only difference between the two, he argues, is in the "species specificity" of the critical period.[38] And, if Bettelheim and other psychoanalytic observers are quick to relate inferences drawn from child development to animal life, from their studies of young animals, experimental psychologists often make the same analogies—in reverse.

While experimental psychology, restricted to the laboratory, has proved its limitations as a means to understanding the psychology of social relationships, especially with respect to the baffling phenomenon of aggression, a new and different approach to the study of animals and their relationships has furnished us with important new considerations bearing on old theories. I am referring, of course, to the innovative and enlightening work in ethology. Above all, the results of ethologists' field research have made mandatory full-scale revision of traditional hypotheses about the role of aggression in animal life.

The facts of aggression among animals in the field have consistently and markedly diverged from the suppositions derived from the study of creatures caged in the laboratory or zoo. The erstwhile observation that a wide variety of animals seemed characteristically to engage in aggression among their own kind has been conclusively challenged with evidence from a wide range of field studies that such behavior is not "in the nature of the beast" so much as it is a function of the unnatural conditions of captivity. The implications of this kind of evidence for the course of academic psychology should be abundantly clear.

The stunning revelation that the incidence of intraspecific fighting among animals in the wild has been seriously exaggerated raises interesting questions about the ontogenetic origins of such a misconception. Its conventional acceptance and popularity perhaps reflects the unconscious residue of childhood fears of violence, embellished in our fantasies, the menace projected outward into images which eventually make their way into scientific works as well as popular culture.

Our fears of animals are a quite common and "healthy" part of childhood reality testing. When these fears develop into phobic anxiety and dread, only in the rarest instances is this attributable to some actual experience. As with all phobias, the source of anxiety is not to be found in the feared object, but in the unconscious conflicts which preempt the fantasy life of the one who is afraid. As we have seen above in the case of Little Hans, the horse he feared would bite him turned out to be a symbolic version (nonetheless real to him) of his guilty, rivalrous expectations of some kind of "attack" from his father. On other occasions, too, in clinical encounters with adult patients, Freud found similar evidence of the intimate connection between a child's fears of attack by a wild animal and his own destructive fantasies. At the time, Freud was interested above all in obtaining conclusive clinical evidence of infantile sexuality in order to refute Adler and Jung who were, independently of each other, attempting to disprove its centrality in psychological development. In the setting of this feud, and as a consequence of it, Freud set aside the analysis of the themes of childhood destructiveness conveyed in his patients' accounts.

Yet, in one of his most famous cases, familiar to students of analysis as the case of the Wolf Man,[39] the patient revealed ample evidence of the demonic role of attacker into which beasts are cast by all too vulnerable children. Before his fourth birthday he apparently had acquired some sort of animal phobia. When he was about five years old, coming upon a picture in a story book of a wolf standing upright, "He began to scream like a lunatic that he was afraid of the wolf coming and eating him up. His sister, however, always succeeded in arranging it so that he was obliged to see the picture, and was delighted at his terror." [40]

On the other hand, he enjoyed tormenting insects and other small creatures. Or, at the circus, he vacillated between excited glee at witnessing the animals seemingly being beaten into obedience and then shrieking terror at the sight which suddenly became so intolerable to him that he had to be taken home. It is the ambivalence of this early identification with animals which is so potent—as children project onto other living creatures their divided sense of themselves as both attacker and victim of attack. To be sure, only phobic sufferers experience this terror acutely enough to be paralyzed by it, but it leaves its residues beyond childhood in all of us.

The crux of the case of the Wolf Man was the overdetermined significance (and its analysis) of his dreaded nightmare of wolves coming to eat him. "There remains scarcely anything strange in the child's conduct in making the transference from the dogs onto his parents and in being afraid of the wolf instead of his father," [41] Freud concluded. As with Little Hans, here in the direct analysis of a neurotic adult, Freud's interpretation of the infantile sexual conflicts explicitly included evidence of the equally unsettling issues of aggression and violence—of the child's crude and confused awareness of possible destruction and harm both to himself and to others—but Freud chose to withhold psychoanalytic consideration of these problems and their bearing on infantile conflicts which were not plainly and immediately sexual.

The creatures we fear evidently accommodate themselves to vast cultural and social differences; however, regardless of geographic setting or historic age, they have a remarkably uniform identity. Their image is threatening: more often than not devouring monsters are ready to "eat us up." The wolf in the patient's nightmare (in all its condensed power) is directly related to the open-mouthed dragons ritually placated in Chinese religious festivals, the ancient Hindu view of politics and the realm of *matsya-nyaya* ("where the big fishes eat the little fishes"), and the ravenous woodland beasts of the fairy tales upon which we in the West "nourish" our children.[42] The fact that we may still suffer such fears as adults (whether in acute phobias requiring clinical attention or in the minor avoidances of everyday life) and that they appear as cultural phenomena clearly derives from ontogenetic sources, from childhood antecedents. Since few, if any, children are spared some period of nightmares and aggravated fears of wild animals—and this includes typical, usually transitory, displaced fears of pets and tame animals which suddenly may seem threatening—there is reason to believe that these are indeed the products and signs of the unconscious conflicts common to all children.

Study has shown that very early in childhood we become deeply interested in what may menace us.[43] Our lives become preoccupied for a while with this all-important question. For we come to know from our daily encounters that what lives may die and, further, that we depend, in part, for our own existence upon the destruction of other living things. They are our victims. It takes scant emotional development before we realize that what we do or wish to do to other living creatures in our self-interest, threatens that creature's life; moreover, little experience is required to make us only too well aware that another may entertain toward us precisely these thoughts or wishes or intentions.

The young child's readiness to attribute his own qualities, his vitality, his needs and expectations to everyone and everything about him is one of his most charming characteristics. His inclination (and, indeed, downright ability) to speak to a leaf as to a frog, or to give life to moving clouds brings him closer to the natural world than any of us. He is part of it, and lives it. The child's natural capacity to animate the world about him, endowing all creatures with a universal language and rapport, also has its ominous aspects. For no less "natural" is the child's self-serving, self-asserting egocentricity. He does not willingly countenance interference with his wants, he suffers rivals poorly, his great expectations seem invariably to exceed his achievements, and he often foregoes generosity and mercy in the pursuit of enjoyable childish torment. His circle of compatible creatures, just yesterday so familiar, now may suddenly be transformed into monsters (ironically, no less like himself) against whom he must defend his very life. As we have observed, this new experience of such a threat, although thoroughly convincing as any nightmare will verify, is usually transient. The persistence of a phobia, which defies all parental and clinical reassurance, is, however, the plainest evidence that the child's unconscious hostility toward someone important to him has turned back, making himself the victim.

As common and serious as this destructiveness and violence are that we feel toward each other, and against which even as small children we must guard ourselves—lest we actually carry them out or find ourselves their object—no parallel among animals exists. In their natural setting, animals are only exceptionally forced either to assert or defend a position among their own kind. The "fittest" animals are *not* the survivors of widespread or intense slaughter.[44]

Essentially two systems operate within an animal species to defend and preserve its existence and the existence of its individual members. One is so-called "social organization," and the other is dominance. How each of these originates and operates is properly a biological problem, beyond the scope of this work; however, the endeavors of some anthropologists and biologists to anthropomorphize the "living" arrangements animals arrive at, and the suggestion that these represent social institutions, fall into that category of fanciful notions conceived to account for the development in each species of the various patterns which operate to secure the animals' existence.

From field discoveries of the exceptional conditions it takes to evoke aggression in animals, we may judge the extent to which the long unchallenged assumptions about violence in animal life represent more accurately a reflection of ourselves than of our fellow creatures. Except in man, behavior patterns which preclude or contain an outbreak of aggression are to be found in all species. For example, many varieties of fish which tend to be highly aggressive (especially in defense of their feeding grounds) during the reproductive season, at other times lose all their aggressive behavior and come together in schools. This applies equally to many bird species which "have the habit of retiring, outside the breeding season, into the anonymity of the flock." [45] Further, as Konrad Lorenz and others have described in detail, "In many animals where only one sex cares for the brood, only that sex is really aggressive toward fellow members of the species. . . . We have never found that the aim of aggression was the extermination of fellow members of the species." [46]

Animals that remain "bonded," whether for given periods or for life, are very aggressive. By definition, "bonding" refers to behavior patterns which hold a troop or flock together or, in some instances, maintain individual animals together in mated pairs. This arrangement is not dictated by sentiment, nor does it express a durable romance. The bonded relationship exists as a defense; its function and purpose is species survival.[47] And within a species the safeguards for individual animals are biologically given.

Unlike all other animals, humans regard no other species as our enemy, i.e. no species naturally prey on us. Whereas among all other animals so-called "socialization" is a defense against natural enemies outside the species itself, our socialization and social organization are directed toward governing our relations with each other and reducing the liability of violence *within* the human species. Nor is our survival as a species premised on circumscribed periods of heightened aggression timed with a rhythm of breeding seasons. Given man's technological mastery of nature, we actually have little need to call upon aggression in defense of our kind—and, indeed, our social order exists only to the extent that we relinquish aggression. Yet, we are the most aggressive of all species and particularly toward one another.

Aggression in the interests of survival, among animals in their natural state, has often been confused by observers with the exigencies of predation. Sharing food in the wild within an area is the rule rather than the exception. Territory is not conquered and parceled out by animals, or held in fee in any "property" sense; such notions apply commonly to men and only exceptionally to animals. Rather, we have learned from the empirical work of ethologists in the field that a given territory resembles a vessel from which to feed; it holds no other known value for animals, any more than a breeding place has an importance beyond serving the ends of survival. Birds, for instance, engaged in feeding, space out their territorial needs over a whole region. Territoriality simply means that a patch of land or sea is a defined area which can support the members of a given species. Under natural conditions, animal social order is sufficiently balanced so that intraspecies aggression is rare even in defense of the feeding. Should a bird accidentally stray from its own flock to where others are feeding, or should a group of monkeys find a strange one in their midst, the intruder would be driven off only in the event that food is scarce. Under extraordinary conditions of privation, the entry of newcomers may upset the ratio of supply and demand to an extent which threatens starvation; at this point, of course, survival is at stake, and fighting among animals of the same species may then occur. However, even on this point, studies have shown that such notoriously vicious animals as rats are not certain to become aggressive even in desperate conditions—they are more inclined to hunt for a means of escape, and in the event none is found, they are known to die from internal stress.[48]

Thus, under natural conditions, herds and groups of range animals do not, as is commonly imagined, struggle to establish territorial "possession." Their discrete and nonoverlapping food requirements and the ranging nature of their daily life afford an ample food supply—without competitive violence. The tremendous aggressive potential of baboons, for example, is rarely manifested in their natural habits. The idea of achieving dominance by fighting for it, particularly among certain primates who are capable of very powerful aggression, is simply not borne out by observations. In the report of one ethologist, "Animals so socially conditionable as baboons have a highly articulated system of appropriate behavior patterns towards each other, within groups and between groups, so that this tremendous aggressive potential is rarely manifested toward species members. . . . Probably the most important point to emphasize is that the inhibitory control system of baboon social organization is so effective that their lethal fighting potential is rarely released." [49] And, in the same symposium on the natural history of aggression, Mathews declares flatly, "The more I have sought examples of intraspecific overt fighting in mammals the less I have succeeded, and I doubt that it normally occurs in nature." [50] The large males among mammals, once thought to have won a place in a hierarchy of their fellows on the basis of their size and power, upon closer study appear to have no such distinction, even within temporary groupings. Their main function is watchfulness for predators rather than the exertion of any special dominance within the group. Social order among animals adds up simply to those arrangements best fitted to particular environmental needs; and it does not regularly require overt aggression to maintain." [51]

There is no agreed claim by ethologists that animals have some latent dynamic reservoir of violent aggressive impulses, only waiting to be discharged or released. Nevertheless, most investigators addressing themselves to the subject of human aggression, psychoanalysts among them, have doggedly worked from a preconceived model of impulses and their release, nerve centers and their activation, energy and its discharge.

Before Freud became a clinician he was a student of neurology, and he had learned and retained a permanent intellectual impression of one of the principal characteristics of all nerve tissue—namely, that a summation of stimuli produces a discharge. It was to be expected that he would rely on this model in his earliest formulations of mental function, the early libido theory and, later, in his theory of the instincts. Indeed, throughout his work it is his classic model: stimuli have a cumulative effect which at a certain point triggers an action. His discovery that our unconscious sends out an endless stream of stimuli, only some of which ever come to consciousness, had far-reaching implications, for it meant that human behavior was no longer explicable merely as a response to our external environment, but that we are additionally subject to the pressures of an *internal state*. Moreover, he went radically further to reveal and demonstrate the revolutionary insight that this inner motivational source could command action independent of—and even at odds with—outer conditions. But, he went on to insist that as with neurological activity, psychic stimuli, too, whether the product of the unconscious or of our circumstances, were somehow cumulative, pooled in a reservoir, eventually to "spill out" as behavior.

In spite of the doubt cast by ethological evidence upon the validity of this traditional psychoanalytic "reservoir" concept of behavior, psychoanalysts today still hold the view, quite unmodified, that energies are cumulative, aggression is retained and the instincts dammed up, the pressure finally relieved only with gratification. Current theoretical statements appear merely to have altered from the language of Freud's 1894 formulation of behavior as the result of "a quota of affect or sum of excitation which finds discharge," to the concept of the manifestation of dammed-up psychic energy pressing for release.[52] These biological patterns of instinctual response, it is claimed, mark our descent from animal life and seal the connection. Given this statement of our natural heredity, some behavior analogous to human aggression should be discernible in animals. Yet such is decidedly not the case.

On the contrary, as we have noted above, only the exceptional circumstance in which survival itself is compromised do animals resort to intraspecific aggression. There is, however, another distinctly different kind of fighting in the wild, namely, the so-called "ritualized" aggression which has held the fascination of several generations of ethologists. Rival stags, for example, meet in combat; they lock horns, yet inflict no real, that is to say life-threatening, injury. A similar instance is to be found among wolves in their combative conduct within the pack; in the "showdown," the weaker wolf exposes his belly and throat to the other who does not rip the jugular vein, but instead walks off bristling. These "engagements" indicate the strictly limited function of open aggression between members of the same species. It supports the social order. It is nonetheless an unusual occurrence rather than a way of life. And, finally, we must be careful to keep in mind that so-called "ritualized behavior," such as the way in which wolves allegedly spare each other when a fight is on the verge of a kill, does not reflect either a psychological unconscious or some social achievement of rules governing aggression.

Whether animals are held together in groups or pairs by the forces of banding, by inhibitory physiological mechanisms, or by hierarchical ranking, the conclusion we are obliged to draw is that these processes effectively govern and control animal behavior. Animals are allowed neither the freedom nor the license to be aggressive. The "ritualized" combat described above—as common to fish and birds as to the powerful mammals—is confined to finely stereotyped aggressive behavior. Whether in the duet of dancing flies, the mating conduct of mallards, or the ultimate restraint of stags or wolves paired in a fight, animal behavior demands no improvisation, no ingenuity; indeed, there is no room for idiosyncratic performance.

All species, even the highest primates, show little if any propensity for behavioral diversity. Animals function on the narrowest base compatible with survival. Where alternatives are minimized, where spontaneity and improvisation in no way govern action, the demands for accommodation are not so urgent. Thus confined, each animal species achieves a characteristic stability in behavior; individuality is minimal. For animals, choices are radically few; furthermore, new ones are neither imagined nor planfully sought. It is in this way that animal life is secured and remains more or less constant. To consolidate and enhance this quality of conservative and conserving harmony, impulsive violence and aggressiveness are left out, and, as added insurance, gratification in connection with aggression is altogether absent from animal life. The prevalent but naïve notion that aggression secures animal existence mistakes this last resort in the interest of survival for the first baseline of security. It is a bald anthropomorphic projection which ignores the function of the elaborate variety of biological mechanisms and so-called "ritualized" behavior. In short, ethological field work has shown the negligible role of aggression in animal life. Animal fitness, survival and the evolutionary course of existence depend upon a variety of factors. Aggression is the least of them. That survival depends upon the bloody claw is an old fiction. The metaphor, sadly enough, more closely approximates the human condition, in which aggression toward others within our species is as prominent as it is absent from animal life.

To sum up, current findings in ethology seem to provide conclusive evidence that aggression is without a natural function. It satisfies no animal need or craving. There is no "reservoir" of aggression awaiting its inevitable "discharge." The long-standing notion that aggression is part of our legacy from our animal antecedents would seem to be a claim without foundation. If violence is a part of this descent and legacy, we have yet to learn its origins. Finally, in this regard, it cannot be emphasized too strongly that gratification in connection with aggression is entirely absent from animal experience, whereas it is an elemental aspect of human life.

The myth of the Garden of Eden, like that of the Golden Age, has man walking the earth pure and exalted, devoid of narcissism and aggression both. It is a durable fable, angrily or wistfully recalled in successive historical periods, as for example in Rousseau's popularized view of the noble savage. This is to say that man strayed from his original path by misadventure. Present-day parlance differs little from Biblical injunction in the strong suggestion that by giving up his aggression—a greater sin than his lust by far—man would be redeemed and welcomed back into "paradise." "To him that overcometh will I give to eat of the tree of life, which is in the midst of the paradise of God" (Revelation 2:7). Now, nearly two hundred years since Rousseau, current scientific theory has taken up where eighteenth-century philosophy left off, with the suggestion of ethologists and others that aggression in man "has become derailed under conditions of civilization." [53] As good Darwinians, says Lorenz, we must recognize—for the sake of human survival—that we have somehow "misplaced" the species' preserving function and "forgotten" the natural defenses which spare animals from mutual annihilation. Since animals of a kind do not attack one another, and inasmuch as we characteristically do so, we have strayed far from the security of animal life.[54] Similar views are presently shared by most psychoanalysts and by many others as well. These interpretations culminate in the affirmation that man's aggression and its intensification, especially in modern times, are due to the repressive cultural restraints imposed upon him, which in turn produce a reactionary increase in aggression.[55]

In this intellectual mood and milieu, Freud proposed a half-century ago the now familiar notion of "civilization and its discontents." It was not as a philosophical consideration but as a scientific theory that he conceived of civilization as an all but intolerable imposition on us, a "naturally resisting majority." [56] The self-curtailments and emotional privations it exacted, Freud thought, formed the kernel of hostility we harbor against that very civilization. Its heavy hand arouses in us more rather than less aggression. The story of the Fall, the humanist tradition, and the modern Freudian theory of our resistance to civilization have in common the idea that man is victimized by his own instrument. To live in civilization is to pay the penalty of foregoing aggression.

Ethologists, recently, rather than behaviorists or psychoanalysts, indirectly have furnished us dramatic, full and convincing evidence which supports the argument that aggression has a role only in human experience. Compared with animals, man is the sole creature lacking any "natural" system of checks and balances which governs violence either toward or among his fellows. Between animals and man, we thus discover that an unanticipated gap exists. It is that our biological legacy of "natural" regulatory devices in relation to each other's behavior is indeed so meager as to be nonexistent. Such reactions to danger as we do have (expressed in signs of anxiety and panic such as racing pulses, diarrhea, sweaty palms, "gooseflesh," blushings and many others) give us no comfort before our enemies. Ironically, these biological responses raise our distress. In the animal world (among creatures of the same species and not under conditions of predation), we have noted, a threatened animal turned helpless may thus be made secure from attack. If such reactions, as a rule, similarly once served us in some period of our animal descent, they have long since failed.

These autonomic experiences in us as infants have a unique function. In all likelihood they raise the earliest sense of the "self." How precisely such a critically central phenomenon, locked in the minds of infants, emerges, remains a matter of speculation. The rapid development of the sense of the "self," we know, appears discernibly early in infant life. It is a time when our existence is closest to our physiology and when our emotional responses find their likeliest expression in physical reactions.

Under administered gratification for the required relief of his fretfulness and discomfort, the "child-self" emerges. Its intensely egocentric nature, with respect to those upon whom the child utterly depends, has no given limits. The curbs which a young child experiences give him no sense of security, but, instead, tend to heighten his anxiety, cause him to increase his demands, and, in short, to warrant aggression. The sense of the "self" manifest in egocentricity is thus promoted. Its needs will not be denied. Only the coercive necessity of a relationship profoundly affects the "self." The foundation for our regulatory devices is a social one and not biological. No creature model for such development descends to man. Without animal precedent, or prototype of pattern, man's unique psychological nature is his narcissism.

The "self," expressive of our narcissism, prized throughout life, is perpetually threatened between expectations left fruitless and circumstances without reward. They constitute an irrepressible source to him of the precariousness of existence and hence jeopardy. For relief, called to the service of narcissism, aggression responds. Man's narcissism, therefore, and not his aggression, is the great menace.

Chapter IV

The Pursuit of Narcissism

A singular feature of human aggression is that gratification is clearly associated with its most perfunctory exercise: in neurotic conflict, in heroic acts, even in daily life. It is this characteristic, together with man's reluctance to forego it, which brought Freud to view aggression, together with sexuality, as the instinctual drives. The close relation between the two, derived from his clinical observations, led to his conception that human instinctuality had a dual nature. It is a view with which modern concepts of aggression have had to contend. He saw aggression and sexuality as our fundamental drives, linked together in some elemental way, the one preserving the species and the other perpetuating it. His interpretations of aggression as being in the service of survival gave it its essential and unique importance, to the species as well as to the self.

The more our wishes are denied, our aims thwarted, or our will blocked, the more we persist, and our aggression is engaged. Impediments, in short, impel us to intensify our efforts. Our needs and wishes, neither readily nor totally relinquished with disappointment and frustration, are not extinguished. And however reasonably "reality" dictates that we submit to its verdict, our resistance persists. We thus begin to associate needs and wishes, from our earliest years, with the significance of a state of want. What remains with us is no mere collection or residue of experiences circumscribed by events, but rather the effects of conflicts into which our needs have taken us, and the failures of gratification drawn beyond and below awareness into the unconscious. They provide the limitless sources from which aggression may issue. The dynamic importance of the effects of the exercise of aggression is obscured by the long-held supposition that it is its own reward. The fact is, however, that we engage aggression to *serve* our ends. Aggression ordinarily is not one of them.

Before Freud's time, only a little more than a century ago, our pursuits were not regarded as revealing the constant press for gratification; nor was the lack of fulfillment viewed as a powerful motivating force beyond the boundaries of disappointment. Our deliberate efforts to find pleasure, or relief from want, were considered self-explanatory, related to circumstances. Aggression was interpreted on the one hand as a natural reaction to the vagaries of daily life, or, on the other, as the expressive discharge of some inner reserve of instinct.

In the medical sciences, less than seventy-five years ago, the ordinary conduct of human affairs, like the qualities of human relationships, were alien matters. They belonged more to the lighter faults of mankind, to the *comédie humaine,* than to scientific inquiry. Human behavior was observed in dysfunction and breakdown; and the data, as a rule, carefully collected, were elaborately classified and systematized into diagnostic statements of symptoms and nervous disorders. Aggression was not among them.

The traditional formula for the study of man—for the pathologists as well as humanists—began with the elements of which he is composed. In medicine, it was believed that since mental states were grounded in the body and its functions, and the seat of the psyche located in the brain, it followed that treatment of the body should affect a faulty or deranged mental condition. Furthermore, the passions of unreason as well as exceptional mental powers were seen to be closely related to bodily states; passions were disorders with ascertainable physical causes and their cure depended upon the correct treatment of those causes. Anger and fear, as well as hope and elation, were seen as elements of physiology,[1] and any change in emotional state was interpreted as a function of change in the physical condition. There was no departure here from the concepts Galen arrived at in the second century. With his death in 200 A.D. the Dark Ages descended on medical psychology. And, as late as 1900 we still find little evidence of a psychology extending beyond empirical observation to a systematic discipline founded on *developmental* hypotheses framing human experience.

Psychology has indeed had a unique passage. It is the last of the sciences to loosen itself from its ancient origins.[2] Its early scientific doctrines were rooted in Pythagorean thought, especially in the idea of the essential harmony of natural phenomena. This, in turn, contributed to the important philosophical conception of a balanced accommodation of opposites, a theoretical notion which not only seemed to explain physical phenomena but which came to be considered a convincing point of reference for interpreting man's conflicted experience as well. Thus, human as well as natural phenomena were seen to follow some dynamic sequence of tension and resolution. This recognition that life is essentially a matter of tension and flux and at the same time is continuous and endowed with a certain stability has engaged the thinking of philosophers at least since the time of the Ancient Greeks.

The rediscovery, many times over, of these principles and their questions put by the religious paved the way for some of the most anguished—and sublime—investigation into the essential quality of "human nature." From the "Sacred Discourses" of the Greek rhetorician Aristeides to the *Confessions* of St. Augustine and the zealous introspection of the twelfth-century mystics, men have indulged in merciless self-observation and revelation in the interests of perfecting the soul. In the same vein, Loyola called the faithful away from the working day to advance their lives and improve their souls through self-scrutiny and "inner discipline." And the aim of this evolving effort toward self-knowledge was to put an end somehow to man's inner struggles, to give him peace. Through this kind of devoted self-absorption, the individual soul became, especially in the context of the Christian religion, infinitely significant, the sum and substance of conscious mental life and of what modern psychologists call personality.[3]

In short, there has been no period in history when the human condition has not been the subject of one kind of scrutiny or another. In any effort to "locate" the subject of aggression as a problem in the history of psychology, the work of Herbert Spencer is of particular significance. We single him out here, not for having independently (and earlier than Darwin) arrived at the conviction of the universality of evolution, nor for extending (as Darwin would in *The Expression of Emotions in Man and Animals*) principles of biological evolution to the realms of mentality, emotionality and behavior, but for the fact that his work represents a significant first step in another direction—namely, self-analysis. Spencer began to suspect that much might be learned from the direct assessment of one's own motives and functions through reflective contemplation of the coercions and constraints inherent in external conditions and social relations.

Before Freud, who credited Gustav Fechner, the late nineteenth-century psychophysicist, with the concept, it was notably Herbert Spencer who endeavored to conceptualize the problem of maintaining a "psychic stability" in the face of apparently endless opposition between the demands of the environment and the direction of our inner inclinations. He believed that through satisfaction we acquire the needed stability, and conversely that discontent as much as guarantees our instability.[4] To what extent Spencer may have viewed this predicament as uniquely human, since, prior to Darwin, he held the view that evolution was universal, is not clear. But with the enormous impact on all thought of the Darwinian theory of our biological origins, the distinction between animal and man in this respect was swept away, if not by Darwin's theory, certainly by the force of Darwinism.

Not until Freud, whose discoveries were just taking shape at the close of the nineteenth century, was there any conception of the dynamic psychological significance we attach, often deeply repressed, to our discontents. That people suffered deprivation and were miserable as a result required no study to be verified. But it was a great discovery that the lack of fulfillment was greater than the sum of deprivation. Moreover, it was an inevitable human state to have less than one wished. Its roots were a source not only of discontent but of a repressed instability and hence vulnerability. Thus, a lack of fulfillment, gradually discovered to play a critical role in emotional development, was also a powerful engine of change. These were psychoanalytic discoveries made within living memory.

From the frustration of everyday life, we learn to accept, more or less, an imperfect world mirrored by our limitations. The failure to "get what we want" is all too commonplace. Furthermore, even when we get it, it is often less than we had supposed, or not quite what we thought we wanted. Fruitless wishes teach us a lesson. Through them we unwittingly are introduced to "reality," and most of us soon enough develop its acquaintance. These vicissitudes of everyday life have always offered man a measure of wisdom. But so long as they were not the subject of systematic critical investigation, they did not enter the province of scientific enlightenment. The psychology of daily life remained merely "household knowledge." It was only in this century, beginning with Freud's work, that the psychology of our ordinary existence became the subject of deliberate discovery. It is still not well illuminated.

In the half-century between Spencer's philosophical-scientific psychology and the appearance of Freud's clinical publications on his discovery of the unconscious as a source from which emotional conflict stemmed, self-analysis of a sort had become widespread among certain strata of intellectuals. Critical self-examination began to be undertaken more deliberately than before. When it was pursued systematically as an *active mode* of contemplation, it proved to be both arduous and fruitful.

Man's motives, however difficult to penetrate, were a constant current from which to fish speculations on his behavior. Indeed it was the very incomprehensible elusiveness of human nature which seemed to sustain the process of self-scrutiny. Sophisticated and thoughtful students of the mind drew upon the work of Kierkegaard, Nietzsche and Schopenhauer, complementing and amending earlier and "more tolerant" guides to human nature, such as those of Erasmus and Montaigne. Yet, sallies into self-examination, in spite of the devastatingly original conceptual work of philosophers like these, remained, on the whole, impressionistic. They did not develop an integrated theory of psychological experience into a science of the mind. Spencer and Freud, then, were not only foremost in representing an intellectual trend, although they were a generation apart and conceptually distant, but they were the lone innovators who went a step further, declaring *themselves* to be the fully appropriate central subject of scientific psychological investigation. The most eloquent testimony is in Freud's *The Interpretation of Dreams, Jokes and the Unconscious,* and *The Psychopathology of Everyday Life.*

It was not until the twentieth century that a substantive theory of personality, or scientific concepts of character development, or a systematic exposition of the ills and achievements of emotional experience were forthcoming. Zilboorg, writing on the history of medical psychology during the half-century between Darwin and Freud, noted the prevalence of a tendency among scientists, including physicians, to reject all psychological formulations. Given the fact that this was a period in which psychological self-examination became a serious popular pursuit in intellectual circles, it is somewhat ironic that in the study and practice of medicine this was an age "which demanded that man's mind be left alone and that only his body be studied. . . . Behaviorism and reflexology (Bechterev and Pavlov) brought this trend conspicuously to the surface." [5]

Freud's discoveries, then, were published in a period of psychological ferment and active self-scrutiny among certain philosophers, writers and generally among many intellectuals. But, they were met with indifference, if not hostility, by the scientific academies and schools of medicine.

When Freud showed, unequivocally, that human emotional development and relationships were susceptible to scientific observation and explanation, and exposed the denial and "escape" from unconscious conflicts, in certain of the rationalizations and romanticisms of the nineteenth century, the furor of opposition was intense.

In medical science and experimental psychology, behaviorism and reflexology, as central to a basis for human motivation, were by no means instantly abandoned for "psychoanalysis." Although early psychoanalysis embraced some ideas from neurology (Freud being first a neurologist), the reverse was not the case. From the very beginning of his work, he incorporated into analysis neurological theories of stimuli, their accumulation and discharge, and their function in providing all animal life with stability. Freud's experience was that another order of stimuli, which he had discovered, seemed to act and were to be explained much as the "outer" ones he knew previously from neurology.

The deeper—that is, unconscious—effect of all manner of stimuli, and the fact that "stimuli" themselves may be "inner" and not merely external phenomena, possibly derived from the hidden conflicts within us rather than exclusively from the environment—of these things psychologists in Freud's time were determinedly unaware. The adherents of behaviorism and reflexology in cognitive as well as in experimental psychology and to a significant degree in clinical psychology, still today, as we have noted in the preceding chapter, are guided by a view which is pre-Freudian. Their work with human subjects fails to consider consciousness in the light of what we know about the unconscious, the "inner stimuli," and thus does not take into account this fundamental distinction between animal and man. Behaviorist experiments remain models of the Darwinian supposition that our mental life represents no break in the continuity of animal existence. Rather, consciousness is translated into behavioristic terms, and products of the unconscious, when taken into account, are interpreted as a "complexity" of conditioned reflexes.[6]

Perhaps no aspect of human conduct is more readily or more doggedly drawn into comparisons with animal life than aggression. Like animals, it is argued, when we are thwarted in our search for gratification we engage in aggression. Although the conventional parallel with animals here is, in actual fact, a weak one (as we have elaborated in an earlier chapter), it is nonetheless quite true that the human striving for relief from discomfort or for gratification of felt needs is powerful indeed. Quite unlike animal experience, it is not left merely to the balance of ecological "circumstances," nor is it regulated by biological patterns of inhibition.

From our earliest moments and throughout our existence, our un-fulfilled needs and wishes, unfailingly meaningful to us however "lost" they may be to consciousness, continually impel us to relieve any sense of deprivation. The emotional logic of it is that the absence of what may be desired—like darkness—is not a reality, but a privation of light. Moreover, the experience of want is not without its further and essential significance, which is that our early experiences of want are associated with a demeaning self-assessment relieved only by satisfaction. Hence, to get what we may wish is not merely to meet some felt need, which is then removed, but it also profoundly affects our self-esteem. And some means of aggression, employed in reliev-ing a want, is no less in the service of redressing self-esteem. Our understanding of human aggression will *remain* insufficient as long as the intimate connection between the pursuit of gratification and *its significance to the self, remains* a neglected phenomenon.

Freud came to see the pursuit of gratification as the first principle of mental functioning. Later, he added the second, equally critical, "reality" principle—his summing up of the way in which we acquire the ability to postpone immediate gratification for a later one. Both require implementation. Freud had discovered that the efforts of neurotic patients to secure pleasure or satisfaction forced them out of real life, "alienating them from reality." Neurotics, he explained, "turn away from reality because they find it unbearable—either the whole or parts of it." The most extreme instances of this break with reality is represented in the hallucinations which often characterize psychosis. He further found that these reactions in adults originate in, and depend upon, an earlier phase of emotional development in which seeking satisfaction was the first and foremost—the primary—mental process. He pointed out as indicative of this "pleasure prin-ciple" and proof of its lifelong power, with active effect both in our dream life and in our daily existence, the strength of our inclination to dismiss and deny and rationalize those distressing experiences, impressions and fantasies which disturb even our ordinary content-ment.

Whatever the relative force and prevalence of the "pleasure prin-ciple" in an individual life, everyday and clinical experience both clearly show that a turn away from it to reality is no simple transi-tion. The process is accompanied by loud and persistent (if some-times distorted and disguised) protests, under the auspices of a vigor-ous wish to resist and not to yield to the demands of reality. Every child accurately sees it as hostile to his infantile aims.

Against all the forces which demand that he "grow up," a child's aggression is mobilized to support his primary wishes which he plainly has no desire to forego. Freud was quick to notice the characteristically aggressive content of the "phantasying" of early childhood and the conduct associated with it. He therefore called attention to its developmental coincidence with the introduction of the reality principle.[7] The small child is an unwilling subject. His powers—he is often forcefully and indelibly reminded—are feeble against the forces he must oppose. Hence, deprived of the gratification he ardently claims, and his efforts to enforce his will weakened by the odds against him, he is often left both unsatisfied and threatened. These are significant, powerful blows to the young child's developing self-esteem. Their effects are lasting. Recovery from them engages aggression. And, it is this point which Freud neglected in his focus on erotic development and which escapes common recognition—that aggression mobilizes to support the child's continually deeply affected narcissism in connection with *both* elementary principles of mental functioning.

As small children, long before we develop that sense of reality which allows us to defer our momentary needs and immediate wishes, we ply our aggression eagerly for what we want. When the "reality principle" no longer signifies for us a deprivation, but rather a consent to defer to future pleasures, aggression, as we commonly know it, abates. The process, painfully acquired, is a long one. It consists in aggression employed in developing skills, mastering the environment and learning—all of which give self-esteem its necessary support. Until it is accomplished, aggression remains the chief instrument in the "engagements" of childhood. Moreover, throughout life, there are occasions when expectations of pleasure are suddenly and unexpectedly disappointed, and when demands for immediate satisfaction are frustrated. In the service of the deeply affected narcissism, aggression erupts often through defenses which had become the rudiments of our character. Such reactions lead us to conclude that the power of our narcissistic needs are scarcely lessened by the successful ways we have found to satisfy them.

Freud saw in the egocentricity of early childhood the epitome of self-containment, and described this state of affairs as primary narcissism.[8] When, broadly speaking, we begin to attach and invest our interest and concern in another, rather than in ourselves exclusively, the primary condition of narcissism gives way. And should this enterprise fail, through the actual loss of a loved person, or through otherwise not being rewarded as we had hoped or expected (as happens all too often), our narcissism suffers. Unconsciously, narcissism when thwarted responds by intensifying, thus signaling a turn toward the primary self-centered and contained condition.

In Freud's theory of narcissism is a conception of a powerful process of unconscious mental functioning which motivates one toward being wholly self-focused. Opposing these egocentric aims is the no less needed social condition upon which we depend. The escape, in order to spare narcissism from the conflict, is by way of a retreat, even at times a flight into increased narcissism abandoning the social gain and denying social need. This reversal, as it were, conveys us on a route which (throughout life, under adverse conditions affecting narcissism, we may resort to taking) seems to by-pass frustrations. It provides us a detour around "reality" in the sense that we do not defer to some future and hence uncertain gain. Instead, we return to a once fabulous time, seen with an inward eye and with a backward glance, when rewards appear to have been more assured and pleasures apparently more fully enjoyed. Such fantasies have an unmistakable familiarity with the timeless beliefs people everywhere hold of a lost paradise which once again may be found.

Freud's clinical material showed that adults, when they resort to their infantile behavior, which is associated with childhood fantasies of unencumbered and unearned windfalls, use it as a means to the ends of gratification. Yet, this course of increased egocentric aims paradoxically increases the actual need for a social relationship. His theory accounted for the means, unconsciously employed, by which the necessity for narcissistic gratification would press to seek its own level.

Freud ignored here the simultaneous and lifelong need we have of relationships which self-interest alone could not satisfy. And he also neglected that the injury to self-esteem was therefore not confined to experiences with frustration or discontent to be repaired by fulfillment. It was also vulnerable to the loss of someone valued or loved as occurs in grief, which he did not know took place. He thought this happened only in severe cases of depression. In short, egocentricity, even when heightened by injury or loss, was not self-sustaining. It required a relationship that supported self-esteem. Freud's view was that regression to some previous level of experience, infantile, was aimed at a return to what once had yielded gratification. It was to retrieve some formerly enjoyed pleasure that would be a respite from a present conflict. But it was also a return to a rewarding former occasion when narcissism was not suffering and regression would then be in the service not only of gratification but in the *recovery* from narcissistic injury. Regression is, therefore, both an infantile and neurotic way to *recover* from injured narcissism.

In the half-century since Freud published his work on narcissism, we have acquired ample clinical and empirical experience to bear out some of his speculation. In the aftermath of early and close relationships—which to some extent all fail a child in that none lives up to his extravagant expectations—it has long been assumed, by psychoanalysts and others, that the loss or injury would be compensated. Some unconscious effort, it was supposed, would redress the balance. Narcissism would, so to speak, right itself. Experience shows, however, that a sustained rise in self-esteem is achieved only through some kind of relationship with another. Self-restoration—the kindling of self-esteem through intellectual achievement, mastery or other "works"—however sustained, pursued in social isolation is a limited course of action. We invariably need our sense of worth to be confirmed by our fellows. In short, without some kind of social approval, self-esteem is not enhanced. To be sure, this inherent need of a social relationship, connection, approval and bond may manifest itself in an abstract, idealized, modified or even pathological form. And, it is never absent. The conventional impression that some individuals appear to thrive in the most austere and harsh circumstances of total isolation and solitary confinement, on closer examination, reveals that their *social need remains intact,* however distorted in symbol, fantasy or hallucination. A heightening of narcissism does not eradicate it.

As we shall see later, a child's narcissism is profoundly affected by the development of his perception and appreciation of reality, as he is forced to accede to it. This is the intricate web which holds narcissism once and for all with the aggression it must summon in its defense. From our early years, the more clearly we perceive reality, the more it humbles us. No child escapes the experience which forces his learning that his existence is finite, his immediate circumstances carry uncertainty, his powers are limited. Against the inevitable blows which buffet his narcissism, a child contends through belief in magic powers and the efficacy of his own wishes. A child's hopeful effort to influence fate, to transcend limitations, and to summon from within himself superhuman powers are not naïve aims which may or may not be molded into wisdom by the force of reality. They are an expression of the child's essential defenses. Furthermore, narcissism is endlessly vulnerable. It does not attenuate and disappear with childhood, but remains a precarious element in our character structure for life. And many of these unconsciously formed defenses, unwittingly employed in our youngest years, continue to serve us into our old age.

In the course of these developmental defenses, fashioned in childhood, self-esteem inflates. At the same time, its typical vulnerability gives rise to an acute sense of inferiority or feelings of ignominy. This seeming paradox is rendered infinitely subtle by the fact that the conflicts which first engage a child should occur in the context of his closest relationships—his family. Thus the inevitable basis of unconscious rivalry with a parent particularly, and also the often open contest with other siblings for favor, the efforts at mastery of his world and the development of the necessary skills, the warding off of anxieties and fears, not to mention all the possible failures which must be either surmounted or succumbed to, are all accountable to conscience. They therefore are closely associated with the fortunes of self-esteem. These are the highly reactive and dynamic, yet commonplace, elements in a child's "normal" existence.

A child's need to act—as an expression of his responses to his conflicts—is far greater than is usually understood. The customary pre-Freudian supposition that children are basically passive creatures, by-standers in their own daily lives, reflects a limited familiarity with their everyday emotional life. In the light of the accumulating data concerning the "ordinary," albeit relative, circumstances and experiences of a child's life, we can no longer presume that his emotional development and the formation of psychological defenses are somehow simpler than the same processes in the adult. If anything, the opposite is the case.

It is all too true that the psychology of a growing child is strongly colored by his sense of his own helplessness, his dependence upon those who care for him, and his natural weakness. Yet these very elements which contribute to the kind of self-evaluation a child makes also generate one of his outstanding characteristic defenses, his narcissism. And it is this consideration which has been overlooked. The underlying developmental significance of the typical failures and aborted expectations of childhood is not only that step by step we must learn to appraise the real world more shrewdly, but also that the extravagance of our narcissism must be modified.

It will be remembered that Freud found his neurotic patients alienated from reality because they found it unbearable, "either the whole or parts of it." In many respects, as we have observed, this is no less true of a child—with obvious significant differences. Confronted by unpleasant reality, a child may resort to a wide variety of emotional reactions which reflect his unconscious store of experiences (often quite elaborate) even more than they derive from his contemporary "objective" circumstances. As we have noted, children can (and do) transcend their real worlds by way of the zesty exercise of their imagination, capacity for fantasy, belief in magic, notions of omnipotence, and their versatile tendency to identify themselves with the adults around them. In this fashion, a child begins actively to engage the uncertainties of daily life which he must master. Aggression plays a leading role in these developments, and, as we shall see, the association is a permanent one.

The two dominant, both popular and common, scientific assumptions about aggressive human behavior are, on the one hand, that it expresses some inherent need and reveals our animal descent and, on the other, that it is a natural reaction to provocative circumstances. Further, it has generally been supposed that the restraints on our aggression are acquired through the exercise of human will and that they are an expression of conscience: the force of the deliberate application of conscience curbs human violence. In the psychoanalytic view, this regulatory process is attributed to the ego. This is one of the critical adaptive processes which govern man's aggressive nature.

Ives Hendrick, during the 1930s, noted that certain of his patients not only manifested symptoms indicative of their limited "adaptability," but seemed actually to lack something more elemental in mental life. He suggested that in such cases there was a devastating quirk in the personality which somehow fails in the task of repressing or modifying "narcissistic thought." To make his point, Hendrick offered an interesting example—the Roman Emperor Caligula. Caligula's entire life was a ruthless violation of all commonly accepted taboos, given over to impulsive acts of rage and cruelty and the compulsive invention of childish games and torments in utter disregard of the moral consequences. Hendrick compared the ancient emperor with patients and other contemporary figures who, similarly, commit antisocial acts, insult people outrageously, and stubbornly (or so it seems) refuse to accept the responsibilities of adulthood.[9] In this vivid illustration, he emphasized the loose moral judgment of such persons, their failure to curb their destructive conduct in spite of an intellectual awareness of its consequences, and the absence of the "normal" dread of punishment or retribution. However, in their efforts to conceptualize this seemingly conscienceless conduct, Hendrick and other psychoanalysts underestimate the importance of the fact that such acts of unrestrained aggression are characteristically self-indulgent and self-aggrandizing, the actors egocentric to a fault—insulting, erratic and cruel. While such behavior is indeed aggressive, violent toward others, and sometimes abhorrent to the aggressor himself, the crux of it, which has been overlooked, is a *narcissism* which allows no compromise. The key to the conceptual understanding of such cases lies basically in the process of narcissism. The so-called "defect" in the adaptive functions of the ego is the result of massive failure in the task of relinquishing egocentric aims. It is not, as has been long proposed, some supposed weakness or incapacity, inherent in the ego, to control aggression or else some sort of overpowering strength of impulses.

It is in the modification of narcissism that we achieve some measure of social—and ultimately evolutionary—adaptive strengths. The destructiveness and antisocial violence of a Caligula are exceptional—for that we can be grateful. Such instances, however, clearly demonstrate that when narcissism must be served, aggression issues.

What inner resistance there is to aggressive acts during early childhood, long before the dictates of conscience are felt, comes from anxiety and fear of the consequences and not from any mere compassion for the potential victims. I have called attention earlier to the child's natural inclination to attribute his own qualities or characteristics and impulses or wishes generously and indiscriminately to household animals, to other people, or even to objects which he may animate. In this way, a three- or four-year-old child's anxiety over his own aggression may not betray itself directly, and he may indeed prove himself fearless—except at bedtime when his dread of the dark and fearful anticipation of attack from a veritable zoo of creatures he has conjured up may overwhelm him. Such apprehensions may affect a child's most innocuous aggressiveness—his need for sheer activity—by intensifying his suspicion and fear of all kinds of dangers in the world around him. He is utterly unaware that the menace he feels himself threatened by represents no accurate estimate of his environment but is by far the projections of his own hostility into the dark shadows and corners of his everyday world—he is thus the first victim of his own violence. Somewhat later in his development, at about five or six years, the rule of his conscience becomes considerably more strict than it was, his fears subside, and the erstwhile nightmares tend to disappear. What has happened here is simply that as the child commences to be governed by his own inner restraints and self-control—significantly influenced by those in whose care he has been—he need fear his unconscious aggressive wishes less. This is to say, as he has less of a need to attribute his hostility to others, he has, naturally, less to fear.

In short, we observe that moral injunctions oppose a "natural" condition. Contrary to conventional expectations, conscience develops in opposition to childhood's extravagantly self-indulgent aims and as a means of curtailing the aggression mustered *on their behalf*. While the injunctions of conscience certainly serve to curb aggression *qua* aggression, this is a secondary, albeit more obvious, consideration. Aggression is not an appetite. It serves the self. Aggression is therefore but a means to the primary aim—satisfaction.

As long as human aggression continues to be interpreted as a biological legacy from our animal forebears, this critical distinction will be ill-understood. As we have noted, according to Darwinians, there is no way to account for aggression except as an instinctual drive which accumulates and requires discharge—sooner or later. But the Darwinian view leaves some irksome issues unresolved. If human aggression is not distinguishable from the aggression attributed to other creatures except for the special "human" quality of the conscience which is called upon to restrain it, human history suggests that this is a feeble barrier indeed, and not much of a distinction. Rather, staying strictly within the bounds of Darwinian argument, one must conclude either that we are mutants of a sort, lacking whatever patterns of restraint effectively spare other animals from mutual slaughter, or that we possess some unique rapacity not found in other species. It must be clear by now that it is the argument of this book that only the lifelong dynamic presence of narcissism can account for the anatomy of aggression in man.

Drawing upon his clinical findings of the decade before, Freud confidently stated in 1911 that emotional development depended upon the exercise of accurate perception and assessment of the conditions which impinge upon our instinctual aims—the pursuit of gratification and the avoidance of pain.[10] Such a hypothesis carried the clear implication that when our behavior conforms to the judgment rendered us by reality, we are "rewarded" with greater certainty than when we act exclusively with respect to our wishes. With any luck, we learn this axiom early in our existence. It spares us, when we adhere to it, the frustration or disappointment which accompany vain pursuits, and the aggression they invariably provoke. These considerations were not paramount in Freud's thinking, however, for he was intent on the discovery of the great, overarching principles governing human psychology. If indeed all living tissue depended for its existence on the maintenance of some kind of stability, it seemed to Freud that this must apply as well to mental functions. Therefore, a *principle* of constancy was as essential to mental life as to any living tissue or biological process. This line of inquiry not only incorporated Freud's first training as a neurologist and his earliest psychological work, but it had the added timely appeal to him that it seemed to furnish another link in the chain of continuity with animal life. Freud, the Darwinian, was naturally eager to forge it.

In his paper "On the Mechanism of Hysterical Phenomena," written in 1893, his earliest explanation of the remarkable data he was beginning to gather, Freud attempted to explain hysterical symptoms in the language of the neurologist and even in terms of neurological tissue. He described, for instance, the cumulative effect of emotional experiences on the nervous system as a "sum of excitation," and emphasized that there exists a constant tendency in every individual to diminish this sum, to reduce and relieve the tension caused by this psychic excitation.[11] More than a quarter-century later, no longer an obscure young neurologist, but working and publishing as the originator of a radically new psychology, Freud the psychoanalyst held to the description of the principal task of governing mental functions as the maintenance of stability—keeping the quantity of excitation low in the service of self-preservation.

If we compare his early writings with those forty years later, we find that in 1933, discussing the relationship between anxiety and repression, he revamped his theory in order to clarify the question of what generated repression. The theory of the critical importance of repression in the etiology of neurotic conflicts in and of itself did not call for amendment, yet Freud at this advanced age demonstrated not only that his mind was ever ripe for new discovery but, even the more difficult task, that he was prepared to revise a long-held theory when clinical findings dictated. Hence, on the basis of his continued study of anxiety during the intervening years (especially in its pronounced instances, the phobias and anxiety hysteria) Freud was prepared to make the statement in a lecture on "Anxiety and Instinctual Life," that "anxiety makes repression and not, as we used to think, the other way around." [12] Yet, he retained the old concept of the "sum of excitation" which transforms impressions into single traumatic moments;[13] thus, in the same lecture, we find side by side with radically altered thinking about anxiety and sexuality, the familiar refrain with regard to the subject of aggression: "Impeded aggressiveness seems to involve grave injury. It really seems as though it is necessary for us to destroy some thing or person in order not to destroy ourselves, in order to guard against the impulse to self-destruction. A sad disclosure for the moralist." [14]

In this late writing we note Freud's reliance on his old models to explain aggressiveness. Above all, aggression is viewed quantitatively. In brief, he says, when effectively opposed by obstacles in the external world, aggression naturally turns inward to find the *necessary* satisfaction. As with all instincts, so with aggression, Freud claimed: regardless of impediments and inhibitions, the inherent aim of all instincts and, hence, aggression among them—gratification and the concomitant relief of tension—is fundamentally unaltered. When its flow is not released, the result is traumatic. Therefore it must not be allowed to accumulate, but must be discharged or "neutralized."

Freud only sparsely developed the idea of the "neutralization" of aggression. He succeeded in showing that there was an alternative to the destructive, violent and antisocial manifestation of man's aggression, that aggression may issue in ways complementary to adaptive functions. The confirmation of this theory was at hand. It was to be witnessed ordinarily when a child in his eagerness to develop skills and to master his environment, and to form rewarding relationships with his peers, somehow had set "neutralized" aggression to work toward such achievements. "Aggressive energy" had been "socialized." This suggested that aggression harnessed, rather than thought of as simply to be discharged, directed man's elaborate adaptive, or what psychoanalysts have since called the "ego," functions. Having thus set forth theoretically that aggression also has a constructive direction, Freud brought into view a new aspect of emotional development. It was the last major item in his legacy. The enthusiasm with which it was received by analysts is reflected in the decade after his death when the substantial development and elaboration of psychoanalytic ego psychology began.[15] "Socialized" aggression, found in its neurotic expression as masochism, had Freud's attention as early as 1905. As a menacing element throughout our life, masochism was plain to Freud. He saw that people ordinarily and frequently are tempted to carry out "sinful actions" which invoke self-censure and the unconscious "need for punishment" at the hands of authoritative power. As Freud saw it, aggression, when not sufficiently absorbed into the channels where it was "neutralized" or "socialized," was followed by human suffering.

In an unusual departure in which Freud considered aggression separately from sexuality, late in his career, he wrote that "if for a moment we leave its erotic components on one side, masochism affords us a guarantee of the existence of a trend that has self-destruction as its aim." [16] In these comments, Freud reiterates a familiar theme that has its roots in his theory of the death instincts. He is saying again that aggression is first (that is, inherently) directed against the self and must somehow be diverted. Either we are the victims, or else others become the objects of our aggression. These notions, of course, are not Darwinian in that they contradict survival as a governing principle applicable to man as to all creatures. Moreover, from his observation that self-destruction is a powerful force, Freud proposes that it follows the dictates of some sort of biological destiny. It is one unique to man. It decrees that man's fate is to destroy himself, and, in the effort to transcend that outcome, he discharges his aggression on others.

In short, according to Freud, each individual carries within himself the process which can destroy him. Aggression is a threat of which we must divest ourselves. That is, we must discharge it. Yet, *social* survival prohibits us from taking action which would reverse the thrust of "aggressive energy" outward. Freud saw this as the most ominous of all human predicaments. "Civilization has to be defended against the individual," he wrote, "and its regulation, institutions and commands are directed to that task." [17] Freud saw the individual inevitably pitted against society which demands a renunciation of instinctuality, or at least which sets limits on the aggressive instincts in much the same way that it places taboos on the sexual ones. "Civilization has to use its utmost efforts," he said, "in order to set limits to man's aggressive instincts and to hold the manifestation of them in check by psychical reaction-formations." [18]

With his customary philosophical gloom, Freud thus placed the moralist, who would exhort us to resist and forego our antisocial and anticultural "lower nature," in an unenviable dilemma. To renounce acts of destructiveness, we will only turn its force back inward upon ourselves. Our inherent aggression, Freud argued, must turn and must erupt somewhere—a "somewhere" which ultimately includes self-injury. Aggression, he explained, rendered innocuous to others by being turned against the self was "internalized." [19] It was his conclusion, supported by the clinical evidence of a "need for punishment" or "moral" masochism, that without such a check the efforts of society to defend itself would be indeed feeble. Our self-punishment, it seems, is well deserved.

Since her father's death in 1939, Anna Freud developed and enriched the Freudian legacy. Above all, she took psychoanalysis into studies of child development.[20] In doing so, her views of aggression run parallel to her father's. Accepting the theoretical dualism between the life and the death instincts,[21] she has emphasized (along with other "ego" psychologists) that we must neutralize our reservoir of energy, employ it for our growth and development, or else risk that such energy, lacking outlets for discharge, will turn self-destructive.

She, too, musters clinical instances of "nonneutralized" aggressive energy which, having no other way out, is primarily directed against the self. Her examples range from easily observable compulsive pulling one's own hair in very young children to the more subtle phenomenon of "asking for it" (the provocation of other's attack on oneself) and to varieties of diffuse or symbolized acts of cruelty or violence, by which children appear to make themselves suffer. Other child analysts have followed in the footsteps of the Freuds, holding that all manner of self-destructive acts can best be explained as ineffectively controlled "instinctual" forces manifesting themselves in a child's unconsciously choosing himself as victim.[22]

The writings of Anna Freud, Heinz Hartmann, and many others appear to have followed closely Freud's guidelines on the subject of aggression. But, as we have pointed out earlier, Freud himself left no body of case material on aggression as he did on sexuality. His important papers on aggression came late in his life. They are chiefly theoretical and speculative expositions which deal in a high degree of abstraction. And the force of Freud's influence upon the profession he founded is perhaps nowhere more striking. Analysts have taken this coincidence literally: the fact that Freud investigated sexuality clinically, by way of case history, and aggression theoretically, by way of speculative hypothesis, has all too often been accepted as methodological dogma rather than recognized for what it was—simply a reflection of the particular course of Freud's professional life.

A review of the psychoanalytic literature shows no consistent work in the direction of developing a *new* theory of aggression based on current clinical observation.[23] With regard to the problems of destructiveness, aggression, violence and hatred, whether in their adaptive and creative sublimation in their common intrusion into everyday life, or in disorder and breakdown, the theoretical task has by and large not been nourished by a fresh review of case material. This may account for the fact that theories of aggression remain the weakest in psychoanalysis. Thus, as we have seen, present-day psychoanalytic efforts to understand aggression revert to the familiar suppositions about "quantities of energy," and still insist on a "pan-sadistic" view of human instinctuality—that is, that sexuality and aggression are indivisible. While it is true that they are conspicuously linked in the course of some phases of emotional development and in certain neurotic states, the assumption of an absolute and invariable connection has been carried over to other kinds of human experience without adequate empirical evidence for such generalization.

Ego psychology—in essence, the psychology of adaptive functions —has yielded a considerable and rich clinical literature, which is nonetheless short-sighted when it comes to the subject of aggression. In charting the ego's adaptive as well as regressive functions, ego psychologists have developed an entire field which Freud at the end of his years had just opened. Yet, even in this context, the explanation of aggression depends upon such ideas as the discharge or "neutralization" of quantities of aggression—or whether or not aggressive "energy" finds outlets. There is no doubt that from childhood on, our ordinary experiences provide convincing evidence that grievances are indeed harbored and hostility mounts, which will find substitute targets when deflected from the original mark. But, explanations based on a theory of the accumulation and discharge of aggression have proved to be a dead end.

Freud's publication of *Beyond the Pleasure Principle* in 1920 marked a major turning point in psychoanalytic theory; for the first time he gave the problem of man's destructiveness an explicit, prominent and permanent place in his theoretical formulations.[24] It was no clinical assessment. Freud emphasized here the many painful and unwanted situations in life which his patients seemed to "need"; that is, they appeared to want to repeat and revive previous suffering. To him this was convincing counterevidence to the pleasure principle. It must be, he supposed, that some elemental process other than the search for gratification or relief from want was being served here. It was one that was perhaps prior to, and maybe more primitive, therefore, than the first principles of mental functioning he had formulated in 1911. Out of this reconsideration and review, he went on to develop the concept of the death instincts.

"The hypothesis of self-preservative instincts, such as we attribute to all living beings," he wrote, "stands in marked opposition to the idea that instinctual life as a whole serves to bring about death. Seen in this light, the theoretical importance of the instincts of self-preservation, of self-assertion and of mastery greatly diminishes. They are the component instincts whose function it is to assure that the organism shall follow its own path to death. . . ." [25] Freud continued in this vein, setting down the guidelines for all his subsequent work on the subject of aggression: "Our views have from the very first been *dualistic,* and today they are even more definitely dualistic than before—now that we describe the opposition as being, not between ego instincts and sexual instincts, but between life instincts and death instincts." [26]

Asking himself to what extent he was convinced of the truth of these hypotheses, he admitted that he was not convinced, or rather that he did not know "how far" he believed in them. With regard to the concept of sexuality and the hypothesis of narcissism, he stood by his formulations categorically. "These two innovations were a direct translation of observations into theory," he declared, "and were no more open to sources of error than is inevitable in all such cases." [27] With respect to the place of aggression in his theory of the instincts, however, he acknowledged outright that "the uncertainty of our speculation has been greatly increased by the necessity for borrowing from the science of biology." [28] And, indeed, nowhere in Freud's voluminous writings does he show more clearly than in his work on aggression that he was a man of his time. It was here that he paid his intellectual debt to Darwin.

With the utmost candor, Freud had written in 1914, "Our inquiry into the various vicissitudes which instincts undergo in the process of development and in the course of life, must be confined to the sexual instincts, which are the more familiar to us." [29] His clinical works bear this out. The sexual conflicts which surfaced among his hysterical patients and demanded his attention as a therapist also attracted—and held—his interest and imagination as a theorist. Freud's references to the phenomenon of aggression in his early case material, however, were peripheral and only randomly integrated into his analysis. By 1914 he was apparently aware of this "monopoly." He explained that the slow development of other considerations in his work was a function of "the course that analysis forced on [my] attention. Of all the slowly developed parts of analytic theory, the theory of the instincts is the one that has felt its way most painfully forward." [30]

Fifteen years later, in *Civilization and Its Discontents,* he puzzled, "I can no longer understand how we can have overlooked the ubiquity of non-erotic aggressivity and destructiveness and can have failed to give it its due place." [31] And he ventured the further self-criticism, "I remember my own defensive attitude when the idea of an instinct of destruction first emerged in psycho-analytic literature, and how long it took before I became receptive to it." [32]

Freud's first lengthy treatment of the subject of aggression actually occurred in 1905, in the first of his "Three Essays on the Theory of Sexuality"; here, elaborating on the phenomena of sadism and masochism, he wrote that aggression seemed to be a component of the sexual instinct.[33] Indeed, it was not until 1930 that for the first time he chose to give separate and special consideration to the aggressive and destructive instincts. And, even then, the question of an original, independent source of aggression still troubled him. In his paper on "Instincts and Their Vicissitudes," he suggested that cruelty may derive from psychic conflicts which had nothing whatever to do with sexuality—perhaps from antecedents in some primeval time when instinctual life was less differentiated.[34] How this impulse of cruelty united with the libido at some early developmental stage of childhood was not at all clear to Freud, even though he had, for some time, recognized it as a common occurrence. In a footnote appended in 1910 to his essay on "Infantile Sexuality," he cited Little Hans as a case in point.[35] It is significant that Freud's references, late in his lifework, to the independent sources of aggression take into account only the instincts of self-preservation. He did not otherwise see aggression as having an independent function.

It is a curious fact, and not insignificant, that historically Freud encountered the first serious, open opposition to his views among his colleagues in the profession he founded, not over his theories about sexuality, but in unanticipated controversy over the separate and distinct role of aggression in human motivation. Alfred Adler, in about 1911–1913, taking a step in the direction of ego psychology that Freud was to take later himself (albeit along quite different lines), risked a deviant view, namely, that aggression is a strong, critical and altogether independent source of motivation—a subject worthy of systematic analysis *in its own right*. Freud opposed him. He regarded Adler's hypothesis as an extreme—and heretical—repudiation of infantile sexuality. Freud conceded that Adler had two good points in his major formulations that human behavior reveals a consistent tendency to compensate for feelings of inferiority, and that the "spur" to do so is reinforced by an innate aggression; but he had to reject Adler's insistence on interpreting everything else in these terms. Ironically, Adler was subsequently to reduce all human conflict to a pan-sexual analysis, thus outdoing Freud; initially, however, his aim was in the opposite direction. A few years after they parted, Freud dismissed Adler with the remark, "Presumably his object is to save the world from sexuality and base it on aggression." [36] *

An important consideration in any effort to understand the persistent difficulty psychoanalysts typically have experienced in dispossessing themselves of Freud's legacy on the subject of aggression—a necessary first step in the direction of theoretical innovation—lies not so much in the manifold and complex issues relating to it which Freud left unsolved (and even untouched), as in the fact that he did not regard aggression *in and of itself* as functional or life-supporting. In Freud's view, aggression yielded rewards only so long as it remained inseparable from sexuality. In that conjunction, and only in that conjunction, was preserving the self—the release of tension by way of direct instinctual gratification or otherwise through sublimation—realizable. When Freud did reflect on aggression as an independent instinct, he focused on it in the light of *thanatos*—the death instincts which carry each of us to his grave. And, in this sense, it seemed to presage a return to our elemental and ultimate origins. It is not that Freud failed to comprehend the enormous and essential part aggression plays in supporting our existence, or that he had not fully appreciated his own discovery of its critical dynamic role in sublimation and hence in our daily lives. The critical flaw is, rather, that he could not seem to relinquish—or modify—his theory of the aggressive instinct as derivative. And although he finally acknowledged his long-overdue recognition of its independence, at the same time this "acknowledgement" unfolded not in new clinical material but in a new theoretical abstraction—*thanatos*. Thus he concluded in *Civilization and Its Discontents*:

> I adopt the standpoint that the inclination to aggression is an original, self-subsisting instinctual disposition in man, and I return to

---

* Adler substantiated his "deviant" contributions to psychoanalytic theory with arguments which drew upon Nietzsche's idea that the "will to power" is the core of human motivation. In a puzzling disclaimer which he felt called upon to make more than once, Freud denied that Nietzsche had influenced his work in any way. Adler's affinity for the German philosopher was thus no doubt irksome to Freud, one more item in the deterioration of their relationship.

my view that it constitutes the greatest impediment to civilization. . . . Man's natural aggressive instinct, the hostility of each against all and of all against each, opposes this programme of civilization. This aggressive instinct is the derivative and the main representative of the death instinct which we have found alongside Eros. . . . And now, I think, the meaning of the evolution of civilization is no longer obscure to us. It must present the struggle between Eros and Death, between the instinct of life and the instinct of destruction, as it works itself out in the human species.[37]

Freud thus saw in aggression no functional role of its own—except as a force opposed to all that supports human existence. His belated consideration of the independence and unique importance of aggression reflected, as we have emphasized, his preoccupation during the last years of his life with metapsychological and philosophical questions rather than clinical ones. And, to a large extent, this coincidence accounts for the fact that his late views, questioning himself on aggression, seem to have had no discernibly significant effect on the work of his colleagues and followers.

The past decade has witnessed a growing trend among psychoanalysts and others to illuminate and elaborate upon Freud's theory of human aggression through animal studies. Ethologists such as Lorenz, experimental psychologists such as Harlow, psychoanalysts such as Bowlby, and popularizers such as Storr have created a lively new literature in this field—but the conclusions about human aggression which have emerged from their work are, as I have suggested in Chapter III, all too often deceptive. Nearly a century of countless experiments in the laboratory and the undeniably innovative field studies of animals in their natural setting have indeed produced an extensive, in some instances astounding, new information about aggression—or, rather, the lack of it—in animals. And yet, from our point of view, the most disconcerting outcome of all these discoveries is that they illuminate not at all the enigma of human aggression and its motivation—except to show that aggression in man has no analogue in animal life.

Finally, as we have observed, post-Freudian studies of aggression, whether "orthodox" or "innovative," although they pay meticulous attention to Freud's metapsychological speculations, give scant and perfunctory notice to his clinical material. The serious challenges to Freud's work, once the novelty of its content wore off, have been theoretical. His actual clinical findings are only rarely contested or reinterpreted.[38] Although Freud's clinical findings on sexuality have been confirmed many times over, his case histories—spanning forty years of clinical attention, care and discovery—remain largely unexamined by those who would seek to clarify the problem of human aggression and its vicissitudes. It is just such a "second look" that I wish to take here and in the following chapter.

Freud, especially in his work, exercised a meticulous caution which he was not known to relinquish casually. Yet, when he applied the psychoanalytic method, both as a scientist and as a clinician, to the published autobiographical notes of a famous judge unknown to him personally, he was embarking on a unique and risky adventure. It was unprecedented for a clinician to quit his own direct observation, let alone to clinically interpret a written account by an author he had never met. Emil Kraepelin (1885–1926), among the outstanding teachers of medicine around the turn of the century and a powerful influence on the development of clinical and theoretical psychiatry, admitted that he could neither follow nor understand Freud, and that if he deviated from his own "accustomed walk on the sure foundation of direct experience and clinical observation," he would only "stumble over the power of Freud's imagination." [39]

Nor were most clinicians of the early twentieth century disposed to take seriously the verbal utterances of their patients, let alone the diary of a mad judge. Patients' words, like their often incomprehensible actions, seemed to obscure more than they revealed. Clinicians such as Eugen Bleuler (1857–1939) and Jean Martin Charcot (1825–1893), as well as others less distinguished, appreciated well enough that the crises and circumstances of life profoundly affected the course of individual lives and in some instances produced serious disorders.

The typical professor of medicine or psychiatry, at the turn of the century and in its early decades, however, stood before his patients unprepared to attend to their disconnected complaints and often bizarre behavior; even when dimly acknowledging that these things must bear some relation to the so-called "complexes" which tormented them, he was at the same time altogether unwilling or unable to grant their utterances the legitimacy of full-fledged communication. To hear in them anything other than the confusion of madness seemed to most physicians to substantiate the imagery of their wild ravings and thus to bring the doctor himself into a dangerously close identification or even alliance with the patients.*

We may wonder, then, why Freud would choose an autobiographical account, the *Memoirs of a Nerve Patient,* written in 1903 by a German judge, Daniel Paul Schreber, to demonstrate important analytic conclusions. There were available to Freud any number of comparable cases from which he might have drawn similar inferences and conclusions by *direct clinical observations.* They would have been severely, if not prohibitively, difficult to manage and to treat outside of an institution. Freud's explanation of his circumstances— that he was not associated with a particular institution, and furthermore that patients like Schreber could not be kept for long in treatment when the prospect of success was so doubtful [40]—however valid —does not fully account for his choosing to embark on this extraordinary venture. It was an undertaking which at any stage in his professional life, and particularly in the first decade of this century, was bound to excite consternation among his colleagues no less than among his lay readers. He may have begun it simply as a *tour de force.* Whatever his motives, the Schreber case has had far-reaching implications for all clinicians. It illuminates the close connection between aggression and narcissism beyond anything Freud himself had deliberately in mind; a connection which, in this case as elsewhere, others have overlooked. And it represents Freud's first significant excursion outside clinical psychoanalysis.

Although the Schreber case is thoroughly familiar to serious students of psychoanalysis, it is not a generally familiar work. Yet, it is Freud's analysis of Schreber's *Memoirs* which unfolded one of his important discoveries—namely, the specific nature of the unconscious conflicts present in paranoid psychosis and the particular emotional conflicts prominent in paranoid ideas and thought processes. Further, this case was an early test—and proof—of the versatility of psychoanalysis as a research method. It showed Freud to be an ingenious master of its application. With it he opened a new field for psychoanalytic exploration. Subsequent students of psychoanalysis have followed Freud's early lead, venturing ever further with his insights into areas of history, letters and biography, mythology, literature and art.

---

* The work of the English psychiatrist R. D. Laing, among others, suggests the immense distance between the clinical frontier at the turn of the century and in our time.

Schreber's *Memoirs* were published in 1903 and widely discussed in psychiatric circles; however, they seem not to have attracted Freud's attention until 1910, nearly a decade after their publication. Freud's "Psycho-analytic Notes on an Autobiographical Account of a Case of Paranoia" were, in turn, published in 1911, coincidentally the year of Schreber's death.

In brief outline, Schreber's illness developed discontinuously in three phases, of which only the first two are related in the *Memoirs*. In 1885, at the age of forty-two, Schreber recovered from an acute nervous disorder at that time labeled "hypochondria" which had crippled him for somewhat less than a year. He remained evidently well for the next decade. Then, about three weeks after assuming his appointment as Presiding Judge in an Appeal Court (*Senatspresident*) in Dresden, he once again became seriously ill and was hospitalized for the next eight years. He was discharged in 1902 and pronounced "recovered" except for certain fixed delusions. In the first period of his illness he felt tormented by his delusions that he was a passive feminine victim of homosexual assaults; in the second, he was no longer the object of persecution in his paranoid attacks, but deluded himself into an exalted sexual union with God, from which would issue a superior race.

Freud had shown intermittent interest in the subject of paranoia since 1895. Although there is scant reference to it in his published works before his "Notes" on the Schreber case, it was clearly on his mind. He knew full well that paranoiacs are among the most resistant of all mental patients, that "they only say what they choose to say." [41] Thus, the astonishingly candid and rich revelatory detail of Schreber's *Memoirs* presented Freud with a rare opportunity to put his method to an altogether new and important test—an opportunity he chose not to resist. And, to our lasting profit. He was indeed able to demonstrate, using only material that Schreber himself had placed "in the public domain," the basis in unconscious conflict for some of the gifted judge's delusional torment. Schreber, certainly, was unaware of the significance the *Memoirs* would have for clinical study. And his motives for publishing them were never clear. They were, of course, considering the time of their appearance, somewhat of a sensation. During the decade after their publication they had sunk from sight, without others, either lay or professional, making much sense of the material—until Freud's analysis. Freud came to think that paranoid patients betray in distorted form "precisely those things which other neurotics keep hidden as a secret." [42] Apparently he also considered that the *Memoirs* yielded insights whose relevance extended beyond Schreber's bizarre delusions to general problems of shame, doubt and obsession in the psychology of everyday life.

Freud's correspondence with his confidant, Wilhelm Fleiss, reveals that he was already tentatively grappling with the theoretical aspects of the problem of paranoia as early as the mid-nineties. There he described the disorder as a neurosis of defense and its chief mechanism as the unconscious attribution of one's own manifestly disclaimed motives to others (projection). The Schreber case furnished Freud with substantial evidence which not only enhanced this earlier hypothesis, but led to a series of important clinical discoveries. He demonstrated incontrovertibly—and, indeed, this has since been demonstrated countless times—the essential connection between paranoia and unconsciously repressed passive homosexuality. Moreover, he was able to clarify the role of repression and narcissism in the unconscious conflicts associated with homosexuality. The specific importance of each stage in the sequence of psychosexual development in childhood and the emphatic centrality of narcissism in paranoid suffering have both been so well documented they have become common knowledge. But sixty years ago this, too, was new ground in psychopathology, and Freud was the first to chart it—nowhere more thoroughly than in the Schreber case.

To study Schreber's story in all its magnified distortion is to recognize that in less bizarre versions we all experience and reexperience unconsciously the conflicts of infantile sexuality, that we "project" inadmissible wishes, dangerous impulses and evil intentions onto those around us. (And, as we have observed in our work with very young children, these phenomena first occur far sooner in development than Freud himself anticipated.) For instance, the "reaction" of withdrawing interest, concern and love from others in favor of an exclusive focus on oneself is a renunciation of the libidinal importance of others and a consequent regression into an intensely narcissistic state which is well known clinically—and not only in cases of paranoid schizophrenia. The similarity of this process to hypochondria, Schreber's diagnosis during the first year of his illness, needs no belaboring.

Since the publication of Freud's "Notes" on the Schreber case in 1911, there has accumulated a profuse psychoanalytic literature devoted to the phenomena associated with paranoia. The most recent and substantial critical review of this literature acknowledged that we still have no satisfactory hypotheses to explain or interpret the most distinctive characteristic of paranoid thinking—namely, an utter inaccessibility to influence. And it is generally agreed that the structure and formation of paranoid ideas is by no means clearly or fully understand.[43] As evidenced in this careful survey by Robert Waelder as well as in other sources,[44] experienced clinicians are well aware of the special potential in paranoid patients for expressing underlying hostility in violent and dangerous aggressive behavior. However, theoretical and academic discussion of this kind of case material, supported by the conventional judgment of many clinicians, tends to focus chiefly on the various "mechanisms" of defense and modes of thinking in such patients; and the question of the relationship between their characteristic narcissism and aggression has been neglected in favor of an exclusive preoccupation with unconscious sexual conflicts. The "typical" aggression of paranoid patients is interpreted as an indication of faulty ego functioning, of defenses insufficient to the task of governing and restraining "instinctual" forces. Here again we recognize Freud's early model—the barrier erected against the eventual eruption of instinctuality—whose preponderant influence has all but obscured the outstanding feature of aggression in paranoid patients—its unvarying association with an unmodifiable narcissism.

The crux of Freud's interpretation of Schreber's *Memoirs* does indeed lie in his careful effort to trace the dynamic development of the judge's delusions to unconscious sexual wishes. By attributing such wishes, consciously repugnant to himself, to his former physician, Schreber succeeded in repudiating them. The *Memoirs* contained ample evidence, Freud showed, for the further analytic hypothesis that the strongly tabooed sexual desires originated in deeper, earlier sources—namely, the young Schreber's relationship with both his father and older brother. The erotic idea of being transformed into a woman was, in Freud's view, "the salient feature and earliest germ of his delusional system." [45] He added that such an idea or wish, regardless of the circumstances of its first *overt appearance* in adulthood, is invariably not its beginning, but is traceable to childhood antecedents. As we have seen in the case of Little Hans, wishful fantasies in the four- and five-year-old child of intimacy with a parent or older sibling (which may or may not find direct expression in actual erotic gestures or activities) are common to the ordinary course of family life.

In the preceding decade, Freud had made frequent reference to the child's wish to engage as a full partner in sexual activity, and had explicitly developed this radical proposition as part of "normal" psychosexual development.[46] In Schreber's case, however, he did not know, and could not clarify, the particular facts and forces of life history which perpetuated and aggravated these wishes to the point of irreversible crises and breakdown. The most he could do—and this with restraint as well as shrewd imagination—was to suggest the probable lines of Schreber's vulnerability and resistance.[47] Thus, during the first phase of his illness his doctor "reminded" Schreber of his own father (a physician of eminent reputation who died when his son was nineteen) and his older brother to whom he was deeply attached. Schreber rediscovered his undoubtedly ambivalent feelings for them in the figure of his doctor, although as Freud pointed out—as often happens in the "transference" of intense childhood feelings and expectations onto those who somehow become important in one's adult life—what may have in its original version been predominantly an affectionate relationship may become a hostile one.[48] The reexperiencing of these feelings and impulses (toward his physician) brought forward into conscious awareness and focus, long-standing, albeit unwelcome and hence unconsciously repressed, passive feminine sexual fantasies. Freud then concluded that Schreber, "as a means of warding off a homosexual wishful fantasy, reacted precisely with delusions of persecution." [49] This is to say that he was threatened by his own desires, constituting a passive homosexual role, and strove to "defend" himself against the delusional enemy. The passive sexual aims once directed toward his father and brother, as expressions of intimacy, were then "converted" into the idea of sexual persecution, coming no longer from his wishes, but from the intentions of his physician. Schreber had to protect himself. Schreber's wishes carried with them an acute sense of ignominy, for him an unbearable humiliation, which took yet another turn. In the form of a "religious delusion of grandeur," [50] he reached the height of his narcissistic pretensions, to be chosen by God. The figure of the physician was replaced by God Himself.

Freud pointed out that in "normal" circumstances and for a variety of reasons, throughout life, we constantly detach ourselves from persons and things we have come to value, without falling ill.[51] In and of itself, the process is not a pathogenic one. Freud suggested that it is rather the *lack of a substitute* or, as I would add, the inability to accept one, which increases conflicts and therefore colors our moods. He interpreted Schreber's megalomania, that is, his conviction of being a desired object of another who was important (the doctor) or exalted (God) as representing a return to a stage of unbounded narcissism. Freud explained narcissistic regression of this kind as a return to the period of early childhood in which parents are not only "important" or "exalted" but also necessary. And at the same time the child's estimate of himself is that he is no less valued by them. Although it is certainly an uncompromisingly extravagant fantasy which young children retain, we have found since Freud's work that a body of such beliefs is essential to a child for the security it provides him. Freud saw in regression an effort at self-healing. It was a hypothesis he derived from the empirical observation that when narcissism is injured, emotional investment is withdrawn from others in order to be entirely concentrated on the self. In his only definitive paper, "On Narcissism," Freud developed this description of the course narcissism typically takes for recovery from injured self-esteem and redress of the psychosocial balance, a restoration effected precisely by the renunciation of esteem for others and a corresponding heightening of self-interest.

Schreber's *Memoirs* gave Freud an early occasion and some arresting evidence with which to test and clarify his concept of narcissism and its particular significance in paranoid disorders. We see that the onset of illness in the apparently gifted judge each time coincided with the anticipation of new public responsibilities of magnitude which would try his competence. They were, as far as we may estimate now, the provoking or so-called exciting causes which heighten the self-doubts of a man vulnerable to proving his worth.

From our experience, we may see in Schreber that his tormenting conflict resulted from a deep sense of self-abnegation. This rests on what we must assume was his conviction when he wrote that his father, brother and his doctor failed to accord him the importance or worth he privately wished. His erotic wishes, floridly displayed in his illness, must have driven him to what we now know is a homosexual panic. It is a state of alarm in which patients are notoriously dangerous and paranoid, and in exaggerating their importance, may become megalomaniacal.

Schreber's deep ambivalence lies in the conflict that those whom he so valued should fail to meet his wishes. The injury to his self-esteem, as a result, is considerable, if we are to judge by the intense reaction expressed in the reckless assertions in his megalomania. In it Schreber, freed from the ignominy he suffered, exalts himself as beyond association with mere men and as a fit companion only to God. Questions of his own value, the key to the feature of Schreber's megalomaniacal conception of himself, taken to the extreme, are settled. Schreber sees himself as a redeemer and creator (with God) of a new race. We see further, however, that his intense self-concern, expressed in the uncompromising wish that first his father, then his brother, and the doctor, and finally God would find him desirable, became more excessive in each instance. Narcissism is intensified, and the more it is, the less sure and confident Schreber seems as he is compelled to demand ever more fanciful and fantastic relationships of fulfillment. Finally, in his excess of self-absorption, Freud saw him as abandoning all interest in others.[52] Actually, this was not the case. Schreber took with him into the psychotic regression the entire cast of characters with whom he was in conflict, coupled with his wishes to establish his worth and thus deny his conviction he lacked value by declaring he was chosen for a union with God. But even this proved to be altogether inadequate as a solution; despite his indignant protests and repudiations, Schreber could not do without the attention, society and care of others. His grandiose delusional representations of their interest in him exacerbated his narcissism, yet it could not replenish his self-esteem in the closed circle of paranoid narcissism.

Thus, Schreber did not recover with the megalomaniacal delusions that his physician desired him, or that God found him an object of erotic interest. A reexamination of Schreber shows us his delusions expressed how valued he wished to be and not how valued he felt that he was. Nor was his self-esteem redeemed in his previous hostile delusions of persecution and attack. In defense of his menaced self-esteem or to recover from the narcissistic injury he attributed to the imagined persecution, he viciously attacked those whom he most valued. Above all, it was wounded narcissism which generated Schreber's massive hostility, which at the same time provided the justification for his violent antipathies. Once he became convinced of his union with God and their superior issue, we learn that Schreber's violent defense of his narcissism softened, as it were, or subsided. Indeed, the link between threatened self-esteem and aggression is nowhere more abundantly clear than in the pathology of paranoia.

As we have noted, the Schreber case is particularly noteworthy in the history of psychoanalysis in that it represents one of Freud's earliest efforts to stretch his analysis of severe mental disorder to include some account of its ramifications in the psychology of everyday life. In addition, he was able to use this unusual "case material" to demonstrate essential characteristics of some serious emotional aberrations which, if we can follow and trace the course of their development, reveal their significance to all of us—the functions of projection and repression. For example, Freud's elucidation here of the affinity between paranoia and homosexuality served to clarify an important characteristic of all such states, whether they assume pathological proportions or not. The role of repression and projection in Schreber's illness are all too plain: the transformation of his intolerable and hence repressed erotic wishes into the angry belief that such impulses were not his but another's, and the resulting bitter accusations of persecution represent a prototypal instance of paranoid projection. In the logic of paranoid thinking, it is only one step from narcissism experienced as demeaned and diminished to narcissism glorified in megalomania.

Schreber's *Memoirs* did not include the details of his early life.* Freud pieced together enough to draw inferences which clarified for him some of the pertinent elements bearing on Schreber's illness, but the basis of his deep and ambivalent attachment to his father remains obscure. We may confidently conjecture with Freud that it was the Oedipal relationship which fed Schreber's subsequent disastrous disorder. Yet, since most men experience this critical childhood relationship in one form or another without becoming psychotic or homosexual, we need to search for further illumination.

Throughout Schreber's story run the invariably coupled themes of "affectionate dependence" and even reverence on the one hand, and on the other, "rebelliousness" and repudiation[53] in his attitude toward authority and authorities. Schreber's original feelings of "cordial" and "warm" gratitude for those he loved "for some unknown reason," Freud wrote, became intensified in erotic desire, and at the same time this change in feeling yielded rueful complaints first that his doctor (perhaps like his physician-father) had no understanding or *sympathy for living men,* that God was Himself "only accustomed to communication with the dead," and "took him [Schreber] for an idiot." [54] With nothing but hostility, criticism and scorn for all the figures of authority in his past and present life, Schreber elevated himself above everyone. Freud called this, in a rather complicated phrase, "a true 'masculine protest,' to use Adler's expression, but in a sense different from him." [55] And, indeed, Schreber's illness was precisely that—a tumultuous and tormented assertion of his masculine identity and competence at outrageous personal cost. For only in the grandiosity of his

---

* In passing, it is worth noting that one measure of Freud's posterity in all areas of intellectual life is that it would now be virtually unthinkable for a contemporary diarist not to include some account of childhood data in his memoirs or to conspicuously omit certain data because of their now recognized significance.

madness was Schreber able to relieve his sense of personal ignominy, to which his passive feminine wishes had brought him and also had deprived him of his masculinity.

While Freud carefully elaborated the erotic content of Schreber's delusions and speculated about their probable childhood antecedents, he did not develop the other side of the struggle, Schreber's constant complaint that he was being humiliated. Whether in the sense of being transformed from an active into a passive creature, subjected to violent abuses or otherwise cruelly used, he felt himself the helpless object of unremitting attack. The problem he presented to Freud (and presents to us) is not only that he felt threatened throughout his life by unaccountably intense, and consciously inadmissible, erotic longings, but that he consistently viewed himself as a demeaned object of hard, hostile and aggressive intentions from those with whom he was (or wanted to be) most intimate.

The lasting effect on a child who is caught in such straits for life, without the respite from such conflicts coming from important relationships, is certain. *Whatever* lowers self-esteem increases hostility. It was in this respect that each of Schreber's intensely wished for affectionate relationships became a hostile one—the more he wanted intimacy, the less he expected he would get it. It was this which carried him to a pitch of hatred and aggression toward those he blamed for his humiliation, which, in turn, provided the basis for his efforts to justify his violent feelings. He was utterly unaware of the extent to which his own affections and hostility were bound up with childish demands which those around him could not have met if they had wanted to. The dissatisfaction of this predicament, unconsciously of his own doing, filled him with fury. Thus, he appeared to quit these painful relationships, defending himself by means of vituperative dissociation from those he especially cared for. As we have noted, however, the repudiated "family" returned to occupy the center of his existence in his hallucinations. Not only were his intimate relationships thus restored to him, but there seemed to be no escape from the violence inherent in them. Like all who experience the torment of paranoid states, Schreber was never alone but, rather, was actively engaged in a bizarre reconstruction of his erstwhile social world.

Freud freely acknowledged that Schreber's narcissism—that is, his regression to its early phase—was at the heart of his disorder. However, Freud had not yet taken up in any systematic way, either through direct clinical assessment or in theoretical discussion, the subject of infantile narcissism. That would come a few years later.

Thus, with neither theoretical hypotheses nor verifiable childhood data to go by, his interpretation of this aspect of Schreber's conflicts remained incomplete. Freud prudently chose to emphasize not so much the intensity of Schreber's narcissism, although that was plainly evident, or the effects of accumulated and repeated injury to it which were also clear, but the recurrence in his adult life of infantile auto-eroticism. He saw in Schreber's total social indifference and his deliberate isolation from everyone around him the signs of some arrest of emotional development, although he was without the data to explain *how* this fixation had actually occurred.[56]

Throughout his "Notes" about Schreber and, as we shall see, in almost all his clinical work, Freud did not fail to notice and describe the hostile wishes, violent impulses and hateful feelings which were (and are) part and parcel of every case history. He did not, however, explicitly address himself to these phenomena as *a systematic expression of the vicissitudes of aggression or narcissism*. In Schreber's case, for instance, Freud recognized the judge's drive and his vulnerability, both somehow occasioned by and in his love for his father, as well as his desperate need to defend himself against his homosexual longings. Freud's single focus, as we have emphasized, was on the libidinal aspects of the case. His revision of the instinct theory, which would include and give appropriate weight to the ego and radically alter his conception of the relationship of libidinal instincts to the ego's defenses, didn't come until three years after the publication of the Schreber case. And neither Freud nor most of his followers evidently deemed it necessary or fitting to review the old case material in the new theoretical and clinical light of ego psychology.

Since Freud's time, the Schreber case has been the subject of extensive published interpretation,[57] for the most part psychoanalytic exercises in deductive reasoning. And, again, it cannot be overemphasized that this literature has been almost totally restricted to analysis of the significance of Schreber's unconscious sexual conflicts.

The opportunity to examine other issues by means of a review of this case has by and large been overlooked. Yet, Schreber's story suggests unmistakably how convincing, overpowering, and intolerable hostility can become. Inner reactions to one's own aggressiveness can be as brutal as its overt expression. Harbored aggression, like repressed sexuality, may yield a host of conflicts and disorders which compromise human vitality and activity. The most notable of these are the obsessional neuroses. And here, of all the examples Freud cited, Schreber stands out: he suffered the divided will and the repetitive compulsions of the severely obsessed. It is interesting and important to recognize that to a greater or lesser extent, *all* Freud's cases reveal underlying obsessional themes, regardless of whether the predominant configuration of symptoms suggested florid hysteria, debilitating anxiety or outright psychosis as in Schreber's case. Whether the obsessions are mild or chronic or the primary source of acute distress and curtailment of freedom, an element common to all obsessive behavior is the proneness to doubting—both in oneself and others. And inasmuch as doubting means an expression of ambivalence between love and hate, doubting is poorly tolerated. The stronger the affect, the stronger the ambivalence. "He loves me . . . He loves me not" has more to it than lovers blithely pulling daisy petals would ever care to admit.

In obsessional states, doubt of someone we love or something we wish, and, indeed, doubt of any feelings or expectations are poorly tolerated, if at all. This is to say that hostility, which is part of all our significant relationships, tends in such states or moods to become utterly convincing. They are the feelings which are denied, or ritually engaged or obsessively obscured, and yet which paradoxically carry the conviction that underlies all the efforts to dissociate oneself from harboring hostile intentions. Moreover, they precipitate a mistrust of all feelings of love. And thus the formation of bulwarks against the corrosiveness of doubts, that is, against the undermining effects of hostility, must be fashioned. Here we have another striking bit of evidence that aggressive feelings toward those we love are unbearable, and that we may go to absurd and ironically self-defeating lengths to defend ourselves and others against them. Unconsciously, any rising hostility touches our conscience, which must now be appeased even as our behavior must be controlled. Devotion to routine, repetition and elaborately detailed rituals, the substance of obsessions, seems to offer those who employ it the promise that events are predictable and relationships manageable, and that the hostility that threatens oneself and others is contained. But it is a contrived guarantee, for these unconscious efforts to undo doubt and restrain hostility betray an inherent contradiction. We all look into an unforeseeable future but the obsessional person regards it with a particular sense of uncertainty and doubt. Although there are wide differences in personality among those who are obsessional in their thinking and mode of life, the basis for the obsessional aspects are similar. The obsessive person is unaware of the foundation of his fears; they arise more from his own unconscious hostility than from his assessment of events yet to come. And to ward off what he manifestly fears, he devotes much of his effort to a meticulous adherence to his various formulae for ruling uncertainty. Unwittingly, he thus supports his conviction that when he can rule his own existence and hence govern himself, he has cause to feel secure. Schreber, the extreme, who proves the rule, by means of his litany of obsessions of persecutions, was able to obliterate his own hostility as he became instead the sufferer and the victim.

Schreber's delusions of persecution reflected neurotic conflict usually traceable to an especially traumatic psychosexual development. Freud showed them also to be psychotic responses stemming from his own hostility toward those with whom he was formerly affectionate. As previously pointed out, we have insufficient data even to begin to account for Schreber's extreme pathological deterioration and isolation. Even with so-called complete and "modern" records, including childhood evidence, exactly "why" one withdraws from "reality" to a world of hallucinations unreachable by others may still remain elusive. We do know, however, that hostility toward any valued relationship places it in jeopardy, and that this in turn creates some of our most disquieting conflicts.

To deny our own hostility by means of a staunch belief that we are the victim of someone else's aggression is a commonplace of defense through projection. It is not restricted to clinical episodes. In the ordinary course of life this process of defense commences in early childhood and remains an open alternative to the ego in any circumstance of stress. For instance, children readily tend to find fault for their failures or blame their limitations on the "unfair" demands of others. A child who stumbles over a stone, on getting up, often kicks it as if it were the offender. Countless similar instances provide every child with a solid experience, to be carried into adult life, in disposing of the burden of his own aggression by "projecting" it elsewhere.

It seems that we tolerate our limitations and our failures more readily when we can somehow exonerate ourselves; regardless of the "objective" pain or danger. To feel the hostility *of others,* originating outside ourselves, is far more bearable than the experience of our own aggressive wishes. This confirms an axiom Freud used many times in other contexts, namely that we never give up anything we value without finding a substitute for it. Hence, rather than acknowledging that we may also hate someone we love, thereby risking their loss to us, we tend to disclaim our hostility along with our faults and limitations and simply pass it all on, as it were. Schreber's story illustrates an aspect of this process. From his sense of being demeaned and humiliated and also very hostile, he developed delusions of grandeur which relieved feeling humbled and gave powerful justification to becoming very aggressive. In short, the same principle holds true whether in psychosis or in the common course of everyday life: whatever injures self-esteem unconsciously intensifies and generates aggression in its defense.

Aggression *always* issues—although unconsciously we may distort or symbolize the form it takes—as a reaction to threatened or actually damaged narcissism, whether the loss of our self-esteem is provoked by our own hostility, doubts and demands, or by some sense that others doubt, hate or otherwise seem to devalue and abuse us. And, as we have emphasized, narcissism is constantly in *double* jeopardy: narcissism, when threatened, intensifies and becomes brittle. It would seem a matter of common sense that injured self-esteem endlessly creates a menace which finds expression in both social and inner conflicts. A live possibility in even our most perfunctory and inconspicuous daily encounters, this phenomenon has nonetheless never received the serious attention it deserves. Its wider dynamic implications are virtually unknown: it is not merely aggression but rather the lifelong corrosive effects on self-esteem that may promote restitution from loss, creativity from a sense of deprivation, and success from failure. Aggression is thus the implement of change. With the possible exception of the work in recent years by Erik Erikson[58] on the youthful agonies expressly associated with forming an identity and taking to aggression in the course of it, we are still only superficially aware of the effects of humiliation on the course of an individual life and, indeed, of its role in the history and fate of human society.

Twice removed to a mental hospital from the world of public affairs, professional responsibilities and household cares, Schreber was necessarily isolated, and yet, as we have seen, in his madness he was never without company. For the hallucinated voices and delusional ideas were, of course, the representation—terrifying and intimate—of his former world. Regardless of how absolutely he quit the society of people important to him or how furiously he may have distorted, caricatured and otherwise expressed his unconscious animosity and ambivalence toward them, he was never alone. Nor did he consider himself alone. Rather, he was engaged actively in a range of significant relationships in which those foregone "in reality" were regained in grotesque delusion of persecution and grandiose schemes of restitution. It has for too long been assumed, by Freud and others, that since "normal" social relations cannot be tolerated and sustained in psychotic states, the need for them is somehow also diminished or abandoned. Upon close scrutiny, however, we find that the need for company is not relinquished—although the form it takes may be altered beyond all recognition.

The need for relationships is a permanent distinguishing feature of human life, for it is here that we gauge our worth, test our mettle, and seek to confirm (and have confirmed) our identity. Nor is this a once-and-for-all proposition, but something we must do over and over again—in all stages of emotional development including its disorders. Even in the extreme instance of pathological severance from the community of others and the exclusive withdrawal into self which is typical in severe psychosis, the need for some kind of society in which our worth is ratified continues. The clinical study of psychosis amply reveals that the cast of characters in hallucinations are none other than key persons from "real life," now masked, misshapen, mistaken—and often bigger than life. Beloved friends become an ever-present menace, a parent transformed to a demon, or a sibling to a saint. These conversions in madness are also reversions to levels of infantile experience and impulse, characterized by all the grandiose self-importance of early childhood. The uncontrollable egocentricities common to psychotic states are expressions of narcissism's regained monopoly of the self. The key to understanding and, of course, the treatment lies in comprehending the narcissism.

Consider the example of an autistic child, not quite four years old. Estranged and withdrawn from each member of his family, he nevertheless kept alive his attachment to his mother by way of a frequent resort to the closet where he would cling tenaciously to her coat, holding on, as it were, to her. Yet the same child persistently rejected any direct overture from her; through her coat, he could "have" his often absent mother. The child's intense need for his mother was thus appeased for him in an object that would neither go away nor be lost.[59]

When we find that the need for others persists even in the extreme circumstances of apparent isolation or solitary confinement, we are obliged to conclude that we exist only as social creatures. While conduct may often appear to contradict our social nature, the most radical alterations in behavior do not dispose of the underlying need. Thus, even those patients who are lost to ordinary society in their psychoses and literally removed to so-called safeguarding institutions have not forsaken social experience, although their means of engaging in it may be obscured. As we have seen, their relations with others may be unbearably conflicted, indeed at an impasse. It is precisely the overwhelming ambivalance toward others which causes the intensification, not the sacrifice of social need.

A very attractive young man, for example, was convinced he was hardly worth a glance. He complained of a distressing sort of amnesia. It was that he often lost his way home from work. He always kept in his possession a slip of paper with his address and telephone number written on it in order to know where to return or whom to call when he found himself stranded in the city. Sometimes he would wander about after work for two or three hours until he managed somehow to get himself home. He was employed as an assistant by an exceptionally tolerant man whose directions he faithfully worked to carry out. At times, however, his forgetfulness became a nuisance, to himself as well as to those with whom he lived and worked. He seemed intent on provoking the anger and impatience of others, and, in the matter of his job, asking to be fired.

The amnesia had apparently been present, in one form or another, at times worse than others, since he was five or six years old. Yet, there was no evident pattern to these aggravated periods. As a young adult, however, the amnesia seemed to take a radical turn for the worse without any discernible cause. Thus, for example, he would forget the evening social invitations accepted that very morning. He wrote reminders to himself on all manner of subjects which promptly evaded his recollection. He would go out on an errand, only to end up in aimless and anxious wandering, oblivious of his original purpose. Through his wife's sociability and her probable neurotic forebearance of him, they managed to acquire a circle of friends. But he invariably tended to alienate them as soon as casual acquaintance seemed to verge on a deeper or more intimate friendship. He and his wife both often despaired of their marriage and at the futility of his efforts to order his existence. The depression he suffered rarely left him. He was confronted at every turn with the humiliation of a will that seemed useless.

Thorough physical examination revealed no evidence of any brain tissue damage or dysfunction, and psychological tests merely confirmed his evident very high intelligence and an unaccountable amnesia. Whatever the source of his disability and the radical interference with his day-to-day functioning, no organic pathology was found.

Shortly after he began psychoanalysis, it became clear that the fact that he had been adopted (as a very young infant) had remained a live source of conflict. This "knowledge" intruded into every aspect of his existence. Although partially aware of its influence in some respects, he was altogether unconscious of its profound impact on his life as a whole—as evidenced in his formidable symptom.

In college, his high intelligence notwithstanding, his peculiar and mystifying disability required that he get special tutorial assistance. After a brief courtship in college, he married his tutor, a girl whom he had known previously, though not intimately. She was very much like his mother, in his view—kind, firm, and managerial. She was utterly tolerant of his lapses of memory. She seemed neither to need nor to want to develop a close relationship, but, rather, to want to "rescue" him; in fact, in significant ways, she had not so much married him as "adopted" him. After two years of marriage, his symptoms became aggravated and he began psychoanalysis.

The couple were at their wits' end; the young man's behavior was as inaccessible to his wife's criticism (whether loving or hostile) as it was distressingly puzzling to himself. He refused to assert himself, to express his wishes or needs, or, for that matter, even to admit that he had any. He seemed without form or identity. His wife expressed a bitter complaint that after two years of marriage she did not know him. Their sexual life was a matter of his acquiescing to her wishes; although he apparently enjoyed their sexual experiences together, he never initiated them. His puzzling symptomatology makes clear that this was not simply an extreme sexual passivity but part of a deeper, misplaced and denied regard for himself.

Two months after his birth, he had been adopted by a family to "replace" a stillborn child. His adoptive parents had two children of their own, a few years older than the new baby. The mother was unable to bear another child; nor did the parents adopt another. In their zeal to be "honest" and also in order to prevent the presumed shock of a later untoward discovery that he was an adopted child, his family persistently managed to give the fact of his adoption a vigorous viability and continuing significance. Regardless of the good intentions in this absolute candor (which is a common convention among the more careful adoptive families), its subtle effects on the child are often not so faithfully weighed as the immediate gains to the parents themselves in the reassuring sense of "doing the right thing."

In the eyes of a child, adoption as a legal procedure gives it no emotional currency. This patient was no exception. As a simple fact, adoption to him was incomprehensible, nor would he wish it otherwise; the idea that someone else could permanently "take" a strange child was unacceptable to him. His puzzled sense of estrangement as he grew up was aggravated by his family's reference to his adoption in the present tense—"He is adopted," rather than "He was adopted." Measuring everything against this all-important fact (or as it was conveyed to him), he saw every relationship as tenuous.

His parents' good intentions were ineffective or even worse in other matters, too. They were, for example, very indulgent of him. Above all, he was to have a fair share in everything with the other children. Yet, it was never entirely out of his mind that his parents' kindness to him even as a small child meant not that they loved him as their son, but that they felt charitable to a stranger. His parents convinced him only of their generosity. Inadvertently, they developed in him neither confidence in his own worth and essential goodness, nor any sense that relationships with others were worth the trust or the effort.

Early enough, he showed unmistakable signs of his eagerness to be valued and loved. He endlessly (albeit unconsciously) tested the genuineness of his parents' interest in him. He was resourceful in discovering ways to exasperate them, to determine the exact point at which they would finally punish him or send him away. He was hardly a likable child; convinced that he was not wanted, he set about proving it. At first as an unconscious means of defensive testing of his importance to others, the determination not to admit that he needed or wanted anything became a set feature of his personality. When things were given to him without his asking, he knew that his needs had been considered, whereas when he had to ask, he couldn't know whether the response was recognition of him or merely an acknowledgment of the request. Only what was freely given could he accept with pleasure. To solicit anything reduced his self-esteem. He went to great lengths to avoid doing it. Furthermore, to admit his wishes openly was to unambiguously identify those wishes within himself— to personalize them. Although he was consistently and generously indulged by his parents, he never lost the fear that the next time he would be denied—an eventuality which would devastatingly confirm his unconscious suspicion of what adoption "really meant." Thus, it was important to keep his wishes secret. The extent of his mistrust is betrayed by the fact that he preferred to depend upon the magic strength of his own wishes rather than upon the concern and good will of those around him. Much later, as a young man, he would imagine delightful sexual encounters in which fulfillment was always the same: an all-knowing woman would discover and satisfy his wishes which he would never need to assert. His wife was a near approximation of the fantasy.

And, indeed, during the months of analysis, it became ever more clear that this man's amnesia was not so much a symptom as a defense which served a critical function. "Forgetting" for him was synonymous with not admitting wishes or communicating intentions; in addition, it served to monitor aggression. For, in his view, wishes were not legitimate—any more than the will and aggressive effort which might be necessary to communicate and obtain them. Illegitimate himself, his long-standing conviction was exposed. "I am not legitimate," he was saying, "nor are my wishes." He felt he had no right to assert his needs, desires or intentions. He did, however, make claims—not upon those allegedly close to him, but upon the homeless and remote creatures of this earth. As a child, he brought home a steady stream and an endless variety of "strays" and mongrels—to a point where he created a nuisance. The minor censure this earned him would send him into a belligerent mood of sullen withdrawal, for, like everything else, he took it personally.

As he grew older, his interest in stray cats and dogs came to include a preference for strangers to familiar persons. His quick wit and a certain kind of generosity found expression in his willingness to share whatever he had with new acquaintances and friends, and to claim nothing as properly his own. He had especially identified these qualities in his father, and he was pleased to recognize them in himself. Even as a young boy, he began to weave a network of rationalizations for his abiding interest in the unwanted and the homeless. The comfortable affluence in which he had grown up seemed to justify his concern and charity for those less fortunate, and it afforded him ample opportunity "to be fair," "to be kind," "to extend pity"—a statement of his social attitudes. But that he was himself a "stray" in this same sense was for a long time blocked from his conscious awareness by his fortunate economic circumstances and the psychosocial purposes they accomplished for him.

As a boy he possessed superior intelligence, and his readiness to learn pleased the adults around him at home and at school; but his invariable failure to live up to their expectations produced only consternation and disappointment, for which he rightly blamed himself. This persistent "underachievement" made him feel guilty and anxious, and drove him to keep ever more to himself. Often contrite, he felt he deserved the criticism and ill will he provoked, but he was helpless to do more than make tearful resolutions to change. As he matured, his social existence paralleled his academic life; he touched off high expectations in others, only to let them down.

His everyday life was devoid of the intimacy and cooperation which characterize mutual relationships, but his dreams and reveries were filled with social activity of quite another sort. In fantasy, he worked closely and effectively with others, and was always actively engaged in worthy causes, rescue operations and all manner of social experience in which his devotion and commitments were unquestioned. Moreover, in this segment of his life, his memory was intact. In fact, it was through the analysis of his dreams and fantasies (which he began to record regularly in a small ledger) and their secondary elaboration in free association that it first became evident that his memory *was* intact. Direct questioning about his life history yielded faulty recollections—or none at all—and uncommonly meager associations. In the early phases of psychoanalytic treatment, however, his entire history was reconstructed through dream material—in this instance the *via regia* was not only to unconscious mental life but to the manifest details and actual events of life history itself.

The unconscious material uncovered in this early work brought out the painful acknowledgment of his enormous hostility, and its heavy burden of guilt and self-recrimination. Above all, the unconscious fury he felt for the unknown mother who had given him away was no less than murderous. Nor was it all that successfully dissembled within his sentiments of outrage at the not uncommon practice of abandoning unwanted pets at the local pound, or in the lifelong fantasy of himself as a mongrel—infinitely superior to pedigreed dogs who were flat, dull and nervous, precisely because of their deliberate fine breeding. His terrible hostility toward this mother who had abandoned him was displaced, however, to the one who adopted him. Even during analysis, he was reluctant to admit that she had ever offered him comfort, warmth and love—or that he had deeply wished for it. His antagonistic behavior as a boy repelled even the most casual overtures, and isolated and insulated him from his family. In his smoldering anger, he usually blamed them. He was convinced none could care for him, and he devised tests—which were cruel to himself as well as to his family—which repeatedly "proved," for example, that tradition and lineage were important and that his siblings had a bond with their parents which he simply did not possess. He was furious that his was an unknown identity. Thus, given his conviction of his ignominious origins, the fact of his adoption came to mean to him not that he was specially sought out, which his family emphasized, but that he was unwanted. With a terrible temper, whenever he was punished for some mischief or misdemeanor by being sent to his room—from which he was allowed to return only when he was ready to apologize—he would become enraged by the imposed isolation. Alone in his room, he would distract himself with fantasies of self-sufficiency and splendid independence in some far-off place. He stubbornly refused to come out until his anxious parents were forced to cajole and plead with him. Even then he would not relent and admit that he had deserved his temporary punishment.

To admit that he had been at fault would have been to acknowledge his having an active part in the unrelieved predicament which his childhood early became. But for this to happen he would have had to stop placing the entire blame for his suffering on others. Only with the greatest difficulty was he able in analysis, finally, to come to recognize his own active role. And only when he was able to take his own responsibility, in part, for the course of his childhood, could he consider the deeper cause of his feeling unwanted—namely, his deeply troubling suspicion that somehow his aggressiveness as an infant had earned him his fate. His own hostility, an intolerable and ever-present menace, placed him in constant jeopardy.

For this child, the customary and typically quite perfunctory punishment of being sent to his room became the drama of his existence. When his parents sent him away, it was an act of abandonment. What had begun when he was very young as a denial of the fact that he had any part in these disciplinary episodes developed, by the time he was about six or seven years old, into the most vehement protests of innocence and that he was simply a victim. It led to a gradual repression so thorough that he retained only the angry conviction that he was mistreated and that "they" were unfair. What is of added importance here is that his need for a close relationship, intense to begin with, given his understandable suspicion that human relationships were essentially fickle, was severely threatened by his own unmitigated hostility toward those upon whom he knew he must depend. Each time his parents dismissed him to his room, he felt that they were disposing of *him,* a conviction of worthlessness he was never able to shake; it was not to be altered until his own hostility, virtually entirely unconscious, which served to demean him, was thoroughly exposed.

From the time of Freud's work on narcissism, psychoanalysts have conventionally subscribed to the idea that our response to humiliation is withdrawal from social relationships into various forms of preoccupation with ourselves. Such a "compensatory" response, however, is rarely sufficient, as we have suggested. A lowering of self-esteem *mobilizes aggression* in such a way that increased demands are made upon a relationship for the relief from the overpowering sense of diminished worth. And yet, as we have seen in the case of this young man, one of the effects of the experience of unrelieved aggression is to further compromise self-esteem, which may, in turn, produce serious depression with an acute sense of self-defeat. Nor does the process end here. Further hostility and ill will, chiefly directed toward oneself and with a further intensification of self-concern, with all its brittle indifference to others occurs. This cycle of contempt, ill will and estrangement was firmly rooted in this young man's sense of his ignominious origins and further supported by his parents' well-intended but misguided candidness in reminding him of his adoption. It was not so much the event of his adoption as its apparently unrelieved significance which, repeatedly reinforced, allowed him no way to be other than *only* adopted.

As the boy grew into a young man, this process hardened into the severely neurotic conduct we have briefly described, aborting all social relations in spite of the fact that he plainly could not live without them. Through his symptoms, i.e. his conduct, he unconsciously forewarned others that he would be a disappointment to them; yet he remained aware that only through friendship and intimacy with others could an identity be confirmed and self-esteem given the stability it requires. This helps to explain much of his persistent, even zealous, pursuit of others. The smaller, the more ignominious, he felt, the more he needed to prove himself in the eyes of others.

Alone, we seem unable to fully perceive our own worth—or to have an enduring conviction in it. The intelligent work, the creative act, the kind overture, in and of themselves, do not accomplish the endless task of self-confirmation. We require social approval and support for our very being. As in the case of this young man, when the grim realities are unrewarding, whether we have had a part in fashioning them or not, we turn to fantasies and dreams in which we ourselves can furnish, or so it seems for awhile, the all-important missing element—the company and concern of others from whom we draw support for our self-esteem.

This young man's marked improvement began as he gradually became aware, in the course of analysis, of the tyranny which the chance facts of his birth and adoption had exercised over his emotional life, and that their significance to him had, beginning very early in his development, deeply affected his sense of worth. He was astonished to learn how much his existence was given over to his enormous childhood fury which he had since carried forward. As he came to recognize that self-esteem, and therefore his identity, did not depend upon his origins or his associations with others as much as it did on those relationships in which he was regarded as worthwhile, the projection of hostility and hatred for himself virtually disappeared. And his disturbing symptom of unconsciously forgetting his wishes and intentions—of obliterating himself while also being a nuisance others suffered—then finally outlived its neurotic usefulness.

Chapter V

A Trial de novo:
Early Classic Cases

Not even Darwin's revolutionary theory can claim the variety of controversies which psychoanalysis for so long has continued to arouse. Both the well-known serious as well as the once popular arguments over the nature of our unconscious sexual conflicts generally have been abandoned in recent decades. But the understanding of man's aggression, explained simply on its biological origins, has foreclosed considerations of aggression that are uniquely human. Despite a large literature, psychoanalytic studies on aggression shed little light on it as an ordinary or common phenomenon of everyday existence.

Psychoanalytic studies of aggression have been (a) abstractions on the subject; (b) analogies with the psychology of primitives allegedly illustrating man's condition with respect to aggression when he was as yet unburdened by civilization; and (c) the psychopathology of serious clinical disorders in children and adults who manifestly are aggressive and border on psychosis, or who in fact are psychotic. There is no denying that psychotic states illuminate complexities in aggression. However, the gap between aggression in clinical pathology and in common experience is not closed by studying the one and inferring the other from it.

The popular assumption, not far behind the present scientific one, is that our aggressiveness is some sort of derivative from our animal ancestors. And, that as it gains its emotional expression, aggression gives rise to conflicts. It is a simplistic view. It parallels the pre-Freudian period when sexuality, not known then to be subject to an unconscious, was regarded as dictated solely by biological drives which responded to given circumstances.

It is chiefly in the philosophical considerations and those about development that there is a plain inclination among psychoanalysts to give more attention to aggression than to sexuality. Freud's remarks on aggression, for instance, are contemplative and far more reflective on the human condition than they are about sexuality, where he is strictly clinical and empirical. He wrote more extensively about the theoretical part aggression had in neuroses than he did of his clinical encounters with it. In no major case does Freud clinically demonstrate his views of aggression in the way he did fully with regard to sexual conflicts. And, as we have observed, contemporary psychoanalysts also direct their interest about aggression into abstraction and theory. They draw heavily though on the meager stores of clinical material. The result is that what may be learned of aggression from both limited empiricism and clinical experience necessarily is weak.

In his clinical research, Freud found that the unconscious conflicts in chidhood that begin to gain expression through our wishes, fantasies and impulses to behave aggressively also lead us to be deeply concerned with putting curbs on such emotional experiences. The restraints we may impose, even if exercised only in respect to our wishes or our fantasies of aggression, define a particular conflict; it issues from the pressing inclination to act and the need to curb it. At the same time, mastery of the environment and the achievement of functions, which make elaborate calls on aggression, are rewarded. Thus, from the outset, aggression, unlike sexuality, is both promoted and prohibited. And both at once! In accordance with the social demands made of us, the emergence of guilt and the development of conscience first are engaged far more with aggression than with sexuality. Perhaps it is for a no more compelling reason than that this is the order emotional development takes. A young child is almost endlessly more capable of being aggressive, even to the point of its constituting a social problem, than he is of being overtly "sexual." In fact, the wide latitude for sensuality given young children throughout the world as an encouragement to the appetites bears out that it creates no significant early social conflicts. But aggression is everywhere rapidly brought to heel.

The morality that we each develop is some of the evidence of what has taken place within us. Morality is first bound to aggression and secondly to sexuality. Inevitably, at least when we are very young, we act on our aggressive intentions. Invariably they naturally will be against someone who cares for us and whom we value. Also at a remarkably early age (demonstrably at about two years), we begin to show that we are opposed to being aggressive by imitating the discipline invoked against us and by directing it as a censure against ourselves. But when we, as yet, alone have not developed our own constraints, we call on others. We do it by provoking punishment at the hands of parental powers. These are not merely complex reactions to circumstance explained as fears of punishment with learned consequences according to some behavioristic animal model. It is the same process, perhaps more dramatically and intensively evident, which begins to appear in later childhood about the Oedipus conflicts. Then there appear elaborate, frequently unconscious fantasies of being beaten. They represent the child's need for prohibitions against sexual wishes when his conscience is not a reliable deterrent. In a period when wishes are equated with acts, the need for prohibitions extends no less to aggression than to sexuality. It creates the temptation to perform "sinful" acts which are certain to be punished, or for which intense guilt will be suffered.[1] These conclusions on the formation of "moral" masochism, Freud completed writing around 1924.

He was concerned with showing that an unconscious sense of guilt developed naturally. And that self-imposed suffering unconsciously went far to satisfy it. This was a need for punishment. Which is to say, that our conscience is brought to function in respect to certain of our wishes no less often perhaps than our acts. We respond thus beyond what circumstances would dictate, to the meaning that they have for us. However, Freud here was attentive to sexual wishes, particularly those of an Oedipal nature which were subject to censure. His conclusions that a need for punishment existed referred to a reaction to sadism, meaning that the erotic gratification of aggressive wishes and acts was in the focus of one's inner self-critical agency. He did not, however, extend its application to aggression alone. With his usual emphasis on libidinal gratification, the relation of aggression to conscience was regarded as a question of somehow satisfying instinctual urges over which invariably there would be conflict. If there were to be distinguishing effects between unconscious aggressive intentions and sexual ones, each imposing different self-suffering, Freud did not include them either in his clinical or theoretical works. As we have seen, separating aggression from sexuality was considered only in theory; and then near the end of his life.

As Freud's early cases, classics of psychoanalytic literature, appear not to have been reviewed in the light of later findings, his cases remain as he reported them, freshly minted clinical documents. They furnish the reader today with the vivid clinical experience Freud encountered more than a half-century ago. And in these cases, the notable lack of comments on aggression, either by Freud or his followers, is all the more conspicuous as we shall see presently. No explanation is even hinted at. Freud's biographer, Ernest Jones, seems not to have recognized the concern Freud had in his last years about this omission. We have only some suggestion of it. In 1937, Freud said about aggression, "The whole topic has not yet been treated carefully, and what I had to say about it in earlier writings was so premature and casual as hardly deserves consideration." [2]

It is both curious and unexplained what little specific reference Freud made to his first cases in his later writings. He often cited some of the theoretical aspects they illustrated but he actually referred to them rarely for purposes of clinical comparison. The outstanding exceptions were the case of Little Hans and the Schreber case. It is interesting that neither case was one that Freud dealt with directly clinically. When he was actively reformulating psychoanalytic theory in the early twenties, making important modifications in basic concepts, the clinical experience he drew upon focused on unconscious sexual conflicts in emotional development and their manifestations in daily life. But there was no review of the important early cases in the light of changes later experience dictated. And while the *theory* of aggression received special notice, as we have called to attention previously, it did not extend to the clinical findings of aggression. Thus, Freud's earlier cases were not scrutinized in the brilliance of his revised libido theory. Neither he nor others reconsidered them then. When he was puzzled and acknowledged his oversight of the independence of aggression in his last, posthumously published writing, it galvanized no reexamination of his cases by others. Instead, they became historical pieces in psychoanalysis to be learned by students rather than clinical ones to be restudied in view of new understanding.

The saga of psychoanalysis may be said to begin, perhaps, with Josef Breuer who became engrossed with his interesting patient, Anna O. She was an unusually intelligent girl of twenty-one years, who, in connection with her father's fatal illness, developed a museum of distressing and crippling symptoms. The problems his young hysterical patient created for Breuer extended to her excessive emotional demands. Between his own alarm over his involvement with this absorbing disorder and his wife's expressed concern at the unusual attention her husband paid to this case, Breuer, during a period when the girl improved, seized the opportunity to terminate his services. However, soon afterward in 1882, Breuer, interested in a younger colleague, Freud, felt urged to share with him the unusual details of his unaccustomed experience. If Freud was not exaggerating when he asserted that the great majority of such severe neurotic disorders had their origin in sexual life, he, Breuer, was ready to pay attention.[4] It was at a time when sexual topics had no more propriety in the clinical practice of medicine than in the parlors of nineteenth-century Europe.

The continuing sensationally popular work, *Madame Bovary,* and the "new women" Ibsen characterized as restless and pressing for fulfillment were harbingers that the repressive society of the period, especially in Vienna, would not for long deny them lodgings. Therefore, when Breuer attended a young woman patient of a distinguished family, whose symptoms were curious and even at times bizarre, who was well brought-up and educated and who exhibited characteristics which he thought contradicted her accomplishments and position, she had made him privy to more than he had previously listened to from his patients.

Three years later in Paris, while studying under Charcot, Freud recounted Breuer's case to him. "But it was easy to see that in reality he took no special interest in penetrating more deeply into the psychology of the neuroses." [5] Charcot was more engaged with the remarkable phenomena hysterical patients presented than he was in giving consideration to what one of his many students was speculating about. Patients of this sort often conspicuously suffered amnesia. It was little understood. And the first focus of clinical attention, amnesia, gave physicians opportunities for the wildest suppositions as to the process of memory. What it was patients forgot had to wait for another discoverer, Freud.

Anna O. through hypnotic suggestion needed little encouragement to pour out to Breuer "streams of material from her 'unconscious.' " [6] Of course, what he could not have known then, and which Freud discovered afterward from his own cases, was that patients under such conditions develop especially intense feelings toward the listener. Anna O. herself demonstrated this reaction. It alarmed Breuer.

The explanation of what happened to the girl Freud later wrote, "The patient suddenly made manifest to Breuer the presence of a strong unanalyzed positive transference of an unmistakably sexual nature." [7] It was generally assumed by physicians of the time that at the root of the disorders hysterical patients displayed so floridly were the trying circumstances of a frustrated sexual life. Such suppositions confined to "the marriage bed," Breuer wrote in discussing the disposition to hysteria, omitted altogether prenuptial sexuality.[8] Despite such conclusions there was no demand for further study of a patient's sexual life. At the turn of the century, much of the theory of hysteria derived from the doctrine that the symptoms such patients displayed were going to be explained as a disposition to the disorder by way of some genetic factors, and ultimately definable in physical and chemical terms. Freud himself retained this view to the end. He explicitly referred to it in his theories that all psychological phenomena eventually would be explained by chemistry. Today there are many who still subscribe to the belief that the secret to human motivation and conduct will be found in chemical elements and physiology.

The first publication, in 1893, by Breuer and Freud represents the beginning of psychoanalysis. It was in this joint paper that the theory explaining hysteria began to be defined as more than amnesia. They had begun to think of it as a disorder in which the patient, finding some aspect of his life repugnant, is genuinely incapable of recollecting it. It marks the emphasis the authors place on the active presence of the unconscious memory of an unpleasant experience, exercising, beyond conscious control, a governing influence over some behavior. "Any experience which calls up distressing effects—such as those of fright, anxiety, shame or physical pain—may operate as a cause." [9] *"Hysterics suffer mainly from reminiscences."* [10]

Thus, the first and revolutionary suggestion we have that hysteria may be founded on other than either unpleasant circumstances or direct sexual frustration was referred to in the same paper (1893). In describing examples of hysteria, Freud wrote about a girl patient who once was described as the victim of savage attacks by a dog, which then caused episodes of later suffering, and another was a man who after being ill-treated fell subsequently into a frenzy of rage.[11] Much is made of these as traumatic events which provoked the hysterical symptoms. No further comment, however, is offered of what possible significance there was in the nature of the trauma that should provoke fury or suffering.

Fräulein Anna O. was the one case reported by Josef Breuer which belongs to the psychoanalytic era. Both he and Freud regarded her as showing a "peculiar kind of psychosis." Besides a marked intelligence, she had a penetrating intuition. An energetic, tenacious, persistent and at times obstinate girl, she only occasionally gave way out of regard for others. She was not suggestible and was influenced by arguments but "never by assertions." "The element of sexuality was astonishingly undeveloped in her." [12] When Breuer first examined her she had neuralgia and pains as well as muscle deformities and contractures from the paralytic postures she held in conjunction with her emotional disorder. Furthermore, she had disturbances which involved speech, vision and hearing.

Breuer reported he observed two distinct emotional states in Anna O. In one she was relatively normal. In the other, however, she was abusive. She threw cushions at people and tore at her bedclothes. She also accused others of doing something to her. She awakened in the morning during such periods with the frequent complaint that she was tortured or tormented.

The frequent disputes she had with her nurse extended to active outbursts against others. They often ended in severe attacks of anxiety. In connection with her father's death, she had visions of "death's heads" and terrifying figures to which she responded with fear. She complained further about her torment by a string of frightful fantasies. And she was "strongly suicidal." While she had many periods when, after Breuer's visits, she would become industrious and cheerful, his absence brought out anxiety and disagreeableness in her. She was often moody, ill-tempered and even malicious. Or she would sometimes tell him "she had no idea what was the matter but she was very angry. . . ." [13] There were also times when she would not hear what he was saying to her and he was obliged to communicate with her by writing notes. "It was especially noticeable in Anna O. how much the products of her 'bad self,' as she herself called it, affected her moral habit of mind." [14]

Two factors, each of immense importance to psychoanalysis, commence with this case. One is the method of treatment of psychoneuroses which begins here with the "talking cure," as Anna O. called her treatment, and the other is the beginning discovery that amnesia has important "hidden reminiscences." There is, however, a third factor. Although amply reported, it is nevertheless to the present persistently ignored.

The neglected material which gives added illumination to the case of Anna O. is contained in Breuer's remarks that "She possessed a powerful intellect . . . under the control of a sharp and critical common sense. . . . Her willpower was energetic, tenacious, persistent; sometimes it reached the pitch of obstinacy. . . ." [15] She could be kindly, but in her unguarded moments she was abusive, "unamenable, ill-tempered, even malicious." [16] These were the occasions when she became deaf and required Breuer to write out his communications to her. The conspicuous part aggression holds in this young woman's disorder is central. Moreover, it is not entirely directed at her nurse and family, but also at Breuer. We are advised that her "Strong suicidal impulses appeared which made it seem inadvisable for her to continue living on the third floor." [17] From this and a few other sparse remarks referring to the anxiety she created over turning her aggression against herself, "by numerous attempts at suicide (though as long as she was in a garden, these were not dangerous), by smashing windows and so on. . . . ," [18] we are forced to conclude they are the clearest and most unmistakable indications of the presence of a serious, self-destructive intention. Whatever other emotional conflicts Anna O. suffered, her strong suicidal wishes and acts are plainly the evidence that a powerful, deep-seated, self-destructiveness and hence aggression turned against herself motivated her.

Anna O. often would refuse to speak to Breuer. He felt obliged to urge her with the plea that she should continue the "talking out." Over a period of time through these efforts she seemed to improve. However, he found she had become worse, more easily angered, and she directed her fury at him. We know now from ample experience that treatment, interrupted by the physician's absence, is certain to risk provoking a patient's anger. Patients often think, why should my doctor go off to enjoy himself when I am suffering. He is neglecting me to indulge himself. Other conditions or circumstances which similarly may interfere with a patient's care may arouse angry recriminations of disregard. Attending other patients or a necessary absence due to the physician's own temporary illness are notorious occasions used by patients to become infuriated and hang accusations of being abandoned on the physician. The patients often freely admit these are not rational demands. But a study of their anger shows they are present with the expectation of fulfillment. And this young woman gave Breuer the effect of her displeasure. She was also very annoyed with him "because a recollection refused to emerge." There were no doubt many such "reminiscences" which must have been related to some painful admission he attempted to extract from her. She resented it, as patients often do. For his pains, Breuer often received abuse rather than good will.

A common reaction to guilty admissions is to direct aggression unconsciously away from oneself to the one who hears them. That is, the guilty one expects that similar censorship to his confessions will be aroused in his hearer. In defense against his own culpability, he attributes accusations to the listener, and resentment commonly follows. Close friendships thus are often strained if not spoiled by hearing confessions. The mutual confession young adolescent girls practice commonly, in which each is admittedly a culprit, in their case suspends the process. The institutional anonymity of the priest spares him from attack and especially when he can dispense absolution. But the physician must be prepared to accept that he will be the target. Breuer, of course, could not have known in his time what we have since painfully learned.

From the outset, in Breuer's account of Anna O., her fury extended to all those about her and she did not spare herself. After episodes of rage, we may note that an increase in severity of frightening symptoms, anxiety attacks, despair, self-accusations and suicidal impulses followed. The young woman directing fury at those close to her and committing acts of violence toward them in the belief that she is a persecuted victim is an extreme reaction to a common experience. Since she was deeply attached to her father, whom she nursed devotedly during an illness to which he succumbed, and since she herself then became worse, questions are raised to which we can only guess the answers. Like Anna O., it is not unusual to find that a girl who is deeply devoted to her father, who cannot seem to give him up, may expect the disapproval of others for her attachment.* Like her own self-accusations, stemming from unconscious sexual wishes, she would expect others to disapprove of them as she herself does. Many instances in Breuer's report indicate that this was the case. However, there are other determinants present which preclude confining ourselves only to the sexual ones. The erotic aspects of the case, within the limits the material permits, have been fully and repeatedly dealt with. His patient's hostility, however, which Breuer did not discuss, laces the clinical material.

A psychoanalytic reappraisal of Anna O. from our vantage point in history suggests that whatever the erotic conflicts were, they fail to account for the violence, hatred and often suicidal course the girl seemed driven to take. She was aggressive, abusive and scornful of those close to her, or else turned the same behavior on herself during her "relatively normal" and depressed periods. Moreover, when she refrained from attacking others, she had nightmares, daydreams and fantasies in which she was the victim. As we well know, conflicts over sexuality may lead to the development of hysterical symptoms. But only conflicts over disappointment and hatred would have led Anna O. into states of acute depression and attempts to kill herself. In short, hysteria is no basis for suicide or violence.[19]

The appearance of euphoria, liberating her from oppressive hostil-

---

* Recall the case Darwin cited (Chapter I, p. 7).

ity—the product of her so-called "bad self" [20]—is a sign which, from our present work, we can identify as a powerfully motivated unconscious denial of impulses and wishes to be hostile and violent. This produces in extreme cases a flight into elation and euphoria. These reactions to one's own deep-seated intentions to be a "bad self" are typically characterized as self-inflating or self-aggrandizing states. They replace self-denigration; the hostility and wishes to be destructive, by repression, are withdrawn from any awareness. Hate and aggression thus become unconscious and give way to an easy affability and extravagant friendliness. However, these responses are notoriously unstable. The good humor of elation is always close to irritability and aggression. And the tendency is to turn on oneself as a further curb to being aggressive; the risk of hostile wishes converted to self-destructive acts is far greater than is generally understood. The similarity of this dynamic sequence in the manic-depressive psychosis to that of the normal-neurotic elations is striking; despair and self-destructiveness are closely parallel and dynamically similar to psychotic depressions and suicide.

Directing toward oneself the hatred of someone loved or valued is the crux of what Freud, twenty years after the publication of Anna O., was to describe as the key to depression in his great classic, *Mourning and Melancholia*.[21] There was some hint of this discovery about despair in another context. In notes written to his friend Fleiss, 31 May, 1897, a few years after the publication of the case of Fräulein Anna O., Freud wrote, "Hostile impulses against parents (a wish that they should die) . . . come to light consciously as obsession ideas. They are repressed at times when compassion for parents is active—at times of their illness or death. On such occasions it is a manifestation of mourning to reproach oneself for their death . . . or to punish oneself in a hysterical fashion." [22]

Two decades later, in 1917, writing on melancholia (i.e. depression), Freud said, ". . . we find the key to the clinical picture: we perceive that the self-reproaches are reproaches against the loved object which have shifted away from it to the patient's own ego." [23] It was his view that the central causes of the lowered self-esteem from which depression issued was to be found only in exceedingly narcissistic people. (This was most likely to be true of Anna O.) Freud was later to make no reference to the fact that she had severe suicidal episodes of depression and that she met his criteria of one who regards the loss of someone loved as an intolerable personal deprivation. The severe blow is to one's self-regard.

Freud's observation that a lowered self-regard is a melancholic reaction to the loss of a valued relationship has led to a large literature in psychoanalysis and related fields confirming his findings. Surprisingly, however, his assumption that such excessive reactions as clinical or psychotic depression apply *only* when the relationship had been a hostile one, and that suicidal manifestations represent a prior hostility which had been repressed and now turned on oneself, has not been reconsidered.

Our studies show that the ones who are most prone to suffer are those in whom loss arouses childlike hostility, i.e. the sense of deprivation which represents not so much *what* is lost as *having lost*. The resistance to accepting that verdict which reality renders, and against which neither wishes nor magic have power, is probably the most bitter lesson of childhood. It is one which actualities begin to teach very early. Those who fail to learn, as their childhood narcissism is naturally threatened and challenged by everyday life, become increasingly enraged. The fury rather than the basis for it becomes a central issue. When a child is not helped to give up some of his egocentricity by those upon whom he depends, the risk is that the serious disorders of heightened narcissism, increasingly resistant to accommodation, will follow.

While it was the nature of Anna O.'s intense relationship with her father that led to the outbreak of her illness, we must add that from her symptoms we may conclude that the relationship was also a very narcissistic one. And it was this element which was to have a critical bearing on her particular difficulties. The death of her father gave her illness its serious turn. We may safely suppose it was this irrevocable loss which she could not tolerate. She became infuriated. And, as we have indicated, the unconscious turn from a grievance against her father, to rage at others, and a turn of it to herself best fit most of the clinical facts. That the young woman's aggression is related principally to narcissism is evident from the persistent indications that self-esteem is an issue throughout. We see it in her difficult course, whether she scorns others or feels herself degraded, abused or persecuted. It is important to keep in mind that when Freud developed his views of his colleague's patient, they were in respect to the girl's unconscious sexual conflicts. Her violence turned on others or herself was seen only in that context. It was not considered as having an independence from sexuality. Nor was narcissism as yet a psychoanalytic concept. Anna O.'s marked aggression was well observed. But it was left unexplained.

It was nearly twenty years later that Freud discovered a determining role for narcissism in neurotic conflict. It was, he found, the unusual susceptibility of some of his patients to the effects of disappointment which gave him the clue to their narcissism. These cases showed little readiness to compromise extravagant wishes and to accept the limiting experiences of everyday life without a sense of deprivation developing. Such events were not regarded by them as realities to be mastered but rather they were viewed as assaults on their being, wishes and aims, and therefore constituted injuries to self-esteem. Realistic limitations led to rage at deprivation with heightened demands for restitution.

Freud thought the increased self-concern, i.e. the increase in narcissism, was a sufficient compensation. These were not concepts or considerations Freud entertained about Anna O. If we take his theory of narcissism one clinical step further, we find that the conflicts over self-serving expectations in his patients are in themselves not extraordinary. In fact, they are like those most of us entertain; that is, our actual conflicts are astonishingly similar. The differences among us in respect to our emotional disorders and from Freud's patients are to be found elsewhere than in our conflicts per se. For instance, when our self-esteem is felt to be jeopardized, it may bring out a tenacious clinging to infantile wishes which may have been long since repressed and even abandoned. The focus of our attention here must therefore be shifted to the nature of our narcissism, the course of what may affect it, the extent and readiness of infantile demands to return and their being relinquished in favor of renewed efforts at mastery and achievement. It has been the focus of analysts to be engaged with what may affect or injure narcissism but to be less attentive to the nature of its wounds and the sequels which issue from them.

When one's egocentricity, expressed in wishes or aims, allows little or no compromise, we may expect the proneness to narcissistic injury to be all the greater. And what might otherwise have been no hurt or but a slight trauma may be discovered to carry an astounding and seemingly incomprehensible impact. For example, a well-meaning, fastidious photographer removed an inconspicuous mole from a portrait he was making for a young woman. Her discovery of what he had done not only brought her to reject the work, but the apparently trifling event somehow precipitated an episode of depression. It was not his having removed the mole, or its symbolic castrating significance which conventional psychoanalytic thinking might assume to wholly account for such a reaction. It was that this particular blemish was an important mark of identification with her father to whom she was deeply attached. He had a similar one, approximately in the same place. The removal of it, a loss, affected her narcissistic identification with her father. It aroused an infantile and long-standing reaction of being deprived, anger with her father she had long forgotten, which, in remorse, she turned on herself and became depressed. The identification with her father, necessary to her self-esteem but which he did not support to the extent she had wished, left her furious. And an event which threatened to reduce what identification she had was certain to bring back old grievances which castration alone as an explanation would not adequately cover.

On 1 May, 1889, Freud took on the case of a woman of about forty years of age, whose symptoms and personality "interested me so greatly that I devoted a large part of my time to her and determined to do all I could for her recovery." [24] She was Frau Emmy von N. His description of her initially fits clinically what we would today call an "agitated" depression. Freud described her as appearing morose and ceaselessly agitated. She so disliked saying anything about herself that he noted two years later that none of the daily visitors to her house "recognized she was ill or were aware that I was her doctor." [25] Among other things about her, Freud wrote at the conclusion of his report, "Frau Emmy von N. gave us [Freud and Breuer] an example of how hysteria is compatible with an unblemished character and a well-governed mode of life. The woman we came to know was an admirable one. The moral seriousness with which she viewed her duties, her intelligence and energy, which were no less than a man's and her high degree of education and love of truth impressed both of us greatly." [26]

Before the treatment actually began with hypnosis, Frau Emmy expressed disgust and horror in relating her tales of distress. Her preoccupation with her own destructive impulses and acts, her violence and contortions, all reminded Freud of similar cases in which "wishes that something bad might happen to her husband and her mother, blasphemies, etc." [27] had a significant effect. From the outset, Frau Emmy's aggression shows, but it was not the focus of Freud's special interest at the time. His effort was aimed at having her speak out the "reminiscences" which he thought caused her to suffer by the fact that they were held in a sort of amnesia from which they needed to be released. The time was not as yet ripe to consider the significance of what she thought so much as it was to get *what* she thought into spoken words.

She had been constantly ill fourteen years since her husband's death, she told Freud, suffering depression, insomnia and pains, and only with some temporary improvement during this period. When she was in an apparently quite normal state, "she entertained me . . . with gruesome stories about animals." She had many tales of horror and death to relate, anecdotes of people being mistreated and tortured. As she told these to Freud, she would suddenly break off and shout, "Keep still! Don't say anything! Don't touch me!" [28] She no sooner spoke of abuses than she acted as though she feared being attacked.[29]

Reflecting on her past, as Freud had her do, she recounted attacks by her brothers and sisters that she suffered as a small child, their terrorizing her, and her fantasies of seeing them in their coffins. Neither she nor Freud remarked on the relationship of her being victimized and her seeing them dead. Later as a girl, when her brother died, the so-called visions of earlier childhood came back, and, much to her distress, symptoms of agitation came also. There were pains and horror stories reported, terrifying memories and the conviction that she would be victimized.

Frau Emmy was an extremely aggressive woman. She hated her brothers and sisters and at times her children as well. She furnished Freud with a long list of grievances; there were accounts of many exchanges of insults and agitations with various members of her family. And yet, she did not escape the oppressiveness of her destructive wishes because they were virtually always followed with bitter complaints of illness, fears of illness and pains, a dread of what might happen.[30]

Freud's attention was paid to the fact that she was "of a vehement nature, capable of the strongest passions," [31] and since her husband's death "had not won her victory over her sexual needs." She had thus exposed herself "to severe mental exhaustion." [32] If he could help her get rid of her "stock of pathological memories," it would make a considerable difference in her condition.[33] He was reminded of "one of the principles laid down by Darwin to explain the expression of emotions—the principle of the overflow of excitation[34]—which accounts, for instance, for dogs wagging their tails. "We are all of us accustomed, when we are affected by painful stimuli, to replace screaming by other sorts of motor innervations." [35]

As in the case of Anna O., Freud was attentive to two major problems. He was attempting to explore the nature of the hysterical features present and to develop some technique for its treatment. As he said, "I tried to disentangle the confusion in her mind under hypnosis." [36] When he inquired into what frightened her, she repeated to him her terrifying fantasies, recounted unhappy childhood memories, and told of her fears, pains and physical infirmities. Freud was impressed with the lasting effect of childhood traumatic experiences producing symptoms at a much later date.[37] Hardly a page of his long report on Frau Emmy is without details of a wretched past, ill humor, hatred of her sisters, fights with her brothers or else with her husband's relatives, and a preference of one child over another. Hardly anyone seemed to escape her hate. In a moment of fearful confession, she admitted she feared she hated herself most of all.

There are two major disorders present in Frau Emmy's case. One is manifestly hysteria. The other, however, is depression and is directly associated with hatred and aggression toward her family, husband, children and ultimately herself. Her destructive intentions toward those who were close to her turned into aggression against herself. Freud published his work on depression twenty years later. If he had looked back on Frau Emmy then he would have said that she would not allow herself to attack those whom she cared about without guilt and remorse and turned the aggression on herself. In conjunction with that she became depressed.

Freud provided us with the material that compels our further consideration that Frau Emmy was exceedingly hypochondriacal and preoccupied with herself to the exclusion of others. We must add, therefore, that she was a very narcissistic woman engaged with her somatic complaints to an inordinate degree. Depression and hypochondriasis, Freud discovered more than a decade later (1911), were characteristic of those who were narcissistic. And hypochondria, for instance, represents self-destructiveness unconsciously, that is, in fantasies of illness and impairment always having a morbid outcome. Hypochondriacs characteristically suffer only serious illness, or at any rate symptoms which are harbingers of grave consequences. Frau Emmy *had* to be ill. She had lost her self-respect, and she must have had good reason—hostility. The point is not whether Frau Emmy's complaints are correct, that is, in accord with some physical syndrome or in accord with those of depression and hypochondria, but rather that she gave a correct, albeit unwitting, appraisal of herself. She was severely self-reproachful for her aggressiveness. And from her excessive self-concern with destructiveness aimed unconsciously at herself, she provides us with a clear picture of an exceedingly narcissistic woman who turned her aggression toward others against herself. This was her illness.

Freud did not here discuss the problem of aggression. In 1915 when he wrote that "various vicissitudes which instincts undergo in the process of development and in the course of life must be confined to the sexual instincts, which are the more familiar to us. . . ." [38] he had even then not discussed either aggression or narcissism specifically in relation to one another, and not at all in connection with his earlier cases. Although he furnished us with ample evidence that indicated both aggression and narcissism were pervasive conditions in his cases, we had no sign from him that they were manifestly part of a "clinical syndrome," or constituted a disorder at some point, or that they produced particular conflicts and suffering. Some suggestion appeared that the aggression he reported was a reaction to untoward, unpleasant or traumatic circumstances or events. That aggression has its own vicissitudes other than those associated with sexuality, Freud considered only later in theory but not in relation to clinical cases.

The most elaborate and probably the most important of all Freud's case histories is the Wolf Man. [39] Many references to it occur throughout most of the psychoanalytic works by Freud. At the time of its publication in 1918, one important consideration to Freud was that the Wolf Man provided the strongest justification for his criticisms of Adler and especially Jung. [40] Freud held that the clinical evidence in this case, added to his previous findings, refuted their arguments. They were denying the primary role accorded by Freud to infantile sexuality. He aimed particularly at Jung, whose chief contention was that mental content could be inherited.

The case of the Wolf Man stands as the principle cornerstone of the edifice of infantile sexuality in mental life. The clinical material of the case is thought to have had a central role in the preparation of such important empirically grounded theories as identification, incorporation, the formation of the ego ideal, the unconscious sense of guilt, and the pathological states of depression. [41]

Freud opened his case study with introductory remarks that indicated that his patient was a young man "whose health had broken down in his eighteenth year after a gonorrheal infection, and who was entirely incapacitated and completely dependent upon other people when he began his psycho-analytic treatment several years later." [42] As a child he was dominated by a severe emotional disorder at about the age of four, an infantile neurosis which became the focus of the case. It was at first an animal phobia which changed to an obsessional neurosis with a religious content. An interesting and important comment by Freud was that his patient had "spent a long time in German sanitoria and was at that period classified in the most authoritative quarters as a case of manic-depressive insanity.[43] The significance of this remark is in the fact, to be shown here, that Freud's study of the infantile neurosis and the disorder in adult life are linked by narcissism and aggression which play a critical role throughout this case. Freud does not make this connection.

The patient's early history tells that as a small child, perhaps two and a half, he was a tractable, easy, good-natured and even quiet child. But, at about this time when his parents returned from a holiday they found him transformed. He had become "discontented, irritable and violent, took offense on every possible occasion, and then flew into a rage and screamed like a savage." [44] The child's unbearable behavior continued. Finally, the persistent aggressive behavior gave way to obsessive piety. Before this occurred, he suffered his sister's torments. They were especially associated with his fear of a wolf coming to eat him.

Other animals also frightened him. He vacillated between cruelties toward them and a fear of them. For instance, he screamed on seeing a horse beaten, yet himself enjoyed beating horses. There were frequent fantasies of being violent and being the object of cruelties. On the streets, when he saw beggars, cripples and very old men, he unwittingly identified himself with them and from that unconsciously developed ritualized behavior that he hoped would be effective in sparing him such a fate. We thus see the child is either aggressive or the object of aggression. Both his fears of attacks and his intentions to be destructive gave way to obsessions with religious ceremonials and piety. In short, the threat of aggressiveness, his own or others', brought on defensive symptoms which served to contain his violence and ward off its possibility which he believed he would be subject to.

In this case, Freud's point was his patient's recurring nightmare of the wolves and the terror of being eaten by them. Freud showed that his patient's obsessional horror contained unconscious incestuous wishes, that they would, by way of fantasied retaliation, bring on fears of castration by the father. His patient's preoccupation with looking on scenes of sexual violence or thinking of them, and conceiving of himself as the victim as often as the one who takes pleasure in cruelty, served Freud's purpose, forming as it did the empirical foundation for the role early childhood sexuality played in the formation of the young man's serious emotional disorder. But sensual excitement and fears of castration are not a full explanation of the patient's becoming like a cripple.

The case need not rest as Freud left it. He wrote in his summation of the young patient that "The blow to his narcissism was too much for him and he went to pieces." [45] Freud referred here to his patient's long-standing fantasy and conviction of his invulnerability and self-aggrandizement that he was a "special child of fortune whom no ill could befall" and which the gonorrheal infection destroyed. The disease, however, was not only a serious reality, which denied the young man his clinging belief in the inviolability of his body, but it meant the magical advantage over illness and thereby over death was lost. The emotional significance of the venereal infection was that it dealt Freud's patient a shattering blow to his narcissism. Together with his other symptoms, in which self-esteem was profoundly affected, we may conclude that the sexual etiology of the Wolf Man's difficulties is shared with a narcissistic etiology.

In each of the various examples cited, in the extravagant fantasies of little Hans, in the vicious egocentricity of Frau Emmy von N., in the bizarre behavior of Anna O., in the Wolf Man's dread of animals which he tortured—in all instances, the patient's sense of worth was particularly imperiled. And, in their efforts to redress the balance by way of the devaluation and destruction of others, conflicts increased and narcissism was not restored.

Since Freud's studies, our clinical experience and analysis show that what is most likely to raise children's anxiety, or bring intensity to their conduct, is their unwitting and obstinate resistance to forego their ego-centered wishes. It is a plain tribute to the power and immense influence of narcissism in respect to relationships. It is not due to some sort of intractable endowment of instinct. The threat of having to give up the deep-seated and heavily invested wishes of an exclusive relationship with a parent, even though only dimly perceived, often evokes fears and apprehensions. The typical rages which mark the failure of fulfillment of such intensely held aims, associated with any period of development, are especially characteristic of the Oedipal period. It is a time of highest aspiration of childhood. The direct effect is to intensify wishes rather than to lessen them. And narcissistic aims parallel the wishes. Yet, a child's daily experience threatens his self-esteem. His narcissism is in jeopardy. His extravagant wishes for himself, whether they are to exercise powers, magically rule events, or to find no limits to his pleasure, are all certain, in large measure, to be doomed. And, as a result, the threatened or the actual failure of his Oedipal aims, like a child's other often boundless and powerfully held aspirations, heightens rather than lowers aggression. And self-regard is then precariously maintained.

It is well within the everyday psychology of children, therefore, to have their aggression kindled with each phase of development. What may have been an adequate defense to exploit, contain or promote aims or wishes, employing aggression to support them, in one phase, is usually not at all suitable in another one. New armaments are required for renewed conflicts. This is what we mean by infantile reactions. They appear inappropriately in a phase which calls for a more advanced or sophisticated forms of conduct.

It is thus no mere abstraction that the Oedipal period terminates with latency. We may recall earlier here that little Hans quit his phobia with the beginning resolution of his Oedipal wishes. Conflicts of the earlier period are but partially resolved and only sufficiently to allow the next period to commence. The old conflicts are continued into latency. There they are subjected to a newer set of developed defenses to be worked through in preparation for the next phase of emotional development, adolescence.

A child's discovery that the great expectations of the Oedipal period come to nothing, forces a sense of despair. It was a finding that impressed Karl Abraham, one of Freud's earliest and most original-minded students. He discovered this phenomenon from his analysis of adults. It supported Freud's theory that the child's experience of the failure of the Oedipal wishes sets a prototype for subsequent depressions.[46] This is to say that as relationships in later life are disappointing, the depression which follows harkens back unconsciously to the serious loss which the failed Oedipal wishes represent. It is doubtful whether psychoanalysis today would want to make the correlation as binding to the Oedipus complex as Abraham and Freud did. This in no way suggests that there is clinical evidence which would contradict these conclusions, so much as there is now a known broader base on which a child's important disappointments rest.

What is not given sufficient recognition is that the child's normal commitment in the Oedipal period to an intense relationship with a parent, necessarily ending without fulfillment, is a colossal disappointment. Its profound effect is immediately on the next phase of emotional development. It is not simply one of a loss. The effect falls on the child's narcissism. In this sense, therefore, the Oedipal debacle represents the most significant injury to self-esteem, albeit both normal and inevitable, that a child experiences. What is of further importance is that, as a reaction, an unconscious severity of self-criticism ensues. This gives the period which now follows some of its unique distinction. It is latency, a time of an increased preoccupation with aggressive wishes, as the child emerges from his great disappointment. And its other chief characteristic is a heightened superego. However, instead of being chiefly directed toward the parent, it is turned on the self. The evidence is plain in the common fears, phobias, nightmares and similar forms of reactions revived in this period from a previous time and given a more sophisticated shape than earlier, wherein the child regards himself as the victim of both punitive and destructive agents. But as we have seen previously, the child is only the victim insofar as he is first the culprit.

As the Oedipus complex ends in its mortifying failure, the child normally, in order to recover, becomes aggressive and employs it in the passionate acquisition of skills and learning. For his further recovery, he also turns unconsciously to seek relationships with peers outside the family. If he is to join others, he must yield a measure of his egocentricity. While limited to the family, he was bound in a way that relations with others outside it were comparatively loose. The new period, latency, signifies that the intensely erotic previous phase has begun to fade, giving way to recovery through a start on the restitution of narcissism. The enormous impetus toward such an aim is best judged by the bursts of intense activity in learning, skill and mastery which characterizes latency. From this aspect, it is the least actively sexual period other than aging.

Freud had little to say about latency. He wrote the least about this period of life. And he probably had little clinical experience with it. Latency does not appear as a study in his clinical cases. Since this period is typically known by its activity and aggression, and in which sexuality is more latent than overt as with other aspects of narcissism and aggression, Freud may have purposefully set it aside. Latency is still the least studied stage by clinicians and carries the least theory as well. The studies of this phase of emotional development as yet are inadequate to bridge the hiatus of our understanding between the Oedipal period and the beginning of adolescence.[47]

The internalized figures of parental authority represent for the child in latency only a crudely formed superego. As such it exacts a severe toll on the child's expectations, demanding that he must strive to gain his place among others. The incentive to thus restore himself is great. And his fears of failure now begin to come from within himself and not so exclusively as before from the expectations of others. With the child's growing abilities to perform, the constructive uses of aggression to promote self-esteem receive an added powerful incentive. Destructiveness, ordinarily censored in earlier periods of development, under the aegis of the latency superego is severely criticized. A guilty conscience in its full sense is now operative as self-accusation with self-punishment.

It is under these conditions that the beginnings of sublimation appear. At the same time, the superego in this period is typically strict and the activities in latency, characteristically vigorous, are a match for it.[48] The child in early latency (five to seven years old, about) is not as a rule generous toward himself, and the means he employs to gain his wishes are not especially self-indulgent ones. With his newly revamped aims he offers himself high social aspirations. The life of the young latency child is not as yet entirely free of the intense and envious wishes of the previous period. From the defeat of his Oedipal wishes, new sources are found through which the child may recover from his injured narcissism. The efforts to restore self-esteem form an immense incentive during latency as the beginning of social achievement. What was lost before personally, may begin to be gained socially.

The intimacy of a child's experience within his family needs no exposition here, nor do we require a review of his wishes and conflicts to recognize that they are characteristically prodigal. However, despite his resort to magic, to a belief in the power of wishes, and to demands to rule over circumstance for the fulfillment of what may be beyond reach, and the persistence of such implements to support the aspirations of childlife, the certainty of their final defeat does not altogether elude the child. And, in fact, central to the sexual life of the child as the Oedipus complex is, its dissolution normally nevertheless takes place. When Freud wrote that it was not clear what it is that brings this about he said, "Analysis seems to show that it is the experience of painful disappointments." [49] "The absence of the satisfaction hoped for . . . must in the end lead the small lover to turn away from his hopeless longing." [50] As a result what followed, he supposed, was a repression of this central experience of defeat. Freud left the unanswered question in 1924. Analysts since then have not taken up what part of the "painful disappointment" and the "hopeless longing" is to be assigned to the child's emotional development.

No foundation exists for our supposing that longings or needs when thwarted bring resignation or an abandonment of them. On the contrary, experience shows the opposite. Yet, it is commonly held by analysts that latency is a fallow period. Our observation is that the termination of the Oedipus complex marks that painful disappointment of early childhood and is brought to its conclusion with a serious loss of self-esteem. It is precisely this condition which gives the impetus to recover narcissism from its injury. It thrusts the child into latency. In folklore, myths and fairy tales, we find countless episodes of desperate struggles which dramatize the adventures into which a child in latency projects himself. The encounters depend for their success on highmindedness, worthiness, great skills and mastery, and finally, triumph over adversaries who, without principle, would subvert a strict conscience. It is no accident that children in the latency period are devoted to heroes like King Arthur and his knights, or the legends of Charlemagne and his paladins, or other similar demigods. Of course, in myths, legends and tales the young generally triumph. What is omitted from such ventures, except through a series of trials, is that the beginning of life's great achievements all follow on a colossal failure. This means that to succeed emotionally, a child must continually recover from the repeated and often deep narcissistic injuries naturally associated with his growth and development.

We have said before, the child who through seduction in fact or in fantasy remains within the intimacy of an Oedipal triangle, that is to say the sexuality of early childhood, is not engaged in a loving and romantic relationship. On the contrary, the child's unconscious aim is a brutal triumph over a rival. Unconscious Oedipal fantasies in a child or those retrived from childhood during the analysis of adults significantly are not recollections of idyllic experiences. They are preeminently characterized as narcissistic relations. And they may represent a savage success. Only when the little "Oedipus" fails can he escape his torment and self-torture. Only when he can see he has done nothing and that what he may have wished for or aspired to he repudiated, can he then look back with fondness rather than with anger on what he quit.

It is not simply the repression into the amnesia of childhood of the deep disappointment of unfulfilled infantile sexual wishes that liberates a child from the Oedipal period, although repression of the wishes and the conflicts associated with them, which would otherwise constitute a source of persistent disquiet, relieve the child to permit the next phase to be ushered in. It is also the beginning of self-governance, of self-regulation, of not depending solely on others for control. This is an imperative in his emotional development.

What of those children who seem to show no such inner regulatory agency? The most authoritative work on the subject is a meager study of a group of exceedingly aggressive children (boys and girls between the ages of approximately seven to twelve years).[51] Their behavior was so destructive and incorrigible that they could not be tolerated at home. They were therefore institutionalized. The chief aim of the study was to show that seriously aggressive children, lacking control over their violent and destructive behavior toward others, were conscienceless, i.e. a superego had failed to develop. They were provocative, hateful and impulsive children. The explanation for their conduct rested on the supposition that there existed in them extraordinary powerful instinctual impulses.

The cases were taken to show that an inability to tolerate frustration produces such aggression. Moreover, that the child's failure to adapt himself was some fundamental instinct gone awry. It is the same argument used by ethologists such as Lorenz and others, to explain all man's aggression, and in particular the violence toward each other. David Beres explained further that it was due to emotional deprivation in infancy. It was on account of parental figures who, for a variety of reasons, were inadequate to the task of being proper models of affection for the child to imitate and thus to make a part of himself. Beres, engaged in expositions of conventional psychoanalytic theory, fails to note that each case he cited shows that the seriously delinquent aggressive child brought repeated injury, punishment and censorship by others on himself. For instance, a violently destructive girl, eight years old, provoked attacks on herself and demanded help from the psychiatrist whose office she would refuse to leave. An eleven-year-old boy carried out serious attacks on other children and was very aggressive toward adults whose punishment he solicited. He could not be tolerated long in any one of a series of foster home placements, where he continued to carry out a series of self-destructive acts from which he could not be dissuaded.

The theories that attempt to account for the serious degree of aggression or violence in such children propose that it is based upon unaccountably strong instincts or drives, or that controls on them are inadequately developed. What is omitted entirely from such conventional reasoning is that the invariable turning of aggression on themselves, neglected in these cases and which each child demonstrated, may be founded on other than some extraordinary sado-masochism. Consideration of their conduct as sadomasochistic presupposes a self-critical internal agency in which the self-punitive aspects of aggressive behavior show an erotic element which finds gratification in being hurt. There is no evidence in these cases for such suppositions. We are obliged to accept the fact that these extremely destructive and violent children, in making themselves objects of their own aggression, are responding to their violence toward others. What is remarkable in such extreme cases of aggression is that there appears to be no place for wanton destruction without turning it on oneself.

One thread pulls all the cases together, Freud's and the others. It is that in each instance *justification for aggression* seems to be indispensable. We may judge this from the fact that it is sought with zeal. And also, in each case, narcissism is defended by aggressive acts, wishes, impulses and fantasies. And then in the final analysis, aggression turns away from others to oneself. There appear to be no exceptions. The serious and even dangerous effects of taking oneself as an object of aggression are plain. Delinquent, destructive and seriously aggressive children like the variety of adults, as we have seen, follow a similar course and menace themselves.

Chapter VI

Aggression: An Engine of Change

Ordinary depression associated with failed effort, disappointment and loss has far more profound significance and effect on our lives than is generally recognized. An immense literature on depression, psychoanalytic and descriptive, is naturally focused on its pathological aspects. But little of this voluminous literature illuminates either the psychology of commonplace periods of depression or its dynamic similarity to the clinical conditions. The bald contradiction between self-denigration and the notorious egocentricity in clinical depression, while long recognized, has not been fully appreciated as holding its central conflict. It is overlooked that the cardinal characteristic of depressions is that the crucial and usually unconscious conflict is a narcissistic one. This unawareness remains true, even though ancient studies of morbid depression did not fail to recognize that a close connection with aggression existed that was often turned on oneself. Attention remained on the consequences of depression: the dramatic dangerous ones, the sometimes interminable suffering, or the fact that it could clear without leaving a trace.

Clinical depression, distinguished by its exceeding self-absorption, has not been related to the depressed states and their derivatives in daily life. Nor has the recovery process from clinical depression, i.e. the abatement of aggression toward oneself, been understood to be indicative of its immediate association with self-esteem. Even the analytic explanation that finally we have flagellated ourselves "sufficiently" to give up depression leaves the question begging; the similar course of transient everyday depression is not understood any better. The reasoning is that self-attack was compelling and therefore having been meted out comes to an end.

Perhaps one of the chief reasons for our ignorance lies in the fact that psychoanalytic research utilizes the concept of masochism to explain self-attacks and the complementary concept of sadism to explain directing our destructiveness toward others. That the erotic role of satisfaction is often a big one in both directions needs no argument. But other considerations respecting aggression should not be ruled out.

The unconscious basis of self-destruction, which contradicts self-preservation, among Freud's important discoveries, is crucial in understanding depressions. He found that it is the functioning of a "self-critical" agency in us which not only makes us guilty but in its severity may seriously jeopardize our existence. From this phenomenon Freud drew the hypothesis of the superego. And, as a result, the unconscious sense of guilt received a new assessment. However, that self-critical attacks, without doubt a curb on aggression, fall on one's narcissism so that self-esteem lowers, has not been fully appreciated.

That self-attacks unconsciously were meant to spare others became plain enough once Freud pointed it out, as he did for the first time in *Mourning and Melancholia*.[1] He continued to view self-attacks, however, from the position of his previous discoveries where he found aggression and sexuality to be fused elements always present in both masochistic suffering and sadistic intentions and acts. The further significance of self-attacks was not pursued. For instance, some destructive aims turn into self-destructive ones simply in the course of everyday psychology, rather than only in "melancholia," as the states of clinical or psychotic depression were called in Freud's time. Transient feelings of depression develop which are founded on other than a masochistic basis.

The sense of guilt that arises from aggressive acts and wishes has promoted the belief that the distinction between sexual and non-sexual aggression may be simply an academic one. In actual practice, no significant research may be cited as a study of the problem.

There is a period in early development when we may regard aggression and sensuousness as indistinguishable for the infant, both in their association with each other and in their consequence. Probably only the first year or so of life passes before aggression in one form or another begins to be singled out by the mother as an element in behavior to be both promoted and inhibited. Important distinctions, due to the differences in meaning between sexual and aggressive conduct, are developed. Those special circumstances in life which grant aggression without the penalty of turning on the self, I shall deal with later in the book. But a main distinction to be made between aggression and sexuality has the most far-reaching implications. It is that with emotional development, sexual aims increasingly depend for their satisfaction upon another person upon whom some value is thus conferred. The aggressive objectives, on the other hand, are increasingly turned from others and tend to be individual. In short, the latter are egocentric aims.

The use of aggression is at first toward the mastery of some skills or functions, and long before we can socially join others with such aims, we are solitary in our objectives. For example, a small group of children up to the age of three years often may be very aggressive in play or some other activity. But they notably, even in the company of others their own age, are distinctly solitary, especially in their aggressive pursuits.

Furthermore, as we develop emotionally beyond requiring others to administer restraint on us for our aggression, we begin to mete out to ourselves what we feel we deserve, and thus take over the function of curbing ourselves. By our fourth year, usually, we start to show clear signs of beginning to police ourselves. And our firm commitment to social aims is thus made. Only after this has begun to function do we join with others in aggressive pursuits. Young children may give encouragement to one another to be aggressive. But they do not band together or jointly engage in more than fragmentary aggressive functions.

We have observed that so long as a child in his natural egocentricity directs his aggression or destructiveness toward others and the things that represent them, he impairs to that degree his social adaptation. Modifying his narcissism therefore constitutes the earliest undertaking of his security. We have seen the extremes which best illustrate the issues at hand. The autistic child, whose egocentricity allows him little social development, or the exceedingly overtly aggressive child, whose menacing conduct permits small social accommodation, are both unable to sacrifice enough of their narcissism to accord a value to others. They remain either pathetically isolated or in a frenzy of profitless activity in which they develop no relationships.

The modification of aggression here is clearly related to narcissism. "Sadism" is not simply transferred to oneself, as the theory of masochism supposes. This applies only when the two elements of sexuality and aggression are fused. I am not proposing that such fusion as Freud described needs to be questioned when so much conclusive evidence supports it. What I am proposing is that when sexuality and aggression are not fused, the theory of masochism is not adequate, and that the problem Freud left must be raised anew—that there is clear evidence that narcissism must be taken with aggression into a separate study.

We need to include in our reckoning that much of a young child's experience is concerned with his egocentric pursuits. And that a good deal of his aggression derives from efforts to realize his self-oriented aims. To realize those ends, however, he needs to enlist the help of those who care for him. He is thus obliged to depend upon others and at the same time to develop his independence. When he increasingly directs his self-seeking through self-employment, rather than by principally soliciting the help of others, he begins to gain skills, mastery, learning and so on. And as the child succeeds thus in harnessing aggression, he is no longer solely following some original hedonistic direction but is engaged in social aims.

The value we accord another person acts as the most powerful deterrent to our violence toward others. Rather than as has been conventionally thought—that it is chiefly the fears of retaliation which turn us from attacks on others—it is the unconscious knowledge that we turn on ourselves which generates the deepest fears.

The concepts that would explain fears of aggression according to retaliation are ideas conceived on the basis of some conditional response, or one which draws principally on a behavioristic model. Such reasoning proposes that human aggression, however complex, is simply a reaction to a situation, or set of stimuli. Those popular and scientific theories of animal aggression applied to us incorporate frustration as the motive. However, all these behavioristic hypotheses fail to consider the sweeping significance of directing aggression toward oneself.

Although Freud's work on "melancholia" showed this to be the key to understanding pathological depression, i.e. turning one's aggression meant for another on oneself, he did not suppose, nor have others, that a similar "turn" takes place in everyday life and that it may account for feeling depressed. And what is more, that it is a course which our aggression normally must take in the interest of social development and no less often perhaps for the sake of later social harmony. This is not to say that the clinical depression therefore lacks pathology, but that the familiar depression occurring in ordinary experience is dynamically similar.

To turn aggression, or "attack" oneself, marks a momentous step in our emotional development. With that an important source of risk to a needed or valued relationship is mitigated; our social existence is thereby further insured. The stride we thus make in our emotional development, sparing others our violence, ironically brings us to victimize ourselves. The price for social gain is the proneness to self-attack. Its value, crucial to fulfill our social need, we purchase through the transfer of some of our narcissism to another. We are saying, so to speak, that the cost of social gain comes in reducing narcissism in ourselves; we are thus less vulnerable to narcissistic injury, and by transferring our value to another or an ideal we are less destructive. And when we repudiate or nullify that credit, we become aggressive. This terrible jest in human experience, that to preserve ourselves we have to value others more, did not escape Freud's notice. However, he saw the dilemma in terms of aggression, biologically driven, which had to be curbed from its discharge. It was therefore, he thought, a doomed expectation.

No biological model explains the wish to spare another our anger, hate or violence, and to take ourselves instead as the object of attack or even destruction. And it is more than some sort of self-serving act of sharp judgment that motivates us. It is the shift in narcissism which dissolves the dilemma. To set a value on another, in certain important respects above oneself, is to relinquish enough of our narcissism to credit it in some sufficient measure to someone else. An enormous social achievement commences. And, as I have shown, the absence of that accomplishment indicates a colossal failure in relationships. The young child (probably after two years of age, when we have demonstrable evidence rather than conjecture) who has begun to make the shift in narcissism from himself to others has started developing relationships on a new basis without which his emotional growth remains seriously faulted. Here is the critical issue in emotional development. Without it, social existence is gravely impaired.

It has generally been supposed that depression ends when self-abnegation and self-punishment are sufficiently exhausted. Observation amply proves this to be the case. Analytic hypotheses come to a halt at this point. That it is the tenacity of egocentric demands in conflict with self-attacks which must be resolved so that recovery may begin is not a focus of study, although it is often in practice at the center of treatment.

The great implications of this conflict as an unconscious experience in our daily life, where it does not evolve clinical depression but probably significantly affects mood changes, also has not been studied. Since the effects of the tenacity of our narcissistic demands begin to be discernible very early in life, and soon conflict with restrictions by others before we develop our own superego, it means they are deeply incorporated into our emotional development.

Freud explicitly regarded the monitoring system by which we come to govern ourselves as essential to our own social well-being. It is the superego, the governing agency to which civilization owes so much. He nonetheless held the view that it limits the human spirit more than it liberates it. "The super-ego is an agency that has been inferred by us, and conscience is a function which we ascribe among other functions to that agency. It watches over our intentions and actions, judges them in exercising a censorship . . . The fear of this critical agency . . . [and] the need for punishment . . . is an instinctual manifestation which has become masochistic; it is a portion . . . of the instinct towards internal destruction." [2]

To whatever heights of social development our faculties may bring us, we mount them only by repudiating direct aggressive gratification by way of the developing superego. In fact, it is remarkable how early in our existence this process commences. In this accomplishment, either the conscience or our parents, as later the dictates of our own conscience, directs us. Freud, however, could not escape his idea that this meant we were inevitably drawn thus to our end. Imposed on us by parents, then by ourselves, others and society, what is instinctive in us is repressed. He held that the instincts thus were turned in part on ourselves rather than entirely outward. It remained his belief that in curbing our aggression we so modify our "natural" impulses that we restrict ourselves in our satisfaction. We thus become our own victims. Destructiveness, he always believed, must find its outlet, and when its flow is impeded by the superego opposing the free expression of instinctual wishes, aggression requiring gratification is then directed at the self. He was not unmindful of the enormous achievements man has shown himself to be capable of by way of sublimating his aggression (i.e. putting its power to social use), but he still saw aggression primarily as the destructive force resulting from thwarting of the original sexual aims with which aggression was inextricably bound.

I am suggesting, however, that the evidence we now have shows that aggression, before sexuality, comes under strong modification as a governing agency. And that what is more, very early in our lives, long before it affects sexual development, we are obliged to modify, yield and govern our narcissism.

Freud admitted that narcissism was a critical element in our relations with others, but conceived of it as playing its part indirectly in man's accomplishments. He did not explore its central role in everyday life. He held that man's social achievements, however great, mocked the sacrifice to acquire them. He was not thinking that our egocentric interests were waived or that narcissism was compromised. Rather, it was man's instincts which were surrendered and as a consequence we were brought nearer to being destroyed by their being thwarted.

Even those followers of Freud who in most respects took exception to his speculation that the death instincts, that part of aggression we do not "discharge," lead us to destruction and our end, continued to support his argument that civilization is the burden the instincts must bear, and that we have paid dearly in terms of instinctual pleasure we have sacrificed for it. No other argument enjoys more support from as many quarters, drawing simultaneously on a philosophical tenet, a popular notion and a scientific doctrine. The weight of this proposition, however, is that the instincts, rather than narcissism, must be compromised. But the evidence points to the fact that it is *narcissism* which must yield.

In the tradition of Rousseau's philosophy, Freud wrote, "liberty of the individual is no gift of civilization. It was the greatest before there was any civilization. . . ." [3] The Paradise myth never had a more eloquent defender. From 1930, the time of the publication of *Civilization and Its Discontents,* Freud's views on how the human community oppressed the individual made many new sympathetic adherents. A persistent protest remains that man has grudgingly had to give up some measure of aggression in behalf of the demands of society or civilization—presumably to his detriment. Everyday life, however, contradicts the claims that we have abandoned our aggression, or perhaps even sacrificed any of it; and when we, the most highly advanced societies, slaughter one another, while some of the most primitive societies have only mock battles in which injuries are rare, or fights are governed by restraint, we may doubt these claims even further.

In 1901, a few years after the publication of his first cases, Freud began to study the everyday phenomenon of turning aggression on oneself. We may glean some firsthand sense of his penetrating interest in it from the observations he made of the underlying motives of self-injuries, in himself, members of his family and others. For example, once when one of his sons was ill the child "had a fit of anger one day because he was ordered to spend the morning in bed, and threatened to kill himself. . . ." That evening he showed Freud a swelling he got by bumping against a door knob. To his father's ironical question as to what had happened, the child answered, "That was my attempt at suicide that I threatened this morning." [4] Freud was certain his professional views on self-injury were not known to his children at that time.[5] He went on to add that the "trend of self-destruction is present to a certain degree in very many more human beings than those in whom it is carried out." [6] He saw this as a conflict between instincts, self-destruction versus self-preservation. However, Freud seemed unaware of the relationship of his own son's fury to the child's self-esteem.

He found that unconscious motivation for aggression gains expression in superstition in "people who are often of high intelligence—that superstition derives from suppressed hostile and cruel impulses." [7] This kind of individual, Freud said, has repressed such wishes into the unconscious and will be, therefore, especially prone to expect punishment in the form of trouble threatening him from without in the form of superstition. But there is no mention by Freud in this context that a troubled conscience reflects a critical self-judgment dictating a lowering of self-esteem.

In a footnote, the editors of the *Standard Edition* call attention to some remarks written by Freud which they found in an interleaved copy. They were that "rage, anger and consequently a murderous impulse is the source of superstition in obsessional neurotics, a sadistic component, which is attached to love and is therefore directed against the loved person and repressed precisely because of this link and because of its intensity. My own superstition has its roots in suppressed ambition (immortality) and in my case takes the place of that anxiety about death which springs from the normal uncertainty of life. . . ." [8] Freud's pact with himself that his ambition was for immortality, ironically, probably intensified his well-known persistent fears of an untimely end. By his narcissistic vaulting ambition to be immortal, he created a certain source of feeling in jeopardy. The premature death that he dreaded threatened to deny him his longed-for place in eternity.

In these remarks, Freud revealed his conviction that aggression turned on oneself was meant to spare others against whom hostility was deemed reprehensible. He shows us that early in his thinking he had begun to discover the course aggression may follow to self-destruction. He was to demonstrate it in 1917 in his work on melancholia. But he also reveals that throughout his considerations of the problem he was not taking into account fully that the self-criticism which occurs, bringing with it self-abnegation and at times actual self-attacks, represents a lowering of self-esteem to dangerous levels and that it might therefore be more than a sadistic turn on oneself.

The injury, however, to narcissism from one's own self-criticism constitutes a menace within us. And as always it provokes our aggression. In our unconscious need to dissociate ourselves from aggression, we may project our aggressiveness to others, claim they hold us at fault, and thus justify our anger, or we may turn it directly to destroy ourselves. Freud viewed all this as the sadism in us, there to be provoked by circumstance. When it got loose from being hobbled by conscience, it discharged. Who would get hurt, Freud contended, would depend upon whom conscience would allow to be placed in the sadistic sights.

In the classic, *The Psychopathology of Everyday Life,* which Freud first published in 1901, we have the unusual opportunity of studying the only work to which he made constant additions throughout his life. To the wealth of material which he himself had gathered, Freud brought not only his multitude of examples, but also illustrations provided him by his friends and pupils. Its importance as an empirical source of the study of aggression, however, has been neglected.

The special significance of the work is that along with the study of dreams as a separate volume, it further enabled Freud "to extend to normal mental life the discoveries he had first made in connection with the neuroses." [9] And, with yet another volume within a few years, not as well known as the other but nonetheless important, *Jokes and Their Relation to the Unconscious* (1905), he brought more riches from the material of everyday life to show still another facet of the unconscious in normal emotional experience.

If we take these three major works together,[10] we may trace in them an unrecognized theme that Freud did not fully illuminate. Aspects of aggression in its relation to narcissism are plainly shown. As though in an unworked lode, they are in the elaborate network of our unconscious. Freud showed that the unconscious often reveals itself, not only to us, but often to others, in opposition to our intentions, and that frequently we expose the uncompromising nature of our self-serving aims. All this Freud showed. Yet, he was inattentive to the direct association of these aims with aggression.

Whether Freud interprets a dream to reveal to us its latent aims, or shows a slip of the tongue unmasking covered intentions, or how we are made privy to some hidden psychological process in humor, he never fails to expose the libidinal elements and frequently the unconscious aggression which is bound up with them. He shows us in what highly wrought mazes of pleasure and aggression we may become lost. But conflicts of self-love, egoism, egocentricity or narcissism, which are clearly evident, received little notice except, for instance, when he commented that as children we are "completely egoistic," feel our needs intensely as a result, and thus strive ruthlessly to satisfy them.[11] Before childhood is over, however, "altruistic impulses and morality awakens in the little egoist." [12] Freud might have added, much as these qualities are enjoyed, that they fatigue easily. In a footnote he commented, "The unbounded self-love (the narcissism) of children regards any interference as an act of lese-majesty, and their feelings demand (like the Draconian code) that any such crime shall receive the one form of punishment which admits of no degrees." [13]

With these and similar sparse comments, we see that Freud has taken narcissism to represent the egocentric expression of the instinctual pursuit of our wishes and acts. He states that egoism is ruthless, but fails to join the issue, when he thinks the Draconian code is enforced only to put down desire and mitigate frustration. What evokes the powerful feelings of narcissism to employ aggression when it is compromised, threatened or injured receives no parallel consideration. The issue is not whether aggression derives from thwarted wishes. This needs no argument. But in paying attention to frustration as a simple direct reaction, there is the obvious neglect of what it *means* to us to have our wishes denied.

Beginning in our earliest years, when we first meet defeat, it is a blow that falls on our self-love, which is to say on our "completely egoistic" aims. The injury is to narcissism. Our self-regard invariably suffers. To restore ourselves we make use of aggression. These commonplace experiences are a far cry from mere frustration. Nor are they adequately covered by the present Freudian theory of narcissism.

The short paper, "On Narcissism," [14] which Freud published a decade after the three works which appeared between 1900 and 1905, is one of the pivots in the evolution of his views. However, in it he takes no inventory of narcissism from the clinical riches he had previously accumulated. Nor did he do so later. Freud did not bring this important theoretical work on narcissism into the light of everyday experience and thus extend our understanding of it in our normal emotional encounters with loss, deprivation and failure. The central functions of a child's self-love, which extend into the egoism of adults in daily life, generally were not appreciated.

Unconscious "mechanisms of defense" against our own prohibited wishes or impulses, especially the aggressive ones, create the ordinary and inevitable conflicts in our daily lives. The persistent need to disclaim aggressive inclinations and to dissociate ourselves from them is common. It is a process which begins in young children. Of necessity, those nearest at hand, usually one's family, are the principal objects of hostility. It may not be voiced, may be kept wholly in fantasy, and may even remain entirely unconscious, yet the child may claim that aggressive intentions are held by others and that he must be protected from that menace. Only then may giving vent to his aggression be justified, guilt be mitigated, and self-esteem be raised rather than lowered.

From these ordinary emotional experiences commencing in childhood we learn that aggressiveness is borne best, and with the least inner conflict, when we are, or believe we are, the victims of another's hostility. (There are exceptions, as I shall show later, when, under special conditions, indifference to the victims of our violence brings no such conflicts.) The strength of our need to rid thinking ourselves to be aggressive is obvious, and the sense of guilt needs no explanation here. But the fact that within us there are responses, often indispensable to our existence and yet which impair our self-esteem, brings these two elements—aggression and guilt—together. The "mechanism" for relief therefore must serve not only to lift the burden of hostility from us, but must also help injured narcissism to recover.

The tendency to disclaim and deny our hostile reactions together with attributing them to others which begins as an ordinary childhood effort is more than a mere response to adverse circumstances. As a clinical phenomenon, characteristic of certain neurotic disorders, it is well known as a syndrome to psychoanalysts. What escapes full consideration is that the effort to dissociate oneself from hostility is as durable as aggression itself, and the need to disengage oneself from it aims at the recovery of self-esteem. The unconsciously formed attempt to divorce hostility entirely from ourselves is to "project" it to others, as it will be recalled Schreber did; nor could little Hans abide his hostility toward his father, and instead fancied himself a victim, the object of attacks against which he had to defend himself. The boy, like the judge, removed the threat of being at the mercy of his own dangerous impulses. The unconscious wishes are feared. The aggression associated with them is poorly tolerated and is experienced in conjunction with anxiety. And self-esteem is reduced. The need to be relieved of the conflict calls for repudiating the hostility. The oldest childhood defenses are often employed, projection and denial.

The unconscious use of "projection" together with a "denial" of destructiveness are among the most developed of early childhood defenses. They are the unconscious means, beginning in childhood and carried forward into adult life, by which we may disengage ourselves from being concerned over wishes and impulses which are a source of conflict. To attribute disquieting aims to others and thus unwittingly deny one's egocentric wishes and the aggressive inclinations that issue to support them affords a measure of relief. Under these conditions a child's fears of what might happen to him, a blameless victim of circumstances, are apt to become prominent. Fears, phobias and nightmares then frequently appear. They are the terrifying forms of the menace within himself which have assumed shape and substance as though they had their origin from without. All the while, however, the child's deep-seated, unyielding narcissistic demands persist. They draw on the aggressive or powerful destructive wishes, impulses and fantasies to get support while at the same time they are also largely the unconscious source of his disquiet. Withdrawn from the child's awareness and obscured by his tenacious fearfulness, his underlying self-serving is unassailed. A child's fears thus have an important function. They may serve to conceal rather than to expose what is underlying them. For instance, little Hans who feared a horse would bite him, like the child who dreaded attacks from wolves, developed phobias which masked the violent intentions each child harbored to abuse and destroy the creatures.*

---

* There is a tradition, especially in psychology, of regarding the formation of emotional defenses and their effective influence in structural terms, i.e. expressed as "mechanism." At the turn of the century, Freud used the language of physical mechanics in the analogies and metaphors he employed to explain his discoveries. In later decades, analysts in some instances replaced his models with their own more contemporary ones. The most recent example is the trend to adopt the language of electrical circuitry from cybernetics. Regardless which of these models is taken for analogizing, the tendency toward a mechanistic view of mental experience remains. The characteristic and natural unconscious action of projection, for example, is a means through which certain specific and burdensome conflicts, particularly those associated with one's hostility, are ameliorated. Concepts of "projection" as an unconscious mechanism employed to disavow one's own unwelcome impulses by simply attributing them to others confines understanding projection to an operation of mental

The child's frequent adherence to a strict protocol of behavior under such conditions provides him with a necessary restraint against his own egocentric aims which would be reckless in their disregard of moderation. These manifestations may appear as expressions of a need to be overly critical and thus herald a premature arrival of governing oneself. Parents to whom this may seem desirable welcome the appearance of the little martinet. But it is the child's imitation of the parents' authority. It does not represent a truly developed superego; rather, it reflects what the child wishes by way of discipline. Often, when he fails to get it from others, because of their permissiveness, he may resort thus to self-restraint. It is the child's attempt to limit his underlying and disquieting but tenaciously held infantile-egocentric demands. However, no significant modification of infantile life may thus be achieved. Instead we find that the child imposes on himself a supervisory behavior, while retaining his child's narcissism intact. Precocious children especially have a tendency to such development.

Our study of children who appear to have acquired social maturation early shows they have unconsciously adopted a role manifestly intended to rule aggression. However, a deeper problem is masked: the child's characteristic self-serving or egocentric aims show an uncompromising resistance to their modification for social ends. Briefly, these children seem socially accomplished and sophisticated beyond their years. But, behind this successful façade, infantile and unmodified narcissistic goals are held. They resist change. Only shallow relationships with others are possible. There is an associated conviction that others are hostile, and whose self-seeking, it is believed, must be guarded against.

The children tend to be almost exclusively concerned with policing their overt aggression, and few other considerations in relation to others have much importance. Therefore, their relationships remain undeveloped. For example, some severe forms of ritualized behavior in the latency period of children (six to eleven years old) give us a sharper picture of the effect of regulating hostility. The necessity for it becomes so overwhelming to the normally strict conscience of that

workings and neglects its significance as an effort to dissociate oneself from one's own strongly held motives which are not relinquished. Moreover, projection taken as a mere mental mechanism places emphasis on it as an emotional device used to unconsciously deny one's aggression and obscures that the necessity to resort to it issues from an intolerable self-criticism for harboring hostility. And by attributing enmity to others, with justification, they may be attacked.

period that it crowds out other functions and brings the child's emotional life to a virtual standstill. Such children often become desperate in their need to control their aggressive impulses. They dread the slightest expression of them for fear of losing all limits to what they might wish to do. As a result, routinized conduct may be extended, either gradually or quickly, to all conduct. The fears of what is unforeseen, unpredictable and uncertain are extended so that even members of their families will not be a source beyond the dictates of control. The result we frequently find is an entire household tyrannized. Fortunately, it ordinarily is a short phase. When it is not, a psychiatrist is often sought at this point to offer a means of relief from the oppressiveness of the child's desperately insistent dictates.

The child's narcissism, for the sake of a relationship, needs to be modified. As it fails to be altered, relationships remain impaired. Such children are too engaged with their own pressing conflicts over worth to modify their narcissism, i.e. to place a sense of worth on others without fears that such a sacrifice, lessening their own value, puts theirs in question.

Guilty feelings ascribed only to unresolved unconscious sexual conflicts have held analysts' undivided attention. It has been at the cost, however, of understanding the child's narcissism, which, normally excessive and with its associated aggression, generates hostility and is thus a certain source of intense guilt. Paradoxically, despite their heightened narcissism, such children do not expect to be valued; unknowingly, it is their aggression which puts their worth in question.

Precocious development in normal young children, so highly admired by adults, while not containing as intense conflicts as those we saw in the two little girls cited in Chapter II, are similar to theirs. The precocity is shown to be directed toward more than achievement, as is conventionally supposed; it is toward the control of aggression. The distinction to be made between normal emotional development and a child's being engaged in overcontrol is not to be found so much in his behavior as in his motives. For example, mastery of a skill may be engendered by fear or by the incentive of the reward of accomplishment. The level of performance in both cases may be similar. The first allays only anxiety; the latter raises self-esteem.

Without a supportive authority over aggression, the child has only his own devices to rely upon. Thus, the child who has been encouraged by his parents through their permissiveness to find his own direction, in short, given his "liberty," tends to be guided actually to hold his inner self-critical functions to the level of a young child. Like one who reaches for what was forbidden by admonitions from his parents, in their voice he imitatively shouts aloud their instructions to himself, "No! No!" But his wish to act or his intention is not given up.

Precocity in very young children illustrates some pertinent effects of an imposed discipline that a child adopts long in advance of the self-critical, governing and judging agency that we are familiar with, and which begins to be manifest about the age of three to four years. Childhood is dependent. It is a state as fraught with anxiety as it is eased with comfort. Premature flight into adult conduct, even though there are the rewards of achievement and accomplishment, offers no stable solution. The adoption of adult ways may become an important source of gratification to mitigate the needs of the child whose satisfaction of infantile wishes is prohibited or denied him. And it may appear that these wishes have been relinquished in favor of adult aims. However, they are a facade over infantilism.

The failure of narcissism to be modified means that the underlying infantile needs are firmly held. They appear characteristically in aggressive demands to satisfy an uncompromising egocentricity.

In fantasy, daydreams and especially during sleep, where everyday ego defenses are least governing, the censorship of egocentric wishes and impulses is relinquished. The ruling wishes of such children are expressed in violence. A common theme in their unconscious productions, appearing in daydreams and in sleep as nightmares, is aggression. The adopted adult role is not secure against the infantile one where the child's egocentric aims have not been transformed. Kept unaltered, they are overlaid, as we have noted, with a veneer of imitated adult conduct. Under conditions which excite anger, this peels off. When the two little girls during treatment are relieved of their adult-like roles, they expose their infantile narcissism. They tell us about the development that failed and the powerful influence of imitation used as compensation. Instead of an identification with adults, the precocious child faithfully *mimics* them. The development that would ordinarily occur, as the child is obliged to yield his egocentricity to accommodate the adults, is arrested. The implications are far-reaching.

The faulty beginning of a self-critical, governing, internal regulatory agency is usually thought to be concerned chiefly with aggression and its derivatives, and the role of the superego over narcissism is not considered. The conspicuous relation of the normal process of identification with parents to gain self-esteem has been neglected. The underlying conflicts connecting worth and self-esteem appear endless. The activities that the precocious child engages in tend to be *performances* to be assessed both by himself and others. When the result is not prized sufficiently to meet his expectations, which are not modest, conflicts over self-worth set off aggressive behavior. This is indicative of the precariousness of a narcissism especially sensitive to injury.

Periodic eruptions of violent conduct have been regarded traditionally by psychoanalysts and others as the result of a damming of aggressive impulses seeking satisfaction, or because such impulses are instinctive; and their release, reducing tension, has been thought to be satisfying. But our study shows that where gratification derives from social relationships, indicative of self-development, the aggressive elements in relationships diminish. And, where relationships are inadequately developed because of a persistent need to support infantile self-serving, aggression issues.

The fact that the demands of narcissism may be satisfied significantly in some measure only by successfully transferring it to another, or involving it in a cause or in the performance of an achievement, assigns narcissism critical functions throughout our existence. Narcissism extended beyond the self gives relief from the oppressiveness of staring at oneself and creates the pleasure of enjoying others.

To hope to satisfy narcissism through being enchanted with one's self-image indeed risks the fate of the Greek youth in mythology—to remain at the pool's edge a prisoner of one's reflection, unable to survive any distance from where one cannot see oneself. To be thus bound to child-narcissism means to hold a commitment exclusively to oneself. It signifies that a social relationship at best is tenuous. And dependence upon another, even though indispensable, remains infantile in character. Self-gratification rules. Whether it is one's beauty, intelligence, skill or proven achievement that narcissism admires, a perpetual reaffirmation is demanded.

A narcissistic image is not self-sustaining. By its nature uncompromising, narcissism requires renewed gratification. It seems to have no inherent stability. Time and circumstance are its adversaries. Narcissism has no allies. It has only enemies. Everyday life, in countless ways, allows no escaping the fact that the image must over and over again be restored. In the course of such struggles, a child's demands or expectations elevate as his fears of diminishing returns grow. The incentive to find restitution is enormous. And indeed, the creative process, in its broadest sense, owes more of its indomitable character to our inevitable losses, failures and limitations than it does to contentment.[15]

The struggle against a reality, which the child may correctly cite as the source of his discontent, convinces him that, but for it, he would not be deprived. That the very nature of his wishes precludes their being realized and is the actual basis for his sense of deprivation is beyond his grasp. The recurrent issue arises from the strength of the opposition to modification which the aims of narcissism endlessly create.

The precocious child illustrates these tensions especially well as he is pandered to. An admiring audience for his notable achievements supports the child's resistance to change. He avoids what Freud called a "narcissistic scar," which comes of being compelled normally to turn toward reality. The precocious child generally is spared this essential humbling experience. Far from learning to scorn his child's condition as a doubtful prize and thus develop a great incentive to give it up, he is readily convinced that the rewards of adult life may be realized without its pains. Here the parent and child may become deeply engaged in a narcissistic folie à deux. To some degree, all parents risk this hazard with a child. When we study such a relationship, naturally bonded by a mutual narcissism, we find it indivisibly associated with intense aggression. It expresses the unconscious resistance to the necessity which reality dictates—that narcissism must alter.

The moral injunctions we offer a child well in advance of his own developed self-critical faculties are rarely received with appreciation since they focus on the compromises he must make. His own characteristically violent wishes, fantasies, impulses and acts, which we compel him to curb and master, plainly oppose the force of our will.

From his first intimate relationships, therefore, the child knows aggression at firsthand as a source of conflict. It is introduced to him far earlier than he knows his sexuality to be an agent of strife. And what erotic gratification he may experience as a young child is not equal to the deep satisfaction that aggression gives him.

Even at the most infantile level of existence, pleasure is not continuous. The infant quickly discerns that often satisfaction may not be found and certainly not whenever, nor to the degree, it may be desired. Pleasure must be sought. And the child's ordinary discontent is, therefore, no mere lack of pleasure, as has been conceived in modern psychological terms from Freud's theory. The search in early life, as it is later, for the relief of displeasure is vigorous. Neither in pursuit of pleasure nor in its implementation by way of adaptation to reality is passivity a wish or an aim.

Analysts generally believe that passivity is the obverse of activity. But if passivity is part of instinctual life, it has not yet been demonstrated. Like Freud's notion of a drive to inactivity or to becoming inert (as part of his theory of the death instincts), his conception was that we are given to passivity. He made a parallel with it to the tissue at rest, to inertia, and to the cessation of all activity—death. Freud and others, supported by the observation of the occurrence of passivity, draw the erroneous conclusion that it is expressive of some inherent drive in man. We are, however, drawn no more by an instinct to passivity than we are taken by instinct to our final end. Passivity exists as a reaction. It belongs to the psychological defenses that form in relation to certain conflicts. It stems from a different source than activity. Passivity commonly masks the most aggressive impulses, aims and acts that are heavily censored as destructive. Hence, as a reaction, passivity is a psychological state without an organic counterpart in living tissue. Nor does it have a parallel in animal life.

As a result of field studies in recent years, some psychoanalysts and ethologists have observed that many animals under the unusual conditions of attack from their own species show an avoidance of fighting or exhibit so-called "ritualized" behavior. It is thought that these are models of passivity, instinctively governed, and that it is a sad commentary on man that he has lost what many animals have so well preserved.[16]

Freud, himself, was not beyond pointing to activity and passivity as a pair of clinical opposites, sadism and masochism, and has stated that they both could be attributed to the element of aggressiveness. He was inclined to connect them with masculinity and femininity which are combined, he said, in bisexuality—a contrast which often has to be replaced in psychoanalysis with activity and passivity.[17] He did not escape the ambiguity of his own making when he explained that early psychological development is active and passive, and that later it may be designated as masculine and feminine. Activity refers, he said, to the instinct for mastery through the agency of a variety of functions and that passivity was its opposite. The endless ambiguity has been continued by analysts since Freud. Activity and passivity, and masculinity and femininity, are used interchangeably, sometimes in the biological sense, sometimes in the psychological sense, and at other times even in the sociological sense.

A commonly held view of infants by psychological workers is that they are passive. This refers not so much to behavior, which may vary from one child to the next, as to emotional experience. Parenthetically, it is a view most mothers would not hold. Perhaps we should not overlook an amusing and pointed assessment of the lack of passivity in infants. According to St. Augustine's direct observation, he thought only their limbs lacked violence. To this he added, "Who does not know this?" [18]

A young child's existence consists in tightly holding to the safety of the familiar and to the rule of what satisfies him. His strict adherence to these patterns of conduct allows scant opportunity for passivity. The child's experience is closely bound up with his mother's care as he is suckled, fed, cleaned, dressed and taught to perform all his functions by her. But the infant is no mere passive object to his mother's care as he has been so often romantically depicted. Common popular opinion of infant psychology, also held by many psychoanalysts, conceives of the child's physical limitations and his dependence upon care as tantamount to furnishing him with the disquieting self-image that he is helpless. Some analysts add that dependence upon what he receives makes him passive. The net effect, it is assumed, is that the young child's assessment of his condition leads him to regard his situation as precarious and even dangerous. And that only by way of some grandiose fantasies and through magical powers does he find relief. Moreover, as I have noted above, a basis for some to believe the child is led to despair is the presumption that the child has a clear perception of reality and that through the pain of his awareness it is repressed. This is thought to form a so-called pattern which becomes the prototype for all later conditions of depression. The common feeling of helplessness in adult depression, it is assumed, refers back to the infant's actual helplessness in caring for himself. In later life, supposition holds; these feelings of helplessness may be evoked by a variety of circumstances and, it is thought, may cast an explanatory light on the condition of infancy as well as on the condition of the depressed adult.[19]

About fifty years ago, Karl Abraham proposed a similar thesis. From his analysis of depressed adults, he thought he could explain their depression as stemming from the earlier and perhaps the first profound disappointment—their Oedipal wishes. He called it the "primal" depression and assumed the depressions of adulthood are a revival of that one.[20] The extent to which the pathological findings of adult life are but a return, literally, of the feelings experienced during infancy is mere conjecture.[21]

The view having the widest currency regards infant life as passive and receptive, even as an extension, in some respects, of "uterine life," which continues into infancy. The conjecture is that our early life as a child, like a blotter, absorbs whatever is presented. This stems from a persistent notion that the infant's so-called "basic" condition is characteristically passive. Then, it is assumed, when the circumstances call for it, aggression unfolds. Others have added to Freud's inferences. Notably Bertram Lewin and, before him, Melanie Klein and her "school," have had a continuing influence on theories of early psychological development. Both former students and later supporters of Freud, yet having marked differences, each represents a strong current of thinking about early or infant psychological experience. Their separate views meet in the belief that in the infant's naturally pronounced oral needs lies the foundation for the human devotion to "hedonistic ends." The child's wishes for such gratification are thus thought to enter into the deep unconscious during infancy to emerge later: "Soon the physiological needs become psychological wishes." [22] In this simplistic reduction, conceived from suppositions of infant experience, the sequence which is imagined reflects the attempts of analysts to give some substance to Freud's prophecy that someday all the complex psychological phenomena will be traced to their origin in physical and chemical sources.

It was not only Lewin's notion; it is a view shared by many others, that we may trace psychology to physiology even now. This idea declares that the remaining problem is to determine which path of the physiology turns into a wish. A linear continuity is believed to exist from physical expression to emotional desire.[23] Although Charles Darwin was not the first to hold such ideas, he was the first to give them a place in science. Applied to infancy, these views are that the young child's state of helplessness, naturally requiring the active intervention of the one who cares for him, results in the reward of being nurtured. And it is supposed that this prolonged experience weds each of us forever to the pursuit of pleasure. Hence, the normally passive child, it is assumed, develops into an active pleasure-seeking creature by way of the satisfaction he receives. The cardinal effect is that he becomes uncompromising in his search. This explanation of the human engagement in the search for gratification is an agreeable formula that conforms to the long-held conception of an uninterrupted evolution from biology to physiology, from need to wish, and from passivity to activity. The concept rests on the conviction that our observations of the infant's condition must coincide with his view of himself. To conjecture thus as to what infants think has been an exercise which has attracted many scientists long before the appearance of psychoanalysts. What family fails to know this? There is always a strong temptation to accept suppositions, especially about a child, for more than they are.

But a child demanding relief and satisfaction, in relation to the one who provides him with these needs, does furnish the key to a principle of early existence. It is that the need for relief from discomfort and finding gratification may be bridged by aggression. The aggression is aroused by want and quelled by satisfaction, through the efforts of another person. There should be no doubt that activity and aggression, not passivity, are important in the assertion of the child's egocentric aims.

Aggression as perpetually present fits Freud's definition of an instinct. It impinges on us from within and "no flight can avail against it." [24] Moreover, it abates only with satisfaction. Aggression so conceived is an appetite. To this biological concept of infant activity is added the notion that the young child's behavior is an expression of energy, perhaps actual or kinetic. The familiar efforts to explain a child's activity in the simple terms of nineteenth-century physics are plainly evident when the frame of reference is to its drives, discharges and inertia, or quantities of energies neutralized, distributed, activated, transformed or transferred.[25] It is as though this were matter imprisoned in our tissues, ready to be dispersed as aggression by some given charge.

The fact that clinical human studies on the development of rage and aggression in everyday life are conspicuously lacking may account for the assumptions that the activities of young children must be similar to those of certain animals. Despite all evidence and regardless of early child development studies, the endless assertions about the motives for human aggression appear not to have shifted from the emphasis placed a century ago, that aggression is innate, instinctive and a drive. These views conceive of aggression as expressive of "instinctive energy that overflows" and that "activates the intellectual apparatus," [26] or that the newborn arrives equipped with "innate discharge channels." [27] One is reminded of a comment by Romain Rolland when once he sat in a philosophy class in which the words to him were "formless, colorless, tasteless and insensible to the touch; words that responded neither to the wooing nor to the attacks of the senses; those mechanical words of metaphysics . . . clever instruments created by the brain. . . ." [28]

As in any scientific study, theorists of psychoanalysis also take excursions into speculation which carry them often far beyond the limits their scientific evidence would permit. The practice is most frequent, however, over questions of the infant's motivations. Perhaps the explanation lies in the frustrating barriers to the motives and thoughts that an infant presents. The psychoanalyst, accustomed to the analysis of his subject's thinking, in order to reveal motivation, with respect to an infant or young child, must be resigned, however, to scrutinizing behavior associated with little or no language. As a result, the analyst, in assigning motivation, is nowhere more tempted by conjecture and gratuitous interpretation.

One important element in hypotheses about a young child's aggression and his so-called passivity is that both are narrowly conceived as simply true to some biological endowment. Such notions allow for little other consideration of motivation than acceptance of destiny. But a study of the play of young children demonstrates that they employ their beliefs chiefly in extending their powers in defiance of a reality they wish to alter; and, in short, they resist the compromises demanded of them. A child does not for long escape the awareness of his limitations. Not only are they palpably real to him, but the efforts which he must make to overcome them, which his play plainly reveals, confirm the correctness of his assessment. Daily life convinces a child he needs more than he has and has wishes beyond what he enjoys.

A child's unconscious and natural belief in magic, easily shown to be present in his daily thinking, supports his powerful hope that he may escape being caught in the web of vicissitudes to which his experiences bind him. It explains why a child's early emotional defenses are extensively associated with a belief in the strength of his wishes and thoughts, rather than in the actualities of his weakness and dependence. Theories that would have it that these activities represent expression of aggression mistake the means for the ends.

Remarkably early, a child discerns that the fulfillment of his needs lies within a relationship. When he can enjoy his dependence, with the care it brings, he may put aside the anxiety and the hostility which is aroused by his condition of being a child. By projecting to others, and to things, what he himself feels, he may thus disengage himself from those experiences which are to him a source of disquiet. But in attributing his impulses and hostile wishes beyond himself, he makes the world fraught with hazards of his own creation. He must defend himself against his own phantoms.

A study of these processes in a child shows that he finds it more manageable to cope with a monster of his own making than to carry about within himself his own menace. The daily life of the child demonstrates the unconscious choice he fashions. He takes elaborate means to dissociate himself, not from his narcissism, but from his aggression. A child fears his aggressiveness. It becomes enjoyable, however, when identification forms unconsciously with others who are aggressive. Thus afforded some measure of relief from the common concern over being a victim, the incentive to become aggressive irresistibly heightens the wish to victimize others. The conflicts over aggression hence are not removed. They are endlessly rekindled. For example, it will be recalled that the Wolf Man as a small child was merciless in his attacks on a variety of creatures who he was terrified would destroy him; the paralyzing fears and phobias that little Hans developed concealed his own destructiveness, which on the one hand he admitted, and on the other disclaimed in his protests of being a victim. The other cases cited here also show directly how nightmares or the veritable "zoo" of creatures under a child's bed and in the dark corners at night express his own narcissism and the aggression that issues from it and of which he is fearful.

A child's aggression, essential to the defense of his narcissism, strains the relationships indispensable to the support he requires. The narcissism to which he naturally clings, founded on no simple device nor on the fact of his mere physical helplessness but on self-interest, furnishes a limitless source of conflict. The elemental concern with self, at the core of the child's existence and only painfully converted to a social experience, is always, as a result of the lifelong vulnerability of self-esteem, readily reverted to egocentricity. Hence, the adult may be rendered once again childlike in his narcissism. It amply testifies to the fragility of social relationships and the strength of narcissism.

In the depths of the unconscious, Freud found our pursuit of gratification relentless. To the degree it was realized, fulfillment reduced tension and carried us toward some measure of equilibrium. He pictured us in our strivings as in some respects winning our reward in pleasure. However, by not more fully considering the significant effect of our efforts on our sense of achievement and, through it, on our self-esteem, he has left us short. We have discussed the profound effects of our failures and frustrations, but may not our success also affect us beyond the mere realization of the gratification of pleasure? We have seen how early in life the mastery of functions, the acquisition of skills, and the formation of relationships may give self-esteem a firm foundation. Taken up in these pursuits, our aggression brings dividends in pleasure profoundly affecting our narcissism.

Whether we examine the extremes of egocentricity, which the psychology of autism represents (as we shall see in some detail later, and not just as a clinical disorder), or the less serious pathological states or even normal conditions of life, we find that the significance of the pursuit of pleasure extends beyond Freud's reduction of it to the aim of relieving tension. For a moment in one's existence Freud's abstract construction about the pleasure principle is conceivable. But in human experience it indeed must be short-lived. Self-reference, which actively begins somewhere in early infancy, does not miss the significance of satisfaction encountered. It is our unique quality, *narcissism,* which carries us far beyond the instinctual limits Freud thought were set for us.

His long journey exploring man's unconscious would end, he believed, in the basic sciences. The final vindication of his prodigious efforts he hoped would be discovered, not in the new science of humanism which he founded, but in the old one of biological chemistry with which he was familiar. And many to this day also believe it. These notions, as though bent on fulfilling Freud's prophecy, show continuing scientific efforts to explain man's mind by way of exhaustive analyses of his juices and ultramicroscopic dissections of his tissues.

It is a nineteenth-century philosophical conception, not separate from a long persistent and still prevalent romantic wish, that science in some not-too-distant time will reveal the "ultimate" secrets of nature. Freud expressed it often. He remained essentially a nineteenth-century scientist. He was also a pessimist. Freud despaired at the human motives he had himself discovered.

The main theme of *Civilization and Its Discontents,*[29] by far the most thorough discussion he undertook of an important problem in the development of civilization, is the so-called destructive instinct. It was Freud's opinion that an irreducible and irremedial antagonism exists between the demands of instincts and the restrictions of society. It is a theme that may be traced back to his earliest writings.[30] But in his last major work on the subject, he seemed even more confirmed. On the one hand, he thought some process unifying mankind brought individuals to combine into families, races, then peoples and nations into "one great unity." [31] And, on the other hand, "Man's natural aggressive instinct, the hostility of each against all and all against each, opposes this programme of civilization." [32] Had Freud been able to pursue his studies further, he might not have had more cause to change his mind or to be less gloomy about man's nature. He would have found, however, that his attention would not be centered so much on the instincts as it would be drawn to a far more unstable and dangerous element that existed, man's narcissism.

As a product of German romantic idealism, Freud was at odds with his own vast discoveries. His optimism, as his idealism, was in science; it was not in the humanities.

An optimism similar to Freud's persists to the present. Its advocates hopefully expect that some simple human essence will finally be found to account for our complex motives and our baffling psychopathology, and that the continuing frustrating search for some deeper understanding of man's nature then will be terminated. Bertrand Russell referred to such visions as a Hegelian illusion. It supposes that there are ultimates to be reached where the process of inquiry ends! He wrote, "This is, however, an unsound view; it seems clear, on the contrary, that enquiry is limitless. Perhaps this circumstance will in the end preserve us from the kind of goal that architects of Utopian fantasies draw up from time to time." [33]

Freud probably had few illusions about man's psychology; nevertheless, he succumbed to Utopian notions about humanity. They, as I have indicated, led him to draw blueprints of the future of psychology. He produced a wry paradox. He proved the existence of a dynamic psychology in man. He removed it as much from romanticism as from animalism and thus shaped twentieth-century psychology. Yet, he himself remained trapped in his own period. He failed to heed his own warning that clinical inquiry should not be given up for exercises in speculation. He succumbed to his wishes that human psychology of aggression was held in some simple secret our fiber would one day yield.

Freud nowhere else abandoned clinical grounds so completely and took more to metaphysical speculation than he did about aggression. There his science faltered. The accuracy and significance of his clinical discoveries about aggression have been amply confirmed. But the suppositions he made about aggression had a minimal foundation in clinical fact. And although Freud himself fully acknowledged the highly theoretical nature of the assumptions he introduced to explain man's aggression, he nevertheless held to them, as have those who followed him. Nowhere in psychoanalysis have concepts been founded on less clinical study or given over more to polemics than in the area of aggression.

Chapter VII

The Achillean Choice

The observation that aggressiveness directed against oneself flatly contradicts self-preservation led Freud, more as the Darwinian philosopher than as clinical investigator, to suppose that some inherent force in life itself must counter the strength of the wish to live. It would explain self-destructiveness and its extreme expression—suicide. It was a view which became more and more prominent in Freud's theoretical works beginning with its first explicit appearance in 1920 when he published *Beyond the Pleasure Principle*.[1] He wrote then that the instincts of self-preservation "are the true life instincts. They operate against the purpose of the other instincts which lead, by reason of their function, to death." [2] The danger in the normal or ordinary prevalence of masochism is "in the fact that it originates from the death instinct and corresponds to the part of the instinct which has escaped being turned outward as an instinct of destruction." [3] And twenty years later in his posthumously published work, "An Outline of Psycho-analysis (1940)," [4] Freud showed that he had held these views to the end.

Freud conceived of the death instinct as destructive and particularly as a force aimed toward reducing complex forms of existence. He hypothesized a life-course of going from the animate to the inert, the reverse of the direction of evolution. Taken to its logical conclusion, this was aggression as a biological process inherent in the tissues themselves, and therefore having no mental representation. Freud was frank in his admission that he had no evidence for these suppositions. He reconciled them, however, on the basis that since man's destructiveness seemed not to be explained by what was known about the strength of the wish to survive, it seemed reasonable to surmise some inherent force existed which opposed living, much as there was one which supported it.[5]

Freud's interest in man's destructiveness extended beyond his clinical discoveries and his philosophical reflections. He was also a humanitarian, and as a parent of two sons in battle in the great war, 1914–1918, he could hardly avoid the question of war. He was deeply concerned and wrote that the tremendous destruction war brought to human life perhaps reflected some inherent element in man's nature that appeared to bring on, if not to hasten, his own end. This long-held supposition of the death instincts evidently was too tempting to forego. Their persistent importance to Freud was especially plain in his famous exchange of letters with Albert Einstein. They appeared under the title, "Why War?" [6] Freud made frequent reference to some instinctual inclination in man to kill. "According to our hypothesis human instincts are of only two kinds: those which seek to preserve and unite—which we call 'erotic' . . . —and those which seek to destroy and kill. . . . As a result of a little speculation, we have come to suppose that this instinct is at work in every living creature and is striving to bring it to ruin and to reduce life to its original condition of inanimate matter. Thus it quite seriously deserves to be called a death instinct, while the erotic instincts represent the effort to live." [7] Freud nevertheless was not to be put off from considering a possible way of ending all wars. He conceived of the necessity for harnessing aggression, inasmuch as we cannot get rid of it. He had a Platonic scheme that an elite stratum of men should be developed, not open to intimidation, who "would give direction to the dependent masses." [8]

It is interesting that the machinations of social engineers appear to be forever engaged in regulating unruly relationships among men, beginning with Plato and extending to such modern planners as Lenin and many others with less distinction than Freud. The proposals all have a remarkable similarity. The timeless scheme, it appears, calls for a small community, or a council of elite and strict governors, or possibly a vanguard in advance of the masses, to exercise control over others whose allegedly dangerous and often blind impulses press to be carried out. It seems that all who govern, or would rule, according to such schemes, fear aggression in others who they expect will resist discipline. The elite is thus self-justified in suppressing those who rebel.

The apparent destructiveness in man, Freud thought, could be scientifically understood when he formulated the idea of the death instincts. It is a curious and an exceptional fact that this theory of Freud's, having so little substance and which analysts therefore have largely dismissed, should find vigorous support among those whose knowledge of clinical psychoanalysis is limited. As a concept it was never a clear one. It was in a sense, however, "so tragically grand that it exhorts admiration, yet so terrible that it seems to make even his most faithful followers uneasy." [9]

During the past thirty-five years or so, the subject of the death instincts has no longer been considered seriously by analysts as a basis for behavior. It seemed destined to live for only a moment in the historical record of the inquiry into man's motives. However, in the last fifteen years the notion has begun to be revived. As some deterministic interpretations of history are being coupled with certain psychoanalytic concepts, both have gained a new sort of popularity.[10] The recent increased interest in aggression has come more from academic psychologists and thinkers than clinicians. Special interest has been shown by such social commentators as Norman O. Brown and Herbert Marcuse. They tend to view the present contradictions and conflicts in society as a direct reflection of some inherent quality of self-destructiveness in individual psychology. The presumption is that armed struggles are reducible to expressions of man's bent toward self-destruction. Freud's death instincts are presumed to be evidence that in man's unconscious is the menace to his existence, and that this hazard to the human condition once loosened, like the Furies, would make our fate certain.[11]

So long as self-destructiveness is taken as evidence of a force opposing self-preservation and is believed to be what Freud meant by the death instinct, the misconception will no doubt persist. Moreover, to take his speculation as a guide with which to search for models in childhood and infancy of some supposed primary destructive instinct fails to be attentive to his specific reference to death instincts as strictly biological. He particularly did not regard them as psychological; his long-held idea was that someday a chemical basis for our conduct would be discovered. He called the death instincts "mute" and "silent," i.e. a force compelling a direction. He said they are not observable. We see that Freud's search was for a theory. It was not a clinical investigation.

To equate, somehow, aggression with self-preservation gives aggressiveness at once a biological caste, supports a Darwinian concept, and makes of aggression a global function in which all manner of creatures employ "the bloody claw" to stay alive. Such prevalent views, a legacy of Victorian notions of man's descent, rest on armchair speculations of animal life, laboratory experiments with various species, and express the narrowest interpretation of aggression applied without distinction to both animals and man. Contemporary field studies of animals, as shown in Chapter III, give no support to such conjectures.

The problem remains. Inasmuch as animals have no demonstrable self-destructiveness, and man obviously does, where shall we begin? Since it is plain fact that self-destruction has a powerful and persistent impetus, we are drawn to the question, what compels aggression to be turned against the self? What has happened to self-preservation in suicide?

The clinical finding that suicide is frequently an unconscious act of revenge, a violent and hostile act directed at others but which takes oneself as the prime victim, Freud discovered half a century ago. This now well-known dynamic process has been familiar to writers and poets since antiquity. But our modern scientific understanding of it only commenced in the early decades of this century.

It is a curious fact that neither Plato's concept of death as the liberation of the soul from its case, nor Epicurus' argument that overcoming the fear of death would relieve us of one of our two great dreads (the other being the will of the gods), nor Montaigne's proposal that we must turn from our fears of dying to the triumph of nature, give us any clue as to how near we exist to self-destruction. Yet, the menace of self-destruction is, while conspicuously distant in the philosophic consideration of the human condition, prominent in the works of Homer and Euripides, in Shakespeare, Turgenev, and in great novels like *Madame Bovary* or the classic Russian novels of the later decades of the nineteenth century. It is therefore all the more astonishing to observe that the great clinicians of the late nineteenth century, traditionally thoroughly versed in the classics, comfortably familiar with Greek, Latin and often Hebrew, and with a knowledge of literature far richer than there can be acquired in most present-day curricula, stood before their self-destructive patients and had mainly philosophic remarks to make about them when the question of motivation came up for consideration. It was not frequent. Henry Maudsley commented that self-destruction showed "a defect of the fundamental energy to live" and that the "act of suicide was proof of wanting in the fundamental wish to live." [12] Griesinger argued whether it was necessary to be insane, i.e. deluded, to kill oneself or whether circumstances were not sometimes sufficiently distressing to warrant it. [13] The writing on suicide before the turn of the century laid great emphasis on the variety of clinical conditions wherein may be anticipated and catalogued the signs and symptoms connected with self-destruction, but it neither recognized nor sought any relationship between this data and the great literature which had long since probed man's motives.

The great French psychiatrist Magnan (1835–1916), whose original studies of alcoholism were rich in clinical material, gave his attention to the serious pathological results of excessive drinking. But nowhere in his teaching or writing did he notice that damaging and excessive drinking provided his patients with a self-destructiveness they seemed unable to relinquish and that it was therefore a critical element in their addiction. Nor was German psychiatry, which led the world in research from the middle of the nineteenth century for seventy-five years and produced such influential teachers as Wilhelm Griesinger (1817–1868), Karl Kahlbaum (1828–1899), and Emil Kraepelin (1855–1926), appreciably different in this respect from what was to be found elsewhere. All were seriously engaged in studying clinical phenomena, classifying and categorizing them. A subject's suicidal conduct, when it was not attributed to some hereditary strains, was reproached as a moral prohibition. It is an attitude which still exists in most parts of the world in the form of statutes or religious interdictions.

Whether as self-immolation or in fantasies of self-denigration, the force of aggression turned against oneself is well known, and suicidal wishes are probably no less common to our experience than they were either in antiquity or among aborigines. Nevertheless, there is surprisingly little in scientific literature to show us that self-destruction is part of the psychology of everyday life and not confined to its extremes and exceptions in suicidal acts.

No aggression surpasses the fierceness of taking oneself as the ultimate victim of one's own violence, and it has held, therefore, a unique and imperishable place in men's minds. It must be just because self-preservation is at the center of our existence that the utter destruction of life carries such significance for us. We have some measure of this in the fact that before our present-day clinical grasp of some of its deeper emotional implications, self-destruction was set forth so completely by Euripides, Homer, Shakespeare, Tolstoi, Mark Twain and many others who could be ranked accurately as great clinicians of their time. Many writers, poets and dramatists of centuries past have provided a rich intuitive understanding of many aspects of the psychology of daily life, and particularly the profoundly moving dynamic elements at work in self-denigration, in the anguish of lost self-esteem, and in the violence of suicide.

But today, well-known scientific works on the nature of suicide or self-destructiveness begin with, and are confined to, the problems swirling about such acts, rather than what they may reveal of their far-reaching unconscious significance.[14] The modern clinician, with respect to understanding self-destructiveness, seems no more ready to use the insight of poets or his own studies of unconscious motivations than the nineteenth-century clinicians.

From legends and myths and literary works we have long known that self-esteem and self-destruction are intimately linked, and that injury to narcissism loosens aggression. It was William Congreve's experience to observe, two hundred years before Freud, that a woman's narcissism when hurt could turn to menace. He wrote that

> Heav'n has no rage, like love to hatred turned
> Nor Hell a fury, like a woman scorned.[15]

But to the present, the exceeding vulnerability of a woman's narcissism and its relation to her aggression and her tendency then to turn it on herself remain more in the poet's lines than in the clinician's research.

However, long before the seventeenth century, Euripides furnished us with one of the most vivid examples in all literature of the violence and self-destruction which issues from humiliation. The terrific power of Medea requires no description. From the outset, quitting loyalty to her father and murdering her brother, who might have prevented her from running off with Jason, Medea is portrayed as allowing no curb to her passion, to be loved. And later, when she herself is betrayed by Jason, her humiliation shows that her narcissism becomes the most destructive force which loosens her fury. She brings all she values to ruin with the dread of being laughed at. This is but her own horror of ridicule, the measure of self-esteem precariously held and highly vulnerable. The effects of injury to her self-esteem are drawn with such accuracy that modern psychoanalytic concepts add little to Euripides' insight.

Exceeding the self-blinding of Oedipus in its force of self-destruction, Euripides presents Medea in Corinth, by her own doing a fugitive from her land, betrayed and insulted by Jason, and possessed of a colossal vanity. For Medea, the great store set by being loved justified both treachery and killing. But now Jason displaced her and favored another, a betrayal and an outrageous insult Medea could not tolerate. Even the risk of being deprived of Jason's love, when she first ran off with him, had not raised such a level of virulence in her as did his betrayal.

Medea shows her struggle is not so much with her maternal feelings or her love for Jason but with her vengeance for being humiliated. Her murderous fury issues from being humbled. But Medea will not endure being demeaned. Her narcissism, deeply hurt, drives her to demonic lengths of passionate violence. Thus acting in revenge, she dooms her sons. The extremes to which she is compelled are justified, even at all costs and ruin, in the name of redress. With Jason abandoning her, Medea's justification for her ruthless treason and murder in order to marry him is gone. Her self-esteem suffers all the more. Yet, above all, self-esteem must be restored.

Much is made by Greek scholars of Medea's disasterous temperament, causing them to regard her as more a tragic victim than a tragic agent.[16] Such interpretations overlook the key which Euripides furnishes us. Medea has a tragic flaw; it determines her fate.

Before the play opens we know that Medea, to satisfy her passion for Jason, exiled herself and destroyed her brother. The opening discloses that Medea's actions were in vain. As Jason now places his ambition above Medea, she is thus rendered worthless. Condemned to a life she loathes, hapless and forsaken, she is blind with rage and goaded by humiliation to violence.[17]

The children's nurse cries in despair:

> Now all is hatred: love is sickness—stricken.
>
> [l. 14]

In her profound loss of self-esteem, she can respond to no one. Grim, she is bent first on destroying herself. The chorus tells of vain efforts to comfort her and the unheeded pleas that she be more temperate. But as the wife once beloved and now abandoned:

> Flung down, she weeps and wastes through all the days
> Since first she knew her lord's wrong done to her,
> Never uplifting eye, nor turning ever
> From earth her face.
>
> [ll. 24–27]

Medea cries out (behind the scenes):

> O hapless I! O miseries heaped on mine head!
> Ah me! ah me! would God I were dead!
>
> [ll. 96–97]

The nurse warns of the virulence to come:

> O beware ye
> > Of the thoughts as a wild-beast brood,
> Of the nature too ruthless to spare ye
> > In its desperate mood.
>
> Pass ye within now, departing
> > With all speed. It is plain to discern
> How a cloud of lamenting, upstarting
> > From its viewless beginnings, shall burn
> In lightnings of fury yet fiercer.
> > What deeds shall be dared of that soul,
> So haughty, when wrong's goads pierce her,
> > So hard to control?
>
> > > [ll. 102–113]

A humiliated Medea cries for death:

> Would God that the flame of the lightning from
> > heaven descending, descending
> Might burn through mine head!—for in living
> > wherein any more is my gain?
> Alas and alas! Would God I might bring to an
> > ending, an ending
> The life that I loathe, and behind me might cast
> > all its burden of pain!
>
> > > [ll. 145–152]

> But me—the blow ye wot of suddenly fell
> Soul shattering. 'Tis my ruin: I have lost
> All grace of life: I long to die.
>
> > > [ll. 225–228]

The chorus warns us:

> Awful and past all healing is that wrath
> When they that once loved clash in feud and hate.
> > > [ll. 520–521]

Medea laments over her lost worth which joins with her anguish that Jason in betraying her has brought the plight of what a woman risks in marriage. It is the infamy of being rejected, she said, and that for the man, "when his home-yoke galls his neck," he can ease himself with a friend, but for a woman, she has only him to turn to. She mourns her own lost hopes of being loved as she cries that life without it is empty. The mockery is unendurable when being desired.

—'tis past—'tis past,
That sweet imagining!
[ll. 1035–1036]

In self-pity at her misfortune, she lapses into a reverie of her exile. Perhaps only death can relieve her. But she arouses herself from such musings with:

—what ails me? Would I earn derision,
Letting my foes slip from mine hand unpunished?
I must dare this. Out on my coward mood
That let words of relenting touch mine heart!
[ll. 1049–1052]

Medea resolves that her only course is vengeance. Only revenge will rectify her being wronged, abandoned. She is determined to regain the "grace of life" she lost, and to recover from the blow that was "soul-shattering" and had plunged her into the horrors of revenge and ruin. Medea's flaw lies in her arrogance. Her tragedy lies in the restoration of her self-esteem.

From Euripides we learn Medea is not revolting because she commits monstrous acts. Nor is she simply blindly outraged and violent. She is revealed as a tragic figure, so tyrannized by her narcissism that even at the risk of her ruin she must attempt to restore her self-esteem from the deep injury it has suffered. What she does to recover it seems warranted. The course she follows begins with her humiliation and feeling worthless. Medea is flooded then with self-destructive intentions; she wishes to die and calls on God to bring her pain to an end. But, her narcissism does not tolerate the terrible abuse inflicted on it, and she turns to the justification she needs and employs. Hence, in full vindication, Medea's sole purpose is, with vengeance, to redeem her narcissism.

Fallen self-esteem, injured narcissism and the issuing deep need for redress through vindication was probably as familiar to Mark Twain as it was to Euripides. The fugitive from Corinth and the one from the Illinois shore hold in common a certain suffering.

In "the small store of truth that American literature has added to the treasury of mankind . . . there is a contribution in Mark Twain's *Adventures of Tom Sawyer* to understanding the deep conflicts which issue from the proneness of self-esteem to injury and clinging to its precarious perch. This book, more profoundly true to the fantasies of boyhood and to maturity's nostalgia for what it once was" [18] than any other piece of fiction, brings an enchantment which is so strong that it beguiles one into neglecting to pay attention to how much of the spell issues from dread and horror.[19] Dark needs are voiced. The vicissitudes of a boy's self-esteem get expression in perhaps one of the commonest daydreams of childhood. Mark Twain wrote about it thus:

> Tom's mind was made up now. He was gloomy and desperate. He was a forsaken, friendless boy, he said; nobody loved him; when they found out what they had driven him to, perhaps they would be sorry; he had tried to do right and get along, but they would not let him; since nothing would do them but to be rid of him, let it be so; and let them blame *him* for the consequences . . .[20]

From Tom's thoughts we see that from lack of love the boy regards himself as a hapless victim of cruel indifference. Thus forced from home, he is resigned that it means he will die. So be it; he is probably to blame for his fate. But at this low ebb in despair and in defense against furthering his gloom, Tom's narcissism can no longer be resigned to a continued ignominy and afflictions from neglect. He turns to vindication. As the one who suffers, he will bring anguish to those who torment him. Tom finds that he is not alone in his agony. All boys seem to suffer as he does. His inquiries among his friends confirm that their discontent is also great—none are fully loved. And for that they would all quit their seemingly heartless families.

To escape the ill-usage and lack of sympathy at home, Tom and his comrades left for the river to be pirates. Each had a special name: Tom was the Black Avenger of the Spanish Main; Huck Finn became the Red Handed; and Joe Harper was the Terror of the Seas. Thus launched, the boys were bent on a reckoning. They were gone overnight on their adventure, their whereabouts unknown, and their families feared the boys may have drowned. As they searched the river for them, the boys watched.

> Here was a gorgeous triumph; they were missed; they were mourned; hearts were breaking on their account; tears were being shed; accusing memories of unkindnesses to these poor lost lads were rising up and unavailing regrets and remorse were being indulged . . .

Tom and his friends were jubilant over the mourning for them. "That was Tom's great secret—the scheme to return home and with his brother pirates, attend their own funerals." [21]

Together, Tom and his cronies set out on an adventure of high crime, piracy. Their fantasy was that through great infamy, beyond the reach of rules and as a law unto themselves on the seas, those at home would be compelled to respect them. This ordinary daydream of young adolescents, of establishing their worth or proving their value, is not to be gained by yielding their aggressive aims but by promoting them; thus violence finds its justification. A passive surrender is not, as is generally supposed, a quitting of aggression, although this may appear to take place; it means taking a narcissistic injury, i.e. a lowering of self-esteem. To prevent such an occurrence violence is allowed. For example, high crimes are extolled, piracy is condoned, and the fiction of a Robin Hood loses none of its currency as authority. Aggressive crimes are perpetrated in the name of self-assertion to gain honor, admiration, and to command respect.

The conflicts of conscience, which appear to be either suspended or absent in such adolescent heroics and publicly a source of despair to the elders, are explained psychoanalytically as indicative of a poorly developed or an as-yet-to-be-formed superego. What is overlooked in such suppositions is that the adolescent's pursuit of self-esteem is one of the chief occupations of that period of emotional development. The need for it is so great that in the name of acts of rectitude, charity or even compassion, the most violent and inhumane deeds may be acquitted. Aggression must have its justification. Without justification it is *not* condoned. Therefore, it is not that conscience is lacking but that self-esteem is more commanding.

Tom and his companions, as pirates, were set on such a course. Much to their surprise, they discovered their absence was taken to mean they were indeed victims, not only of drowning, however, but of not having been sufficiently loved. To their great pleasure, the boys overhear the villagers make a complete confession of guilt. And the comrades' aggressive measures to gain favor are fully vindicated. Their self-esteem seems thus assured.

Tom's secret, however, is not simply attending his own funeral, which is another daydream of childhood. It is his longing to be loved, not so much for what he may do or not do, but simply to be loved, solely for himself. By secretly attending his own funeral he hopes to observe the mourners who in their guilt confess their selfish crime of not having expressed their deep love of him. These wishes, mainly unconscious, are at the height of childhood's narcissism; the aim is to be loved merely for the majesty of one's existence; and as the need to prove one's worthiness becomes unnecessary, what remains is the enjoyment of being adored. It is often a deep-seated longing that is never relinquished. And in later periods of life, it continues to generate discontent with any love which cannot fulfill this narcissistic prerequisite. There are countless fragments of daydreams and fantasies and instances in our daily lives in which we would, like Tom Sawyer, wish to destroy ourselves to deprive and thus to punish those whom we fear love us too little for our liking.

Mark Twain well understood the nature of those egocentric conflicts which give rise to ambivalence when he described this episode beginning in a boy's loveless gloom. Only as a wretched victim and through suffering does the boy enjoy revenge for the humiliation he endured. While Tom Sawyer is no Medea and the scale of the drama in the one cannot be measured against the other, the agonizing conflicts are nevertheless remarkably similar.

In our classical literature the most illustrious case of humiliation, grief, suffering and revenge, and the recovery of self-esteem is that described by Homer. In *The Iliad* [22] the brilliant Achilles and the powerful Agamemnon quarrel over a prize of war, a girl. The king appropriates her and refuses to give her up or to take a ransom for her, and

> raging, the heart within filled black to the
>   brim with anger
> from beneath, but his two eyes showed like fire in
>   their blazing.
>   [bk. I, ll. 103–104]

draws from Achilles the remarks that Agamemnon was

> greediest for gain of all men.
>   [bk. I, l. 122]

> . . . for the present give the girl back to the god;
>   [bk. I, l. 127]

Agamemnon replied:

> . . . good fighter though you be, godlike Achilleus,
> strive to cheat, for you will not deceive, you will not
>   persuade me.
> What do you want? To keep your own prize and have me sit here
> lacking one? Are you ordering me to give this girl back?
>   [bk. I, ll. 131–134]

Achilles spoke:

> O wrapped in shamelessness, with your mind forever on profit,
> how shall any one of the Achaians readily obey you
> either to go on a journey or to fight men strongly in battle?
>
> [bk. I, ll. 149–151]

He went on to say that the Trojans had done no wrong to him; he and the others followed the king to do him favor, to win him honor from the Trojans.

> You forget all this or else you care nothing.
> And now my prize you threaten in person to strip from me,
> for whom I laboured much, the gift of the sons of the Achaians.
> Never . . . do I have a prize that is equal to your prize.
> Always the greater part of painful fighting is the work of
> my hands; but when the time comes to distribute booty
> yours is far the greater reward, and I with some small thing
> yet dear to me go back to my ships when I am weary with fighting.
>
> [bk. I, ll. 160–168]

His final words denounce the king as cruel, heedlessly sacrificing his men in battle and humiliating his subjects. He withdraws from Agamemnon's service, outraged. As he nurses his injured self-esteem, he warns others against being swindled by the king whom he further accuses of dishonesty and cruelty toward those whom he beguiles with words. Betrayed, he goes off in the most illustrious sulk in all literature.

With Achilles absent, Hector in battle kills Achilles' friend Patroclus. Achilles finally puts his "gall of anger" aside when he learns of this loss. But not before in deep mourning he pours ashes "that befouled his handsome countenance" over himself, allows no one to comfort him in his sorrow, and blames himself for not having been present to prevent the death of his dearest companion. His guilt is all the worse in that he believed he was negligent through serving his own ends. This makes him all the more eager to avenge Patroclus. Only this justification will permit him to rid himself of self-reproaches and regain his self-respect.

Achilles, before he sets out to "overtake that killer of a dear life, Hector . . . in the dust lay at length, and took and tore at his hair with his hands. . . ." He finally turns to his enemy when Iris comes running from Olympus with a message from Zeus. The time has come when remorse and self-pity have to give way to shame. And with that Achilles' fury increases. The greater his anger at Hector, the readier he is to give it substance. He at first held himself accountable for his friend's death, but as the self-recriminations mount so does his sense of outrage rise.

Burdened with self-reproaches, Achilles reflects on what he is set to do.

> I must die soon, then; since I was not to stand by my companion when he was killed. And now, far away from the land of his fathers, he is perished, and lacked my fighting strength to defend him.
> [bk. XVII, ll. 98–100]

As his thoughts of his own death are vivid, he turns more and more to wishes for revenge. As Hector glories in his shining armor, Achilles observes:

> Yet I think he will not glory for long,
> since his death stands very close to him.
> [bk. XVII, ll. 132–133]

Revenge and his own end seem indivisible. The oppressive memory of the dead Patroclus is weighted with relentless self-accusations. From self-blame Achilles rails at Hector, on whom he pours accusations he shortly before inflicted upon himself. As they faced each other on the field, Achilles spoke:

> Come nearer so that sooner you may reach your appointed destruction.
> [bk. XX, l. 429]

To which Hector answered:

> Son of Peleus, never hope by words to frighten me
> as if I were a baby. I myself understand well enough
> how to speak in vituperation and how to make insults.
> [bk. XX, ll. 431–433]

In destroying Hector, Achilles gains relief from the burden of his guilt. And Achilles not only kills Hector, he utterly degrades him. No one can persuade him to do otherwise. And through this violence, Achilles is redeemed. His guilt, through the justification of hostility, is expiated. Only then does the ritual reconciliation with Priam, Hector's father, take place. *The Iliad,* having opened with rancor and humiliation, ends on the note of honor restored.

The heroes of *The Iliad* are caught in tragedy. Their jealousy, their conflicts, their loss of face and subsequent vilification and rage, their self-reproaches for another's harm—all are heroic versions of familiar experiences. Our grasp of the conflicts requires no special effort. These are the conflicts of everyday life, in ancient Greece or anywhere. The human condition does not alter in this respect. Central to Achilles' character is the human vulnerability of self-esteem and the compelling need to repair its injury. Even though god-related, Achilles does not escape its hazards any more than did Medea. Achilles is the chief of Homer's heroes, graced with beauty, swiftness, strength and valor. According to legend, as a youth, the choice between an early death with undying fame and a long but inglorious life was given him, and the fate he chose was renown. Despite his proven heroic qualities, he nonetheless is prone to the mortal agony—suffering injury to pride. He succumbs to the humiliation of a vain king, he reproaches himself for nursing his own wounded vanity which costs his friend's life, and he deprecates himself as he despairs at his shortcomings. With each narcissistic hurt Achilles receives, the aggression it evokes turns first on himself. Recovery from these injuries only commences when, in the name of justice, he finally launches a murderous attack on Hector. Hector then becomes the victim of Achilles' loss of self-esteem, the object on whom his severe conscience pours abuse.

Mythology, the world's literature and history furnish examples of the tragedy of a great man who through a fault in an otherwise noble character brings disaster upon himself. Homer in *The Iliad* cites such a case. The events which took place before Troy were set in motion by the quarrel between Agamemnon and Achilles. To Greek scholars, and eminent among them Richmond Lattimore, Achilles is the tragic hero "great, but human and imperfect." [23] And while Homer shows Achilles to be "prescient beyond others," [24] he has limitations, and his character is invaded by the human emotions of grief. He plainly is neither semidivinity nor superman; he is, above all, subject to anger.[25] Although both Achilles and Agamemnon are regarded as men of great pride, the king demands "recognition of his kingly stature," as if afraid of losing his position if he lacks what others have;[26] and Achilles, great though he is, nevertheless is enraged by the king's conduct. It is here that the two meet. The key to the tragedy is neither in the circumstances of the quarrel or that Achilles' heel deprives him of immortality, nor is it in the fuming anger which issues. It is in the confrontation of each man with the other's pride, before which neither yields. The hero's humiliation initiates the train of events which leads inexorably to the tragic end. In short, Achilles is vulnerable and the chink in his glorious, shining armor is his narcissism. When it is hurt, he is infuriated, goes off sulking and nurses his humiliation. Odysseus warns him of the danger and urges him to give up his anger on account of it. Achilles refuses. The damage to his pride is too great to give up being angry. Redress is imperative.

The lesson in the epic is not that a great man can become so angry or that in sulking he succumbs to a perverse stubbornness that leads to his being done in. It is that to be exceedingly narcissistic is as much a menace to oneself as it is to others. And to be unable to yield one's narcissism somewhat for the sake of another's need places us in double jeopardy.

Legends and myths illustrate our common conflicts even though the characters are greater than life-size and their feats superhuman. For instance does not Prometheus' fate actually contain the ordinary story of a youth who defied authority? Despite warnings, he persisted in his mischief. The punishment was severe.

Prometheus, one of the sons of a Titan and a nymph, was regarded as the wisest of the brothers. One day a dispute took place as to which portions of a sacrificial bull should be offered to the gods and which should be reserved for men. Prometheus was invited to settle the argument. He prepared the portions in two bags. One contained all the flesh which he concealed beneath the least tempting part of any animal, and the other contained the bones hidden beneath a rich fat layer. Zeus, offered the choice, was easily deceived and chose the bag of bones. He punished Prometheus for humiliating him. And since Prometheus had passed on to mankind various useful arts, Zeus went further in his admonishment by ordering fire to be withheld from mankind. "Let them eat their flesh raw!" he cried.[27] But the youth was still not to be restrained. In defiance of Zeus' authority, he broke off a fragment of glowing charcoal from a torch he lit at the fiery chariot of the Sun, stole away undiscovered, and gave fire to mankind. Zeus swore revenge.[28] The punishment was severe.

Perhaps Prometheus hoped he would be rewarded for his altruism, if not forgiven for his delinquency. In any event, his deeds are rationalized, according to legend, as serving the greater good, and he succeeds to martyrdom through his suffering. That he brought his agony on himself through his youthful, impetuous arrogance tends to be overlooked in according him honors for his gift to man in the face of defying the highest authority, Zeus. In our gratitude for

Prometheus' gift to us, for which he paid with perpetual agony, we must not neglect that Zeus would not tolerate having his powers challenged or his position demeaned. And, as the youth's accomplices in receiving stolen goods, our punishment was to have the beautiful and beguiling Pandora offer us the contents of her jar.*

The need to be enthroned and the wish for the advantages which that position affords is found among the most primitive peoples as well as among ourselves. Such pressing wishes are evoked not only in the crises of life and in those circumstances which arouse fears and apprehensions but they also derive from the "quite ordinary events of everyday that leave their dissatisfactions, unrequited wishes and unfulfilled expectations." No great mishap is required for us to feel troubled, hurt or anxious and, while awaiting the unpredictable outcome of an event, to wish and pray for a favored solution.[29]

For instance, the Dani are a contemporary primitive society in the mountains of West New Guinea. They are an industrious, belligerent, proud, independent tribal people. They regard themselves as the original humans. All others are viewed as aliens, are enemies until proven otherwise, and are designated by their word for excrement.[30] Similarly, a very primitive tribe of South American Indians, the Yanomamo of Southern Venezuela, "believe that they are the first, finest and most refined form of man to inhabit the earth. All others are inferior because they developed later by a process of degeneration from a pure Yanomamo stock, explaining their strange customs and peculiar languages." Yanomamo, in fact, means "humanity," or at least the most important segment of humanity. "The characteristic reaction of any group to a tape recording made in another nearby area in which the language differences are slight was met with: 'They speak crooked; we speak straight, the right way!' "[31]

People everywhere and always, whether the Dani, the Yanomamo, Old Testament Hebrews or ourselves, inescapably are confronted by an identically inscrutable future. To the inevitable apprehensions it arouses, we find a remarkably similar remedy. We all make the same claim to priority, with only superior descendants issuing from

---

* The symbolism of fire, central to the myth of Prometheus, was familiar to Freud in connection with one of his earliest cases in the analysis of dreams; it came up again later in connection with the Wolf Man case and also in respect to later papers on sexual conflicts. His hypothesis suggested interpreting the Prometheus myth only in libidinal terms. The psychoanalytic literature since Freud, although having elaborated on his theory, retains his quaintness.

us, while others are at best inferior collateral relations. Our assertions seem to emerge more from doubts than certainties and more from anxieties than confidence.

Every generation stages the same familiar encounters. And hence the myths, legends and tales are easily carried over the millennia. Only the forms and the styles presenting the indentical conflicts undergo radical change as they reflect differences in cultures.

Thus, this rich store is a universal legacy. At a safer distance than autobiographical accounts would allow, we retell and at times directly refer these materials to our own experience.

No better illustration confirms this human phenomenon than the myths of the origin of our species. As I have shown here, people in New Guinea and in the rain forest of Venezuela each make the claim that humanity sprang from their own ancestors. The ancient Hebrews and the Buddhists today make similar assertions. An imperative emerges. It is that to be held in highest regard by the greatest authority, our gods must spare us what we otherwise fear we cannot escape. To be a chosen people appears to be a universal narcissistic claim against ignominy and fate.

The Iliad, remote as it is in time, conveys to us with fidelity the perpetual conflicts we encounter in our efforts to maintain self-respect. A loss of self-esteem and the mobilization of aggression to defend it are confined to no boundaries, to no period, and to no people.

In a nearer time, through the creativity of another genius and with a dramatis personae having scant resemblance to the players in Greek drama or epic, a sixteenth-century Elizabethan play, drawing on an Italian story published a half-century earlier, presents us with similarly deeply rooted and shattering conflicts.

Othello begins with the humiliation of an important citizen, a Senator of Venice. In the night, he is aroused by an alarm that his only child, Desdemona, is missing. Following a search, she is found. To her father's shocked disbelief, his devoted daughter has secretly married. The father is appalled by this totally unexpected news. But that the man is a Moor has made it a scandal. The father is certain that the girl could not have married Othello without having been stolen or enchanted by him. Moreover, the Senator is certain his daughter would neither flout convention nor "fall in love with that what she feared to look on" [32] and run away from her father to a "sooty bosom." From the outset, the marriage meets with the strong disapproval of a father betrayed. The fact that Othello is famous, a general and a noble who has done a great service to the Venetian state, and that the couple are in love seems not to matter. The objection stands that Othello is a Moor; he is black. He is alien. And Desdemona in marrying him acted "against all the rules of nature." She debased her father and created a scandal.[33] The tragedy opens and closes on humbled pride.

Othello's prowess carries the man. He disclaims other assets. His great exploits have fascinated Desdemona. She scorns fortune for love. And it is for this that she marries Othello. We are warned at the outset by the father's words—"look to her Moor, have a quick eye to see: she has deceiv'd her father, may do thee"[34]—that being esteemed can be a precarious rank.

With so much of Othello's reputation owed to achievements rather than to his qualities, and the least of it to his person, being a Moor in Venice regardless of his distinction as a general, leaves self-regard in peril. Othello is therefore especially prone to what others think of him. Furthermore, he is thus particularly and sensitively dependent upon his own severe self-judgment. Iago's villainy is certain to succeed when this vulnerable quality in his general's character is strained. The fatal flaw is thus in Othello's highly vulnerable self-esteem.

We have confirmation of Othello's flaw in the readiness with which he doubts his worth and that his worst suspicions convert to convictions. Othello's narcissism, excited by a "jealousy so strong, that judgment cannot cure,"[35] brings him to acknowledge that out of his smallest fears come his greatest doubts. They weaken him. But for the moment he takes some assurance in Desdemona's having wanted him. "For she had eyes and chose me."[36] His narcissism briefly secured gives him comfort. But Iago's plot nevertheless succeeds as he exploits the flaw in Othello's character. He recalls for Othello his father-in-law's ominous warning that by marrying him Desdemona had deceived her father and that she might in turn betray Othello. Incited thus by Iago, Othello's fears of humiliation magnify. They bring him to charge Iago with the collection of evidence against Desdemona. ". . . if more thou dost perceive, let me know more."[37] As he demands more proof of betrayal, Othello's course on his tragic end is set. The prestige his prowess carried is abandoned; Othello becomes engaged solely in suffering deceit. And with that his self-esteem ebbs. He turns to his blackness as indicative of his lack of grace. He confesses it as his inferiority. He has suffered abuse and "my relief must be to loathe her."[38] Now even his proven accomplishments no longer have value. His being a general had once assured him of his worth; however, being deceived cost him its value.

Suffering deceit and scorning oneself are monstrous agonies. Othello's character cannot tolerate such humiliation. His violence emerges. It protects his afflicted self-esteem. Othello welcomes Desdemona's end. Nowhere in the play is he more coherent or cool. Killing her is doing justice. But Othello is no mere instrument of moral rectitude. "For nought did I in hate, but all in honor." [39] To recover from his humiliation he must destroy Desdemona. It is not through murder but by redressing a wrong that justice is done. And with it his self-esteem is restored. That he discovers he must in the end blame himself brings the tragedy to its conclusion. Othello turns his fury, as the final humiliation, on his own life.

Othello and Achilles, like Medea, suffer deep injury to their self-esteem and become violent. And, in each, self-destruction also emerges. When honor is ravaged, recovery demands redress. In the name of so high a purpose as honor, self-esteem or respect, aggression is merited. Whoever has offended must be destroyed. First, however, the betrayer must be demeaned. Only then can the final debt be cleared. Hector, Desdemona and Jason are each devalued and then killed that honor may be restored. None escapes.

Each hero appears to hold an essential discordant element in the fabric of his heroism; each appears to defy self-preservation. For the sake of his narcissism he may be prepared to die. Narcissism is powerfully defended. Yet, paradoxically, it is also sacrificed. In order to reclaim her self-respect Medea must destroy Jason, and in so doing she ruins her own life. Achilles must redeem himself because through his self-indulgence, nursing his wounded narcissism, Patroclus is killed. He kills Hector knowing his own death will consequently follow. Tom Sawyer is ill-used and heroically must go off to restore himself. Those who made him suffer now are grieved. Like the others, Tom is a victim first. And in his resurrection, which reinstates honor, worth or self-esteem, violence as an instrument appears to be justified. One's narcissism may be recovered from injury, but in the process death, ruin and suicide may occur, even if only in fantasy, as in the case of Tom Sawyer.

It seems that even the most unclouded justification to preserve narcissism from threats, or to restore it from injuries, risks turning the same force on ourselves.

Studies of motivation on the turn of hostility toward oneself do not extend significantly beyond Freud's discoveries a half-century ago. The most authoritative review today of psychoanalytic concepts of aggression states, "The bulk of what we can identify as self-directed aggression in mental life seems to be related to the superego." [40] And further on aggression: "In general, discharge is associated with pleasure; lack of discharge with unpleasure." [41] These current views are still a page from Freud. Are we only deterred from pleasure in aggression and from our destructive purposes by prohibitions? Were all the earlier examples given here simply instances in which the superego dictated that one should destroy oneself rather than someone else? Aggression, rather than being discharged, or somehow held in a sort of reservoir, is a *reaction*. It issued from a deep injury to self-esteem. Some deterrent acted, however, to turn the violence away from its mark. Once violence was justified with regard to self-esteem, i.e. reconciled with narcissism, aggression was unleashed, often without bounds. The full brunt of violence was vented on Hector, Jason, Desdemona and even Tom Sawyer's family, once the justification for making them miserable was set. The little girls, Peggy and Katie, it will be recalled here, were as relentless in their attacks on discredited infants as they were on themselves for their repressed infantile wishes. And the scientist was without compassion, nor would he be deterred from attacking himself, so long as he judged he lacked value. *What we render worthless we may attack freely. We grant no exception and suffer self-attacks when we rate ourselves paltry.*

To make the self secure, and to keep it as a preserve for personal use, consists of more than remaining viable and serving one's germ plasm, i.e. appetite is more than simple hunger, and sexuality is not simply copulation. Commencing at birth, the aim to fulfill oneself and to master the environment in the course of it requires aggression, and it plays no less a part with respect to unconscious conflicts in relation to others. In effect, aggression represents a widely varied and diversified spectrum of activities throughout our existence, always carrying a mandate to serve the self.

That portion of the personality which enforces elaborate emotional defenses, exercises voluntary thought, and discharges emotional tensions through behavior is defined collectively by the conventional psychoanalytic view as "ego functions." These activities are regarded as a series of complex interactions which have been formed into a theory of systems of mental mechanisms. Such models of our emotional life, however, omit the consideration of aggression as an engine of change. Aggression in human experience plays a dynamic part in altering conditions and resolving tensions profoundly affecting the self. Moreover, its ubiquitous presence in our emotional development and experience compels us to assess it in all considerations of emotional functions and their disorders.

Freud's discovery that aggression turned against oneself held the key to understanding the enigma of depression carried implications he did not develop. He wrote, "We have long known, it is true, that no neurotic harbours thoughts of suicide which he has not turned back on himself from murderous impulses against others. . . . the analysis of melancholia now shows that the ego can kill itself . . . if it is able to direct against itself the hostility" of its reaction to others.[42]

I shall show that turning murderous impulses away from others to ourselves is not confined to those emotional disorders in which such conduct reaches pathological levels. It would be reducing literary works to clinical pathology to take the trials of such characters as Achilles, Othello, Medea or Tom Sawyer as illustrative simply of neurotic behavior rather than as profoundly revealing of some of the passionate conflicts of daily life. Moreover, the timeless quality of the human struggles portrayed is borne out by the fact that one need have no direct encounter with ancient Greece to appreciate the great importance to Achilles of his pride, the depth of his grief, and his conflicts. Nor is Medea's sense of outrage or her need for vengeance any further beyond our understanding than Othello's deeply hurt vanity and feeling of inferiority which demands relief. And, as we shall see, only under certain conditions can hostility be mounted against others without the consequences which bring on depression or self-destructiveness.

Freud succeeded in showing that clinical depression was more than normal despair driven to madness. He placed, however, the chief emphasis on the role of the erotic elements. Freud's conception of the dynamics involved in suicide was essentially a view of childhood ruled by sensuality: instinctual aggression bound to the inordinate demands of childhood sensuality creates pressure for relief and gratification against a severe conscience. The result of his equation was no surprise. It was that in depression a conflict rages between sadistic wishes toward someone valued which press to be satisfied and strong prohibitions which issue from conscience. The result tends to bring a reversal, taking oneself to be the object of deserved abuses and in the extreme—suicide.

Freud supposed that the dynamics of melancholia with its typically lowered self-esteem and often-serious self-destructiveness were unique to pathological depression and did not apply to states of "normal" grief. Neither he nor others extended his study to the actual analysis of grief or to the many other aspects of life which evoke depression of short duration. There is little scientific literature to be cited demonstrating that quite ordinary disappointments, losses, failures and grief may have many unconscious conflicts characteristic of clinical depression.[43]

On examination the same key to understanding depression applies to these common experiences in which self-esteem suffers. As the tendency in them is to direct aggression at oneself, the essential conditions for depression are fulfilled. The important question, therefore, is what determines whether the depression will be severe or transient, dangerous or not, lasting or fleeting.

The course of depression in daily life, as in clinical disorder, is governed principally by the direction aggression takes. With the fall in self-esteem, without which depression does not occur, hostility begins. Whether it is directed at oneself or is aimed at others is mediated by the superego. When justification is found for hostility, the license for aggression toward others issues as legitimate. On the other hand, without such a grant of permission, aggression may still arise, but then it is directed inward and the self suffers.

Rage at frustration or deprivation, or at pain, hunger and fear, without involving conscience, occurs only in early infancy. What is remarkable is how rapidly in human development the governing self-critical agency begins to operate. For only about two years in our existence is aggression not under the surveillance of the superego. In the young child, for some time, it is not his own conscience which acts as a governing agency over his hostility but that of those who care for him. And in his "borrowing" of that conscience he promotes the development of his own. Aggression in human affairs is thus neither left to chance nor free of surveillance.

The important point is that aggression is not mobilized principally for defense against an opposing world. When it is not urgently called on for defense against feared or actual narcissistic injuries, it is allowed to be freely engaged in a variety of functions such as mastery, skill, invention and creativity. But those aggressive activities which arouse guilt encourage self-attacks. *And in them self-esteem is not raised;* the depression which often occurs does not readily come to an end. Even immense achievements under such conditions may not erase the sense of worthlessness indelibly stained with an aggression a developed conscience will not condone. And underlying such a tissue of self-abnegation is an unconscious infantile narcissism resistant to sacrificing its aims. It also demands its pound of flesh in the fulfillment of egocentric wishes valued at the cost of relationships that would require its modification.

No condition of life is as simply experienced as it is formulated. To pursue gratification through aggression does not avoid the burden of self-criticism. Aggression often entails a defiance of prohibitions and taboos. The inevitable guilty reactions for such violations, while rationalized, may not be unconsciously denied. Such victories usually are Pyrrhic. For example, a small boy, Rusty (nearly three years old), whose mother is deeply devoted to him, appears unable to reconcile himself to the birth of a brother. At nearly every opportunity almost two years after the brother's arrival, he continues to tease him. He wants to see what may please the baby and then deprive him of it. To satisfy himself, he persists in such conduct despite his parents' strong disapproval and at times their punishment.

The mother's preference between the two children is toward the older one. It is neither obvious nor is it her deliberate wish to be partial. Her awareness of the older son's jealousy brought out her reassurances to him that his younger brother was no serious threat to her affection. Her efforts succeeded only in bringing out the boy's rage. He demanded to know the need for another boy. Was he not sufficiently satisfying that his parents should add a further child to the family? Until his brother's birth, he had been a relatively placid child who rarely gave way to temper. Since the new arrival, he began to have tantrums. Also, the tormenting of his brother extended to the family pets and he often spoke of his fear they would die.

Before long he became unshakably preoccupied with fears of being separated from his parents. He clung to them with alarm regardless of their reassurances, and they became anxious about him. Their concern was brought to a head by his refusal to go to sleep. He used tedious and repeated pretexts to remain near his parents. Their suggestion that he play outside near the house often brought a flat refusal that led to his not going outdoors for days. The affirmation from his parents that he was safe was ineffective. When he was forced to go out, he held his father's hand or his mother's skirt with a tenacity that revealed his fear of separation. His sleep was frequently interrupted by nightmares. He later developed a fear of the dark spaces under his bed. He imagined monsters would emerge from there and attack him. Only a light in his room during the night dispelled them.

This boy had become a miserable child. He lived in dread of attacks, certain that he would be lost or forever separated from his family. No assurances relieved him. He wished for his brother's death, that the brother be sent away to where he came from. It turned out, however, in virtually each detail, that he feared the same fate. His fearful convictions were as strong as his wishes. His parents' efforts to give him the security he lacked could not touch his destructive wishes toward his brother, which he then unconsciously deflected to himself. In the course of treatment, he finally abandoned his satisfying destructive intentions because they also made him anxious; he could see that his wishes for his brother became his own fears. His fears commenced to subside and the shadows in the corners became empty of monsters.

With the brother's birth, the beginnings of normally intense jealousy appear. The child's question as to the need for another plainly shows that he sees the infant as compromising his unique and favored place in his parents' affection. Narcissism is hurt and self-esteem is lowered. The attacks launched against the brother as a devalued, unwelcome arrival were aimed at destroying him. And the parents' efforts to persuade their older son to grant a place to the younger one demanded in effect that his egocentric wishes must yield. He could no longer enjoy his narcissistic exclusiveness. As this was made increasingly evident, the boy's loss of self-esteem continued and brought on an intensification of his rages. Their emergence as destructive behavior toward the baby coincided with his own tantrums. They marked a new turn in development, in that tantrums are rages to which self-destructive elements are added. The older boy became a victim, not only of jealousy, but, as his self-esteem did not rise, of the consequent attacks on himself. To this misery was added the eruption of fears of being abandoned, the dread of being separated, the dreaded attacks by monsters he had begun nightly to anticipate. All indications were that the fate he wished for his brother had become his.

Recovery came when the infantile narcissistic demands failed and thus finally forced the employment of aggression for achievements. Achievements serve as narcissistic rewards; they raise self-esteem and represent a turn from aggression aimed at destruction of the offender to a force for acquiring skills and mastery. The shift is not in narcissism, as is generally supposed, but in the aim of aggression. As we have seen in other instances, justification is needed for the pursuit of aggression, and in this little boy, with help, his justification found an ample basis in the turn to constructive activity. With it self-esteem can thus be raised and the recovery from the injured narcissism is gained. The persistence of such aggressive conduct, without the turn this child made, results in continued narcissistic impairment from which an entire series of disorders develops.

Another example of injured narcissism in daily life, parallel to childhood, comes from old age. An elderly lady throughout her life had had ample means. She had lavished them freely on her large family and many friends. When they angered her, she soon offered gifts to make up differences or mend rifts. She was deeply attached to her family and to her many collateral relations and friends. What ambivalence she experienced consciously was difficult for her to admit. Yet, as she witnessed in others the greed in taking her countless presents (I had never heard, in the years I knew her, anyone refuse to accept what she offered), she denied the hostility aroused in her. But her reactions were betrayed in the attacks of anxiety she suffered at such times. She had heightened fears that she had inadvertently provoked the fury of others. These were the projections of her privately held anger of which she was not aware. Her fury was further masked by her many acts of real kindness. Not being thanked adequately for her generosity was a long-standing grievance with her. It was not that others failed to show gratitude, but that she could not be satisfied because her discontent was fed by her hostility; this was the unconscious source of her doubts about her value that no amount of reassurance would relieve.

Now, late in life, deprived of much of her income, with many of her friends and relatives either dead or dying, and her children engaged with their own lives, she could not diminish her anger except for short intervals. And she could no longer buy it off, i.e. placate in others the hostility which she had attributed to them, as she had done for many years past. With her real losses, and without her previously functioning defenses against her hostility, she became increasingly both aggressive and anxious. Moreover, her failing memory and minor infirmities became a source of hypochondriacal complaints. She well knew her limitations would only increase. And each new development of them represented expanding narcissistic injuries. The knowledge that she was quickly becoming socially isolated further added to her anxiety and aggressiveness. She felt unable to control either. And, as she had before, only now with greater intensity, she turned her anger on herself. Her recovery from depression was modest, precariously held, and was gained with some understanding of the jeopardy her narcissism placed her in. Her improvement also depended on her family's active efforts not to neglect to express their interest in her.

This woman's conflicts are commonplace. As I have shown else-where, old age is a period of real psychological impoverishment, paralleled by physical depletion and a corresponding rise in narcis-cism. There is no lessening of it as is often supposed. The proneness of narcissism in old age to be hurt is all the greater.[44]

Losses and discontents in a wide variety of experience through-out life begin in childhood. We tend to forget how painful some of them were in that period. The vicissitudes of childhood need to be considered in the light of the narcissism of that period. An infant or young child who mourns the loss of his mother, or who suffers from a separation, has been understood by an entire psychology of "sepa-ration." [45] The focus on these often critical or traumatic experiences shows a rising tendency among analysts and others to overlook the quality of a child's everyday life. His precarious self-esteem is sub-jected both in fact and in fantasy to experiences which compel the tempering of his defenses. We will not understand a child's behavior without scrutinizing the route his egocentric concern follows as well as the features of the adaptation his narcissism obliges him to take on.

The child's helplessness and dependence, like his ignorance and inexperience, do not fail to impress him. To an extraordinary degree, however, they are mitigated by his narcissism which embodies his great expectations and the fulfillment they promise. The discrepancies between his wishes and his rewards, a perpetual source of discontent, are an engine of change. His value of himself and his sense of being valued help him to pursue his egocentric aims, in the course of which his achievements develop. However, a child quickly learns that he alone cannot fulfill himself. And, the extent to which he understands this dictates how much his narcissism must give way. Others must be brought into the orbit of his narcissism. The im-portant point here is that the development of a child's narcissism is profoundly influenced by the nature of these earliest associations.[46]

The child's first experience in a relationship naturally is one in which his physical needs are met. To be cared for means to be valued, rapidly and permanently becomes an emotional dogma. What narcissism a child may give up with the discovery that he is neither omnipotent nor in command of magic is compensated for by the conviction that he is valued. And with that his self-esteem is but-tressed against erosion. When a child's sense of his own worth is supported by the value placed on him by someone else (his mother, for instance), a loving relationship is founded. It becomes, *quid pro quo,* a model for all subsequent intimacies. Only when we love ourselves less can we love another. This is a process and not a quantity.

The solitary effort to sustain narcissism or to develop self-esteem is difficult. It is also dangerous. It tends to develop a variety of serious aberrations of egocentricity often of psychotic proportions. Extraordinary circumstances may either accelerate the process,[47] or give the appearance of it in precocity, or bring about a regression to a more infantile level of narcissism.[48] We have seen earlier how a child's narcissism may remain fixed. Recent studies of infants furnish dramatic examples of how early in life circumstances deeply affect narcissistic development. It was found that infants, although provided with excellent physical care in institutions, were, however, deprived of individual attention and affection. They were seriously retarded.[49] Limited to their own resources, young children fail. That is, confined to themselves, their egocentricity is exaggerated in just the opposite fashion from the precocious child.

In the child, growing awareness that neither fantasies of omnipotence nor the intensity of wishes nor the power of thought are adequate to his wants forces some realization that others are indispensable to him. It is not that the child thus simply commences to learn the reality principle—which indeed occurs—but rather that this lesson is indivisible from another one. This is that he accords a value to whomever he needs to do for him what he cannot do for himself. At first, this is not sharply defined. Within a short time, however, the development of the delineation occurs.

The beginning transfer of value from oneself to another brings the earliest phase of narcissism to a conclusion. This occurrence involves no dramatic moment or circumstance. Rather, it is a process through which the child acquires his attachment to his mother. We begin to recognize this period by the end of the first year. Theoretically, some of the narcissism a child holds entirely to himself he is obliged to transfer to his mother. The clue to the process is in his intense engagement with her to give him what alone he cannot provide. Hence, she comes to hold some of his narcissism as though it was in escrow beyond the control of the grantor. Since she has her own narcissistic needs which he as her child is called on to satisfy, narcissism bonds each to the other.

The quality of the ordinary happenings of a child's life, rather than of the moments of crisis or trauma, defines the essentials of existence. Much of self-preservation for a young child is in the hands of another. The jeopardy he may anytime encounter and from which he is extricated by another is his everyday experience, in which the relief from threats or the reassurance that another may be trusted quickly come to have far-reaching importance. They convey some of the sense of his value to another and thus to himself. With the earliest phase of narcissism ended, these carriers of one's worth make the child's next period of narcissism dependent on a relationship. Physical care alone, even when it is very good, does not meet this issue. In the extreme, autistic children who often have received indulgent physical care, further confirm that the experience of one's value and self-esteem only appears in the course of a relationship. Without an endorsement of worth a child's self-esteem amounts to little.

The following event was not pathologically traumatic, yet it reveals a young child's fears of dying, his questions of his own worth, his efforts to master his fears, and how he won an important round in the struggle for self-esteem.

A much-beloved first child, Willie, not quite three years old, came running to his father one day with the announcement that he was about to catch a bird or perhaps a squirrel and get its bones—that is, kill it. His thoughts centered on what happens when familiar creatures are attacked or destroyed. Such queries from a child this age are invariably autobiographical. He wants to know whether he is in danger, if he is liable to some attack or even to be killed. He has learned from sitting at the table and eating, from comments he has overheard and observations he has made, that living things are killed. And he wonders what his own chances are. The father, knowing something of his child's possible motives, said that he had no intention of joining his son in pursuit of or in inflicting injury on anything or anyone. He aimed to tell his son not to be afraid of what his father might do, or that his father would act on his son's wishes. In the end, the boy said, "I'm going anyway!" and ran off to play.

The following morning when, without warning, Willie declared to his mother, "I don't want to die!" he showed that his thoughts of the previous day were still with him. Rather than being the hunter, he was now the quarry. His mother was startled. He had never before indicated even an awareness of death, and that he should have an anxious concern over it astonished her. She reassured her son saying, "You won't die for a long, long time." He began to whimper, "I don't want to die. Hold me! Hold me, Mommy!" She sat down with him and he, still sobbing, began to recite the names of members of the family, adding vehemently in each case that he did not wish them dead. All the while, his mother tried to comfort him by repeating that he would not die for a long time and adding that he would always be cared for. He seemed unconvinced. Throughout the day he became increasingly active. There are two main courses open to a child in such revelations of truth as this: one is to retreat into a state of helplessness and demand more care, i.e. to "regress," and the second is to attempt to master his new-found fears and thus gain some independence. From the game the boy had invented by noon the same day, we know it was an unwitting play aimed at mastering his fears.

The child pretended he was a bird flying. He would strike the wall or some object quite deliberately and shout he was broken. He lay on the floor motionless. After an interval, he jumped up and flew about again and repeated the same sequence. The intensity of his play increased until his mother distracted him by taking him with her on errands. That evening he played a similar charade. The mother reported to the father that the boy during the entire day had from time to time thrown himself to the floor or over a couch shouting he was dead. He would lie immobile for a few moments then run and go through the same play again and again. His behavior finally upset his mother as she saw how obsessed with death her child was. She made a point of asking the father to help distract the child from his game where she had not succeeded. The father was no more than momentarily able to engage the child in another bit of play.

The day following, while at work, the father telephoned home. The boy answered and while chattering on he added that he did not wish to die. For the remainder of the day, he whined to his mother that he wished to see his father, wished him to remain at home and referred to fears his father might die or that his mother would. When the father arrived home, the child firmly demanded that he not leave the house again. To both parents the child addressed his questions on what it is to be dead. The mother's explanation was matter of fact, that it was when the heart stopped. It set the child off on a renewed round of play. He would suddenly drop to the floor motionless for a few moments and declare he was dead; or he threw himself in awkward postures over a chair, lay still, and said his heart had stopped. He began asking more questions as to what else would make him die or stop his heart. He seemed tireless. Songs or ditties on either radio or television that made reference to dying, death or mourning brought out his strong objection.

After about a week, our little boy's playing at momentarily being dead came to an abrupt end. He came in from outdoors with a rock in his hand and announced to his mother he "deaded" a bug. He brought it to show her. She turned away saying, "No, I don't want to see it!" The child was delighted—with what he had done and with her reaction. He was in good spirits, he no longer played dead, and waited impatiently for his father's arrival from work to tell him, "I did a good job!" The child had become the aggressor. Rather than the victim, the little boy was the assailant. His self-esteem rose.

What trifling circumstance may have set off this three-year-old's struggles with fate is not directly recoverable from so young a child. Its significance, however, is not lost. Neither a momentous happening nor a serious trauma was required to call out the sequence of events we have just described. Long in advance of superego formation or the development of masochism, but when he is fully capable of identification, a child wishing to kill a creature reflects a concern for himself, and an attempt to solve that conflict.

He is not motivated out of retaliation, an issue of conscience, or a reaction to being thwarted, although all these conflicts are no doubt present. Nor is he simply discharging some accumulation of so-called instinctual aggression which self-criticism will govern. The boy wants to know what protection he may count on. Beginning very early in life, it is an assessment he endlessly makes, as he perceives with developing clarity how precarious existence may be.[50] No child fails to consider his chances when daily life, even under the most peaceful and protected conditions, requires the sacrifice of living material. A child's natural tendency to project himself into another creature's place and to refer another's fate to himself is inescapable. What is remarkable is how early in life this process commences. It is common among children this age to refuse to eat meat, or to chew it, but within a short time, as a rule, they identify themselves sufficiently with the aggressor to quit their role of victim to become predator. The entire process is not a conscious one, yet it nevertheless is present in some measure in us all, and we soon adopt the part which carries us with the least conflict and gives us the justification we require. It is small wonder, as we shall see in the last chapter, that violence and destruction toward others require that the identification with the victims of our aggression be dispelled. Designated as foreign, alien and strange to us, the first mark of hostility, our enemies must be lacking in our humanity and thus be without the values we support; our objects of aggression must carry no resemblance to us. Thus, devalued, we have an unbounded license toward them.

While the boy's father assured his son that he himself would not engage in destruction or wanton killing, he unknowingly failed to answer all the questions asked of him. Although it was important for the boy to be secure in the knowledge his father was no menace, the child had still another concern. He knew that other creatures were killed or died. He feared his own fate, and how could he be assured his parents would see that he was spared? He also knew that what was valued was protected. His own worth was his real question.

The next episode is the dramatic one in which Willie returns from his adventure to a sudden, sharper awareness of the fear of his own death. Directly associated with this, he denies all hostility, repudiates aggression toward anyone; vociferously he wishes each member of his family and, by implication, himself, to be spared from death. His wish is that by disavowal of aggression fears will be dispelled. The boy, however, does not rest his case only with a reliance on such magical influence. He then plays a charade in which he pretends he is the object of destruction. He plays at dropping dead, yet he cannot tolerate to be reminded of death. In the final sequence he is no longer a victim. Instead, he mounts an attack and kills an insect. In this role he asserts himself. It gives him relief. As his confidence is restored, self-assurance grows.

Contrary to most suppositions, a child is not necessarily convinced of his vulnerability, or persuaded of the precariousness of his existence by some *particular* experiences which may cast doubt on his sense of omnipotence. Nor is it simply through frustration that he learns his wishes lack power. In this instance we have seen that a little boy, by way of his natural penchant for self-reference, directly applies to himself the ordinary dangers or hazards to life that he perceives. He thus forges the sense of his own jeopardy. Without this inclination, we might suppose a child would be either a mere witness or a hapless victim of the swirl of events he encounters. And, like all other creatures, he would respond only to the immediate circumstances which engage him. Since, however, by means of our consciousness we humans refer what happens to others to ourselves and then respond vicariously but intensely to such experiences, we are given an immensely wide spectrum for self-reference.

Insofar as we tend to remember experiences, some of which have their sources only in our fantasies, we regard them as belonging to our inner environment. In small children it is not known with any certainty when the distinction comes to be made between dreams as belonging to inner life as from the outer one. In any case, our reality is made up of both components. Willie repeatedly played out his death and return to life as though the representation of the conflict would magically dispel it. In his efforts he carried the exercise to a point of extravagance. No longer earthbound, he flew, pretended he quickly mended grave injuries, and even rose from the dead. Moreover, in the rehabilitation, he became grandiose. Undoing what he pretended had happened he ruled as circumstance. With the unconscious employment of the powers of magical thought, wishes and omnipotence, the significance of the child's conduct goes beyond a mere aim at mastery over the environment; he also would thus influence fate. To the extent a child is persuaded that he succeeds, his narcissism appears to have won. However, Willie still despairs at dying. His parents' reassurances offer too little consolation for what he dreads. His fears persist. And his aggression associated with it is progressively heightened as he repeatedly plays vignettes of his desire to live and to overcome death. Simply to be assertive, to master his fears of death through play, by coming alive from the dead, gives the child small comfort or relief. His play with its underlying grim purpose goes on for days. Finally, only with an additional change is escape possible, and the tyranny of his fears for a time ended. When the boy himself became the one who "deaded" the bug, he found relief.

To view this play as simply a little boy's version of early Oedipal conflicts, the turning of his unconscious intentions, his death wishes, away from his rivals toward himself has some validity. But this boy is barely three years old, rather young to have that phase and intensity of infantile sexuality we have come to know and expect as appropriate to a child twice his age. To suppose he turned the aggression on himself, or that he unconsciously was offering himself in some passive fashion to his father, whom he feared may wish to castrate him as he anxiously inquired into the fate of those who are attacked, expresses the sexual conflicts we attribute usually to an even later period, the passing of the Oedipus phase.

Psychoanalytic concepts of the unconscious conflicts in a child of about three years characteristically focus on the phases of psychosexual development. Consideration of the meaning to the child of his common needs and the conflicts over his being aggressive, which he ordinarily acts on, and their significance with respect to his relationships tend to be omitted when reconstructed from the psychology of the adult. The best-known analytic explanation of a child's unconsciously motivated aggressive behavior is Anna Freud's, which appeared in her further development of her father's study.[51] She showed that a child's fears of being hurt produced a particular defensive emotional reaction. The child will identify himself with the aggressor: "By impersonating the aggressor, assuming his attributes or imitating his aggression, the child transforms himself from the person threatened into the one who makes the threat." [52] "In 'identification with the aggressor' we recognize a by no means uncommon stage in normal development of the superego." [53]

Freud's discovery of the identification with the aggressor is indeed, as we have seen here, a powerful defense against being a victim. But it is not confined to mastering fears of anxiety or attacks. Its far-reaching importance is in the role of recovery and surmounting threats and injuries to narcissism. Without doubt, the boy's fears will be revived on countless occasions throughout his life. The same process of self-reference will be aroused and circumstance will repeatedly give support to the jeopardy he is bound to suffer. And in principle he will resort in the future to identification with the aggressor, albeit in more sophisticated forms than he did as a child.

To quell his fears and reduce anxiety, identifying with an aggressor leads the child to find a way out of anguish. He is then no longer identified as the victim of destruction. Employing what mastery he has acquired, the same self-reference which brings him in his belief to the brink of death is also his deliverance. Self-reference may also turn toward an advantage. The oppressive necessity for relief from his dread of what may happen, the obsessive concern with the future, may bring the child's triumph. Aggression may be made an engine of change. As identification with the aggressor is unconsciously formed, fears are fended off and uncertainties of everyday life may thus be mitigated. The significant effect is to enhance self-esteem. Aggression thus comes to function in us as no simple reaction to being thwarted, but as a demonstration of the force we may release essential to our own support. The process of identification with the aggressor is, therefore, not limited to child's play nor, as is generally supposed, to a child's mental mechanism against experiences of hostility. The gain in identification with the aggressor serves, in the course of becoming aggressive oneself, to enhance self-esteem. Aggression thus commences in early childhood to assume a major role essential to the protection of narcissism. In fact, in its relation to narcissism, aggression gets its clearest definition of function. In the formation of emotional defenses, in achieving skills and mastery, in adaptation to the environment, aggression performs a role in all aspects of daily life. Employed in the permanent service of restitution of our narcissism, which the conditions of everyday life tend to erode, aggression becomes its indispensable arm. When it fails, narcissism suffers.

As an example, Willie's father, my patient, brought upon himself the same conflicts his three-year-old son had begun to master, along a neurotic course and hence to no resolution. The father's fears of death were not an engagement with the problems of dying but with the recognition that one dies without relevance, i.e. without worth. To him, the loss of life meant to forego what he held priceless. The effect in him may be read in his defying death, in his exercise of magic, and the search for secrets to cheat death. In short, his life of aggressive pursuits unconsciously was aimed at the pleasure he gained in challenging and eluding fate. In each successful encounter his narcissism was promoted, giving him the illusion of extending existence so long as he turned the bold face of the aggressor toward death. This is what the father was unwittingly engaged in; so long as he thwarted death, he prolonged life!

It was during the period of his son's active struggles with fears of dying that he himself discovered that after work he wanted only to watch comedy on television, to be entertained, and distracted from the thoughts he was certain he would become preoccupied with. An adventure program he had previously enjoyed, in which the character had but forty-eight hours remaining to live, became so distressing to him that he turned it off. "Somehow, I couldn't stand it. If I thought I was to be killed, I'd get so scared. It's that there is no afterlife that makes death so frightening. I wish I believed in heaven the way I once did. Now, I get upset. I feel frightened. There is no denying it. When my son talks about death, he gets me too in a sort of panic over it. I just had to get up and walk away from him. It's curious. I can't even say the word 'death' and not get some reaction. When you don't deny death, you can't act in dangerous ways. I've got to be cautious. It's essential for myself as a pilot. I sometimes get compelled to act dangerous. Like I am always testing and have not accepted inevitable death. I really know how inevitable it is. But when I do what's dangerous, I save my life! I prove I won't die!

"As a child of about seven or so, I could read well by then. I heard about the Fountain of Youth that Ponce de Leon was after. And I remember how interested in that I was. I was worried about dying. And my later interest was in the same thing, but in trying to find out the secrets of the past that might prolong life. Thoughts about extinction always hurt and saddened me. The dinosaurs saddened me when I learned about them as a child. There was nothing they could do but die. I hoped there was a valley somewhere of dinosaurs where you find out it's a place where you may not die after all. I suddenly had the thought I had better lose weight. I am too heavy.

"One day when my boy was getting wild throwing himself around playing dead, I got very bothered. I went out driving later that day and had him on my mind. I felt I had to drive wild. I opened my car all the way for a short stretch of road. I went as fast as I could. I remember thinking. Here I am! Come and get me, if you can! I really felt wild and aggressive and like doing a lot of destruction. I would do nothing to avoid death. I thought, I don't have to be careful. I have no fear of dying! I defy caution! I really drove at very high speed. I was reckless!

"What I would like to hear too is precisely what my son wants to know: that death can't get me. I want to hear I won't die. As a little kid, I thought my father was big and strong and old. He didn't die. I'll be like him and then I won't die. I wasn't going to be like my mother. She was always afraid of dying. I knew it even as a little kid. She refused to talk about it. You couldn't mention it around her. She was so afraid of what would happen if you did. My father wasn't like that. He liked going hunting. I liked it too. Maybe, I got my interest in guns that way."

My patient's fear of death, never far removed from consciousness, needed only his son's encounters with the same conflict to fan them into intensity in himself. And, like his son, he could not resist throwing himself about recklessly in his car, becoming very aggressive and entertaining destructive fantasies. In the course of it he was exhilarated. His reactions, like his mother's, who could not tolerate the mention of death, led him to test his mother's fears—now his own. Death is a sad loss to him. To prove his mettle he must defy it. Through aggression, like his son before him, he aims to prove death will not catch him. His excitement gets high in his rash experiments with danger. He is pleased with himself and his self-esteem gets restored. Although, with regret, he cannot believe in heaven and a life after death, he still daydreams of a secret place; as a dinosaur hunter he hopes to find a valley without the shadow of death. He also identifies himself with his father and his aggressiveness increases, and the identification with his mother recedes with repression. Self-esteem gets high. Both father and son turn to aggression to defend themselves, and the fruit of their triumph is self-approval.

Jean Briggs, the anthropologist, in her study of a small remote settlement of Eskimo families in the Arctic who lived by hunting, described the play of small children.

> Crouching in imitation of the adult hunting posture, they would stalk the clucking ptarmigan that ran ahead of them over the uneven ground and that finally stood stupidly waiting to be stoned. They chased lemming and ermine with wild torrents of giggles in and out and around their stony burrows, prodding the animals out with sticks whenever the cowering little things thought themselves under a rock; or else they took turns at being caribou, stalking, 'shooting,' and 'butchering' each other in the field behind camp. They played at being dogs . . . holding the fish on the ground with both 'paws' and tearing at it fiercely with their teeth . . . and pretended . . . to snap and snarl at each other.[54]

Eskimo children, like our own, enjoy identifying themselves with aggressive adults. In that role the children are hunters, tormentors; and if they pretend to be prey, they also are predators. As Eskimo dogs, the children play at being very fierce with each other. In these vignettes of child life in the Arctic, an Eskimo child's play is not to be distinguished from what we may at any time find in our own children. The everyday life of a young child, whether native to the Arctic, the Kalihari or Boston, similarly calls for mastery, skill and accommodation, regardless of culture. And insofar as a child's narcissism is continually challenged, it must also be constantly defended.

The fantasy from childhood of a secret valley of no death, like beliefs in the Elysian Fields, or joining our ancestors or the company of the immortals, is eloquent testimony to the strength and influence of our striving toward a narcissism which eludes the reach of impairment or injury. But as threats to self-esteem inevitably happen and as there is ultimately no escape, aggression is mobilized in its defense. For instance, Achilles' humiliation by the king, Medea's by Jason, or Othello convinced he is betrayed and Tom Sawyer unsung have in common with the three-year-old boy and his father that narcissism is assaulted. Moreover, the target is oneself. And in each instance, therefore, self-denigration appears first. Only with justification is aggression turned from oneself to be unleashed on others.

Neither the beloved child nor the favored heroes of legend, any more than a people chosen by God, are spared outrageous trials. The flaw and the virtue in all is in the peril to self-esteem. Its defense may bring the highest honors and justify the lowest violence. But its loss risks our extinction.

Chapter VIII

The Tyranny of Narcissism

The tyranny of narcissism, associated in its earliest forms with hostility and profoundly affecting emotional development, has been the emotional phenomenon least directly studied. Freud's clinical observations of adults led him to conclude that emotional development normally proceeded from childish egocentricity or narcissism to an adult maturation of relationships. The sequence in our development went from hate to love, aggression to altruism, and from a natural resistance to change to a rewarding adaptation to altering conditions. And, that yielding the narcissistic focus on oneself in order to value a relationship with another is the highest form of adaptation—love. His explanation was in the terms he knew best—those of sexual conflicts. Studies of narcissism and aggression were aspects of psychological life with which he was least familiar.

He was not inattentive, of course, to what supreme narcissists little children are. He did not, however, study them. An understanding of the nature of a child's early relationships on the basis of direct studies is only of recent origin, within the last thirty-five years. Hence, as with the studies of adults, the most familiar aspects of a child's life are the libidinal ones. There are no authoritative references to cite of studies of the development of a child's narcissism.

The failures in a child's early relationships—the most serious emotional disorders they experience—have been variously designated as "autistic," "psychotic" or "atypical." Which aspect of a child's psychological functions is impaired determines the designation given. If the child's adaptive development is bizarre, referring to the erratic course of social adaptation in which there is a strange admixture of achievement and the simplest failures, he will be termed "atypical." [1] "Autistic" is a term which refers to the manifest signs of the child's intense self-absorption to the exclusion of others. [2] And "psychotic," the most loosely conceived aspect, chiefly aims at describing such a child's growing impairment of his reality sense. These children display, in varying degrees, a wide assortment of signs and symptoms. In none of the many studies of this subject, however, has serious consideration been paid to the role of hostility or aggression. Where these elements have been remarked upon, they are regarded as reactions to frustration or deprivation. And although in some instances this may appear to be the case, attention generally is drawn to the results of the libidinal disorder or of the indications of the faulty ego development.

Autism,* without parallel as a grave psychological disorder, fortunately is not common. Its importance as a phenomenon derives from the fact that these children irrevocably repudiate, forego or fail to develop the relationships upon which a child usually depends. A study of autism provides us with bold, unmistakable lines with which to illustrate the central role narcissism commands. Except for the inadequate descriptions of the rare instances of feral children, who very likely are a special example of autism, we have few opportunities to study the developing human condition in which necessary relationships are so tenuously maintained. There are no other conditions in either life or laboratory which parallel such a pervasive concern with the self, in which a compromise or concession to another person is excluded. There is no clearer instance of a primitive or rudimentary narcissism than in childhood autism.

The seeming indifference of an autistic child of two years (in some rarer instances a younger child) toward his care and the one who administers it is used by many authors to support the assumption that the young infant somehow recognizes or attributes certain characteristics to his mother.** The child is alleged to be hostile, or to display indifference born of hostility, and on this basis he may turn away from his mother to become absorbed so deeply in autism that he later cannot be persuaded to relinquish it. However, it remains mere conjecture in which period of development the disorder of autism may be

---

* I shall use this term in its least cumbersome sense. Simply—autism is the exclusion of interest in external reality.

** No emotional disorder, when the speculation of possible constitutional and genetic factors are set aside, has been more completely attributed to a mother's personality than autism. It is an understandable assumption. An emotional disturbance, which as a rule begins in early life when the child's relation to his mother is closest, naturally will implicate her. Another added consideration is a mother's normal tendency to heap blame on herself for what happens to her child. This willingness on her part has probably led many to accept her claims of culpability without more than a cursory study of her motives.

said to commence. Since normally, in his growing awareness of his dependence, a child turns to his mother, to that extent, at least, he moves away from his natural self-absorption. The beginning of his social experience thus represents not an interest in her so much as an extension of self-interest which includes her.

Autism is thought by some to indicate a reaction to the child's natural but sometimes futile search for gratification other than mere physical care. And, as a result of such deprivation, he directs his attention to himself rather than toward others. In the early descriptions of autism,[3] a special point was made that autistic children were known to have received good physical care. But the early and erroneous assumption was that the autistic child was the issue of upper-middle-class intellectual or professional parents who, while providing generously for the child's care, did so at the expense of a loving relationship. Such a possibly empty experience for the child led Bruno Bettelheim and others to the belief that the autistic child mirrored his bizarre emotional experience, i.e. the actual impoverishment he encountered. Many suppose that the child's discovery that his demands are ineffective "discourages him from interacting with others and hence from forming a personality through which to deal with the environment." [4] Infantile autism ". . . stems from the original conviction that there is nothing at all one can do about a world that offers some satisfactions, though not those one desires, and only in frustrating ways." [5] "Because of their immaturity and basic vulnerability their chances for taking action in their own behalf are severely limited and their motivations grossly inarticulate, obscure." [6] Bettelheim, observing that the autistic child appears to be "terrified by relations because they all seem destructive to him," [7] suggests that the child perceives hostility in the important relationships about him. That he may project his own angry wishes to others is not considered by writers on the subject. Nor is there taken into account that the unrewarding existence of bleak and shallow relationships affects character formation in a particular fashion. Autism gives us a window into some of the deeper recesses of absorption in the self.

Margaret Mahler, who has attempted direct studies of young autistic children and infants, has the most extensive experience with them. She says that conclusions about observations of infants' behavior based upon hypotheses that are deduced from observational data of later phases of childhood become precarious positions to maintain.[8] Despite her warnings, which she herself tends to dismiss, the most widely held theories on autism and psychosis in infants rest principally on extrapolations drawn from data that Mahler herself would consider insubstantial. It has been proposed that autism is due to some sort of "structural limitations" or perhaps a "cultural deprivation," possibly an "organic dysfunction" or finally "some combination thereof." [9] Such guesses, in all directions, conclude by begging the question.

The autistic child belies his apparent indifference and contradicts his evident isolation by the fact that he displays his utter dependence on those near to him. His egocentricity is a tyranny to others, defining his relationships with them. As a rule, he neither responds to teaching nor to entreaties to assume what seem the simplest responsibilities for himself. He takes them on only after great resistance and within narrow limits. In that state, others necessarily are pressed into service. It is a quality of relationships which he ordinarily does not relinquish.

Studies of the autistic child's intelligence show it is erratically employed and that his learning is consistent with other aspects of his behavior. His egocentricity is served so exclusively that others are compelled to support the heavy burden of his care. His well-being, such as it is, rests with those toward whom he keeps no commitment. Since the process is not deliberately contrived, the obligation that this disorder incurs on the part of those who may take care of the child is all the greater. The excessive permissiveness which the exasperating care of an autistic child demands supports, in effect, a course in which the least modification of his narcissistic aims or demands is necessary. The result is that he becomes progressively more distant and isolated, and retains his egocentricity.

The autistic child may often master a few remarkably sophisticated functions, which prove his capabilities but do not lead him to take satisfaction in knowing that, through their performance, he fulfills a need in someone else. Normally, the child begins to enjoy parental pride in his accomplishments, as a modified extension of his own vanity. In this way the child's narcissism begins to have social importance to him. The parental wish usually becomes the normal child's achievement; the parent's and the child's narcissism is thus mutually engaged. However, the autistic child does not participate in such an enterprise. Moreover, it is likely that the signs of his failure to do so are the first indications of his serious limitations. The most common concern is in the parental lament that the child is socially unrewarding, unresponsive and indifferent to his parents. Lacking the smile of recognition, the response to reward, there is often instead the inscrutable expression which reflects no receipt of a parental gift.

A parent's vanity, exceedingly sensitive to the injury a child may inflict, suffers especially from autism. An autistic child may learn with zeal and often with a seeming desperation. For instance, he may learn the dimensions of a variety of airplanes, the sequence of street signs, the statistics from an almanac, chemical formulas, or to distinguish from the first notes played whether the concerto is by Handel or Bach. All such accomplishments superficially show precocious growth, especially when these are achievements of a child less than five years old. His performance, however, reveals that he is indifferent to needs other than his own. His knowledge, like his achievement, is exclusively for his own consumption. What he learns he does not share! And although he is frequently insistent on exhibiting it, he does so only to an audience from whom he awaits no response. The repetitions that he endlessly, frequently and tirelessly drills are carried on with a total disregard for others. The rituals, like his conduct, are almost wholly esoteric. Neither his favor nor his gratitude are won by acceding to his often adamant and bizarre wishes. Only *his* satisfaction is met. None but the autistic child is so impervious to everything but his own appetites.

We find that autistic children do not discover that the world is rewarding, despite the fact that they live an existence that brooks little interference with gratification. Paradoxically, they live by the pleasure principle yet enjoy nothing.

To the autistic child, the world lacks the stability he demands of it. The passing of the clouds, the rains that fall, the snow that piles up, the winds that blow, the very transience of the day are not the facts of everyday life to him. They are the unwelcome harbingers of change. Nothing seems reliable when circumstances cannot be turned to advantage and the element of surprise is cause for alarm. Constancy, sameness and endless repetition create a desirable monotony that to the autistic child means stability. In the simplest satisfaction, without deferment, he finds security; an unchanging predictable experience is fulfilling, and means contentment requires the least of his efforts. The serious obstacle to learning that is common to these often intelligent children is that they would solve their problems of daily life by bringing everything to a halt.

Since we know that we are ignorant, or that we have limits defined by what we do not know, learning is an emotional experience. We do not need conscious boundaries or estimates or conclusions arrived at by virtue of some penetrating insight to prepare ourselves to learn. We need not indulge the omnipotent fantasies of young children, and instead we may turn to reality in order to mitigate our inner fears of helplessness or of what is strange, alien and hence unpredictable. Learning is a cast of mind. It is an attitude that uncertainty or unknowingness may be tolerated and, what is more, it may be overcome. A child encounters humiliation in his ignorance of everyday life. He is furnished with countless occasions in which he experiences the discrepancy between what he comprehends and what he fails to understand. Whether he bridges the gap by learning is determined by the intensity of his grip on his childish narcissism. Recovery from common narcissistic bruises takes place through the gratification of learning, solving problems, and acquiring a mastery over functions and the environment. To follow instead a course from which recovery is attempted through resorting to increased exhibitionistic qualities, fantasies of grandiose powers, and wishes that support a belief in magic and omnipotence is to promote narcissism rather than learning.*

It is typical of the autistic child to take such a direction. The defenses which form are not adaptive, i.e. they do not reduce conflicts and allay anxiety, but function to maintain narcissism in its resistance to the threat that change poses or suggests. To accept change is to give up resistance to change; it assaults narcissism. The autistic child responds with a fury that dictates: no changes are permitted. And, as a further reaction, he may intensify his rituallike behavior and become even more isolated from others. For example, it is typical that an autistic child on his return to my office from a short absence of a weekend or a month—the time interval actually does not matter as a central issue—takes a quick inventory while looking about and has a tantrum. It requires some effort to discover what set off the anger. The explosion of fury may be over nothing more than a wastebasket that was not precisely in the place he last saw it. The astounding memory for such trifling details, we discover, has an important unconscious function. It unwittingly keeps an accurate record of what

---

* What often appears to be a genuine interest in music that has been observed in autistic children and thought to show some characteristic of them, I have noted on closer scrutiny, reveals the autistic child particularly enjoys the precise sequence of notes and time that music contains. His interest in music is directed unconsciously to the fact that he can reduce it to a predictable regularity of performance. In those uncommon cases in which autistic impairment is not so severe as to preclude university training, creativity nevertheless is relatively as absent as it is in younger autistic subjects. But, sometimes through remarkable feats of rote memory, diligently applied, noteworthy achievements may be realized.

is familiar. It serves as a defense against the fears that arise from what is out of place and that therefore represents change. Turning inner fears and apprehension about uncertainty and change into an intense and slavish preoccupation with keeping articles in some pre-conceived order, not to be varied, is an indication of the tenacity with which the autistic child holds to his abhorrence of change. If only all uncertainty could be reduced to a banal order, fears would leave.[10]

The autistic child's similarity to obsessional neurotics has been observed since autism was first described in 1943.[11] Both cases may have their origin in the normally observed need for some order which very young children display (at two or three years of age) as transient phenomena. Children notoriously rage, on occasion, that articles are out of their usual place, or show devotion to keeping some routine; for instance, in the telling of a familiar tale, they demand verbatim adherence to what was previously told. In the course of normal devel-opment this is a brief and passing phase. In those individuals who develop an obsessional neurosis, the typical exaggerated caution, fears of change, and adherence by preference to known wisdom seem to be the normal neurotic aspects of emotional experience carried forward from early childhood.

Beyond the limits of obsessional neuroses (carried to a heightened degree), we find the autistic child has all these characteristics. Autism in children and the severe obsessional neuroses in adults thus have in common signs of being tyrannized by their egocentricity, and dem-onstrate remarkably similar defenses formed to favor narcissism.

Those who are restricted to an autistic existence are limited to a large extent to autoeroticism. The development that sexual life nor-mally takes has no place in autism. It permits no allowance for a relationship to evolve, no person other than the self with whom to contend, no value placed on another at a cost to oneself. The autistic child thus holding fast to his egocentricity does not develop his sexual experience. This is to say that he is bound by his rudimentary needs to gratify himself. Such children exhibit masturbatorylike activities and infantile oral erotic excitement as in smearing spittle and mouth-ing articles, a self-sustaining process that neither requires nor permits intimacy. The sexual aims of the autistic child are active but they remain at a level that precludes all but self-centered needs. No plea-sure in giving satisfaction beyond oneself develops. As he grows older, the autistic child may in some instances adopt a manner, even marry, as if another person was important. But in fact there is no real change. The other person in the marriage remains merely an instrument in the autoerotic aim. Thus hobbled, no modification of narcissism in autism develops.

From these highlights of abnormal emotional development, we may observe the exaggeration of ordinary anxieties and conflicts. They show us that the autistic preference for a bizarre choice of defenses aims to resist a reality which normally compels us to an accommodation with uncertainty. The autistic child commonly is infuriated and may explode in a rage when his bladder fills and presses to be emptied, or when his bowels become distended by his refusal to relieve himself. He may become enraged that his eyes involuntarily blink and the saliva that collects compels him to swallow. He would govern all but his wishes with the strictest control.

We are perpetually required to adapt, to accommodate, and moreover to constantly renew our commitment to change and to others. If we are to meet these requirements, we must be able to modify, and even at times relinquish, our egocentric aims without a resulting pathological sense of deprivation. This complex process begins in childhood. It is opposed by the child's strongly held self-serving aims, by his adherence to what is pleasurable, and his rigid resistance to its postponement. The reward we normally earn is in mastery of reality, rather than a narcissistic and, in the extreme, autistic, repudiation of it. And, as we have observed, when narcissism fails to be modified, maturation is arrested. The result is that aggression, without the aegis of ego development, remains as the menacing arm of the narcissism which it serves.

Aggression, hostility and hate are older than love, and the development of a relationship is conspicuously impaired when our oldest reactions remain unmodified. Countless experiences in daily life impress on us that a needed, valued and intimate relationship requires that rage and hate often must give way. The cost to us is in giving up some of our exclusive aims for the sake of satisfying the needs of someone else. Immediate gratification must be modified and aggression, its commonly used instrument, governed. The failure to develop these changes gives all elements and people an aura of hostility against which we must defend ourselves.

Freud's references to autism are to its appearance in adults as a sign of their retreat into highly narcissistic, severely neurotic and psychotic states. His theories on autism, however, have an applicability to the childhood condition even though Freud had no clinical encounter with it. The autistic exclusion of others by a fixation on oneself, he thought, further heightens a child's normal autoeroticism.

It thus promotes a restriction and impairment of relationships. We have found that in most children the excessive concern with themselves is a troubled experience. This is to say that as the child's narcissism becomes extended, rather than modified, it increasingly resists change; narcissism thus intensifies and autoeroticism increases reluctance to change.

From studies of fixation in later periods of life, in which we find similar autoeroticism, we know there is a stubborn persistence of aggression from earlier periods which continues to challenge modification. It is directed at others in defense of the tenaciously held self-gratification. "People who have not freed themselves completely from the stage of narcissism—who, that is to say, have that as a point of fixation," [12] are in danger from their autoeroticism and a heightened narcissism, and meet any threat to either one with hostility.[13] The finding of satisfaction within oneself, especially in one's own body, perhaps our oldest of pleasures, has the effect of pushing back reality.

However, the need for another is in such circumstances only apparently annulled. Since one's own narcissism is not adequate to the task set for it, the need for another persists, even though the form may be difficult to recognize. Freud supposed narcissism would be self-fulfilling. But, after a temporary withdrawal into oneself, the "pseudopodia" of narcissism continue to reach out to become attached again to another. The infantile wishes for omnipotence or extravagant powers are not self-fulfilling; they, in fact, are self-defeating. Paradoxically, if a child's aspirations for himself were more modest, his narcissism might then be more intractable; as it is, however, a child's exorbitant demands are beyond ransom. And it is this very fact which makes naricissism normally yield to actuality.

Autism attempts to take the opposite course, and reality is turned away. And the autoeroticism, the sexual activity of the early narcissistic period of development, Freud identified with "self-preservation." [14] He meant that autism as clinically illustrated, in its exclusive focus on oneself, was probably the earliest and hence most primitive form of self-preservation. Since Freud's writing on this subject in 1920, we have discovered that no incentive has been found to induce the autistic child to give up his heightened egocentric aims or to reverse the course of his autoerotic activities.

Bound to narcissism to the extraordinary extent that he is, the autistic child defines a perspective of normal mental functioning that is often very difficult to demonstrate. Autism means not only to repudiate what is real, to turn away from what circumstance may demand, but it shows the renunciation of an emerging principle of mental functioning. In the growing infant, the effort to reach beyond the mere search for gratification indicates there is no longer a focus solely on what is satisfying but includes that which is even unpleasant in relation to its mother and others. Arrested in its development, self-interest, however, resists this encroachment and mobilizes aggressive reactions against the demands of concession. Since so much of the child's early care is a mother's, she is the most likely and chief focus of the hostility of the autistic child. What effect this hatred has upon a young child has not been studied. Hate affecting the formation of character defenses, as a factor influencing the child's development and relations with others, has had limited study. Young children who are known to be sadistic, destructive and jealous tend not to be studied from the point of view of hatred.

When not dealt with simply as a reaction, hate, like aggression, tends to be viewed as inseparable from erotic life. Psychoanalytic studies since Freud have continued to regard the two only together in spite of the fact that Freud himself commented that he should have considered them separately. And as hate and aggression are not understood to be intimately associated with narcissism, the psychology of self-preservation, self-reference, the self before others, aggression over altruism, and thus the separate rule of egoism are lost sight of. All are lumped together as expressive of libidinal life. As a consequence, the central role of the self expressed in narcissism, consciously realized in terms of self-reference and defended by aggression in a spectrum ranging from destructiveness to mastery, remains unexplored.

The conclusion continues to be the conventional and simplistic one, taken in its modern form from animal psychology—that frustration leads to aggression. There is no question that this often is the case. But it applies only narrowly to us. The supposition that all dissatisfaction brings out aggression is a limited formula that all too often fails. The equation omits the enormous incentive and the rich resources we may draw on to serve our aims. When we satisfy our aims, we have done more than merely remove an obstacle to gratification.

For example, the entire gamut of the common and typical obsessiveness with its slavish devotion to routine and rituals is unconsciously employed to resist the unpredictable, and serves to defend oneself against what is unknown and hence threatening. The unconscious expectation is that an entrenched order will stand effectively against fears of the unforeseen. All these pursuits resist interference or interruption with aggression. Here is more than aggression released by frustration.

The plain psychological evidence of unconscious wishful conflicts over cleanliness and dirt, order and mess in the ordinary obsessional character poses no question. But his typical aggressiveness is not fully understood until it includes his defense of his devotion to order and thus to predictability. He dreads what may happen, and, as a defense against what is unforeseen, he would hold everything in place, repeat what he knows, and devote himself to routines. The fact that this extends to include such physical functions as the passage of stools, and is associated often with a lifelong syndrome of constipation, is no mystery. We find such fears arise early in childhood when demands for bowel training are enforced; this period as a rule coincides with a phase of a child's development when order and predictability in others are a comfort to a child's need to make himself secure from his fears of what is unfamiliar, foreign or alien. The stand against such dreads is in some measure an endless problem. The fear of what is unforeseen is thus more than frustration turned to aggression, nor is aggression explained by the psychoanalytic observation that anal-eroticism is conveyed forward from infantile conflicts.

The direct resort to varieties of aggression, carried to a bizarre excess in autism, employed at times by those who have an abhorrence of change and who dread differences, may be seen in the obsessional adult and in autism. Both oppose accommodation, passionately resist yielding, are fearful of what is new, and relish the old for the fact that it is known. The wish is to hold all together what can be palpably accounted for. The category and the pigeonhole, to the obsessional, often acquire an importance over what they contain. The ready use of aggression enforces those tightly held egocentric aims.*

But an additional source of disquiet is the disturbing presence of violent wishes and impulses. These are ruled into submission by fears, which are then dispelled with fixed and slavish attempts to impose order on everything. An example taken from the treatment course of an autistic child illustrates this. "There was an intense preoccupation with establishing a fixed order about himself. He attempted to achieve one by stabilizing everything. There could be no changes,

---

* In an important respect autism differs from the obsessional states. Autism allows no value to be invested in another person. The obsessional neurotic, on the other hand, forms valued relationships, but unconsciously demands heavily guarded defenses such as fears and phobias to ward off the outbreak of aggression which readily issues from a narcissism which is easily bruised.

no differences, dissimilarities or strangeness. Everything had to be reduced to a stereotype. This contented him. Monotony, tedious repetition and stereotypy became his comfort as he reduced the world around himself to a fixed, lifeless and, therefore, highly predictable static system. His concern, however, was not limited to the environment. Everything within himself as well had to be static." He raged at the rain he had not anticipated; he was furious that his stools urged passage or that tears flowed and spittle collected.[15]

To unravel all that there is to autism is not yet possible. However, it can be made less of an enigma. Autism, rare and statistically a negligible disorder, has no demographic significance. The hypotheses which seek its cause in actual emotional deprivation fail to take serious realities into account. The extensive wars of the past half-century, in which the worst sufferers are children, whose physical and emotional privation are beyond all calculation, have not produced autism in any remotely corresponding numbers.

The argument that perhaps in a multitude of casualties autistic children would tend to be overlooked, or that the recognition of autism somehow may be missed, is not supported by the fact that autism, when it is present, is conspicuous. Autism is a condition of such obvious social isolation and simultaneous dependence that it calls attention to itself. For example, a group of very young children, aged six months to about twelve months, although spared extermination by the Nazis, were held in a concentration camp between two and three years. "The children had grown up in an atmosphere laden with fear and anxiety. Tereszin was a transit camp, and although some people remained there from their arrest to the end of the Nazi regime, thousands of others, adults as well as children, passed through it on their way to extermination camps in Poland. . . . Arrivals and departures took place continually." Anna Freud and her associates studied a group of these children who had been liberated by the Russians, and who, after a series of subsequent transfers, were finally brought to England and taken into a newly established nursery where they remained for about a year and then were individually adopted.[16] Her study shows that the children were not lacking in a variety of psychological ill effects, some of which were serious disorders. Aggression was a common symptom.

Current theories on the origin of autism rest on privation and maternal rejection. According to these theories, this group of children should have produced a number of such cases. Anna Freud's researchers would hardly be expected to overlook such a conspicuous disorder. None was reported. The emphasis on a mother's character to explain autism neglects the role to be assigned to the child's egocentricity and the course of its development.

The importance of autism is not in its incidence. It is rather that autism reveals in elaborate detail, and by its long persistence, elements of narcissistic processes of mental functioning. As a disorder, it follows a protracted difficult course and then as a rule it is not responsive to being altered.

Clinical examples of adults whose childhood history of autism may be documented are relatively unknown and none are available to be cited here. Perhaps this is because the clinical condition has been under psychoanalytic study less than forty years. Descriptions of autism are familiar to only a few. The instances that I know of directly show that the autistic children now grown to adults remain bizarre regardless of long and painstaking efforts at their treatment. Some twenty years ago I described a case of a three-and-a-half-year-old child.[17] After a four-year period of treatment the final results were poor. During the first year there had seemed to be favorable signs that promised a modest measure of success. The expectations were that the child's social development would continue. The patient is now in his late twenties. Throughout life he has been generously indulged by a large family of sisters and brothers, parents and grandparents. He has kept himself aloof from them and they too have kept their distance after many attempts in years past to keep him within the immediate family. He has held to his seeming indifference to them all. The only rapport with him has been through the indulgences which the whole family has from time to time allowed him. That is, he, as always, may do as he pleases. He insists that his wishes be promptly gratified, and when they are not, he is easily angered. He has never been openly aggressive to others, but when he is provoked, he finds some valued or necessary article to destroy. He continues to live a hand-to-mouth existence, occasionally working at a simple job for a short time. Without plausible excuse, he walks off to spend days in idle preoccupation, engaged by his bizarre whims which are usually associated with some past experience. The sudden thought to visit a farm he once stayed in is enough to set him on a journey to visit it. If he is curious as to what the weather is in some place where he once worked briefly or where he may have once slept, his wish to make an inquiry by telephone to some remote or distant place is promptly carried out. For similar unpredictable reasons, he from time to time visits me or telephones me from a distance and resumes a conversation we may have left off years before.

It may be tempting to ascribe this odd conduct simply to a childish self-indulgence pandered to by a family who wishes no disorderly conduct thrust into its midst. And that this young man's impulsive and aggressive behavior and tantrums remained essentially unaltered since childhood is a clear indication of his infantilism carried into adult life, where he tolerates no more interference with his wishes than when he was four. But such an oversimplification conventionally neglects the impressive fact that it is his narcissism which is impervious to modification. It is borne out by relationships which are held shallow and a readiness to become destructive or violent, both of which speak for uncompromising self-seeking interests and being easily angered as a reaction to some quickly imagined slight to his self-esteem. The more tightly held the narcissism, the greater the vulnerability of self-esteem.

An underlying severe narcissism, even under the unique conditions of analysis, is resistant to being uncovered. Because the analytic process itself is aimed at disclosures, in the course of it self-esteem may be threatened. Such a difficulty was presented by a man who, the more successful he became, the more fears he developed. He had a recognized career in business. It was founded chiefly on his exploiting a natural ability to correctly assess his clients' needs. He became scrupulously attentive to their wishes and made a success of having them properly fulfilled. His position thus became permanently secure in a large business in which he had been made an officer.

The more he was advanced to positions of greater responsibility, the worse his fears became. They were known only to himself. He had the growing concern that something about him which should not be exposed would somehow be revealed. He knew it was an irrational fright, but he was increasingly on guard against something he could not identify that would betray him.

Physically attractive and socially skillful, he hid his natural shyness by easily making small talk and asking questions of others in a discreet fashion, effectively forestalling inquiries about him and masking his reluctance to engage in many subjects he preferred to avoid. It was not that he had actually anything significant to hide. It was that he was loath to make personal references. "It would be like giving away your thoughts." He could not bring himself to share them. He was jovial, witty, and confined himself to talk of current events. Nothing of his private or past life was referred to.

He has a companionable marriage. There is no intimacy with his wife. And although this is not a serious issue because his wife is herself frigid, despite their many children, there are some occasions on which she complains of the distance he keeps between them. He is tirelessly devoted to their children. He patiently understands each one of them like his clients, and they in turn seem devoted to him. Each child is like another facet of himself. His fears of intimacy extend both to his wife and their children.

After a considerable exploration of his fears, he developed the following verbatim account. It represents what he repeated in countless ways on many occasions during his treatment. The context concerns the nature of his relationships, i.e. the conflicts over the modifications he is obliged to make in order to sustain them. We observe him weighing and measuring what allowances he must make for the sake of relationships, and his resistance to place a value beyond himself on others. The hostility which is constantly held in check as the alterations in his narcissism are called for is unconscious. He fears unconsciously that his egocentricity will be exposed, that he is only self-serving, and hence a menace to others whom he would not hesitate to sacrifice for his own aims. The reactions to these wholly narcissistic intentions were fashioned into a career. His reaction to being self-serving is to carefully provide for the needs others may have. His clients, like his children and to a degree his wife, are convinced of his attention to them. His own wishes and thoughts, he feels, would betray him, and he is thus careful and rarely divulges them.

"My self-centeredness is that everyone else has to be pushed down. If my wishes or daydreams were real, I'd be in terrible trouble. I need people to be kindly disposed to me. Then I know I am safe. I need them. I admit to wanting to feel safe. What I mean is that when they are around me, I can see that I have nothing to fear from them. But if I acted as I want to, I'd be miserable. Because I want to give nothing and to have to, makes me want to be destructive. The way I want to be, I'd be in danger. I have only one question: when will danger come? And I have to be ready for it. Any system that reduces danger interests me. I think of all the possible ways to eliminate it. It means that sometimes I have to be nice to people to get that. But the trouble is that I come back to the same thing; I have to pay for being nice. I hate that. What anyone gets from me like affection or consideration for another means less for me. To take someone into my life makes me weak; I can never give gratitude. I give nothing. Oh, I give presents, but that covers that I really don't want to do it. I want to say the hell with them and the trouble with that is it turns into the hell with you! To take others into account is only trouble to me. I fear being excluded because I think how mad people are at me. I am determined not to be social. I have to act as if there will be no change; part of me believes that there will be none. I hate change. If I am forced to move, I will. I have to contend with the world that changes. I have the idea that if I accommodate to the world, it's a deficiency in me. Kindness, gratitude, affection are all dangerous. These things might take me over. For instance, if I liked someone, they'd have free access to me. If someone gets pleasure from me, it feels like I have less. I hate to give gifts; I refuse to adapt or to civilize. Oh, I do it at work but I really have to think that way I win. Or else, if I adapt because I want to, someone else wins. I want no knock on the door, no telephone to ring. In a sense, I have to be drawn out. I want only to watch myself and not have to have humans about. If I let myself rave and rage away as I'd like, I'd hurt everybody, so I have to be careful not to go too far. I should be able to do as I please, and no one to get angry while I do it. All this I have to keep secret. What I want would make people furious. I want to be so aggressive. I am afraid to expose it. I sometimes lie awake at night and think for hours, how to escape the law. It all comes from hating and not giving. I always get uneasy, uncomfortable and I want to go and defy the laws. The hell with all! The idea of punishment bothers me."

Each of his children embodies some aspect of the characteristics he has recognized in himself. One child is rather stoical. It is a quality the father prides in himself. As he observes this in his child, he attempts to foster its further development. Much as he does with himself, he sets trials for the child to pass. It is done in a kindly way but its purpose is clear. He privately thinks of himself in the child's place and, through the child, adds to his own sense of achievement and reduces his anxiety. Another child shows a precocity in mathematics. By promoting this talent, which to a degree he has himself, he feels he is cultivating his own garden. And so on with his other children. What he sees in himself and finds similar in his children reduces the distance between them. As he helps to develop their talents or capacities, he is doing as much for his own. All parents take a narcissistic pride in what their children may accomplish. This man, however, shows his additional narcissistic need which, although illustrating what we all enjoy in a child's achievement, demonstrates that each child is a narcissistic extension of himself.

How much of this man's existence is autistic, however, is pointed out when we see that there is little else that is significant to him other than the reflections and extensions of himself. Whether in his work or at home, his relations with others are virtually exclusively autistic. He sees in everyone only reflections of himself. He has put into words what we have often obtained from autistic children with less eloquence. The stubborn resistance to change, the lack of accommodation to an intimate relationship, and the threat posed at having to give up self-serving aims are remarkably like characteristics of the autistic child. Obviously he is not so egocentric that he sacrifices all relationships. It is part of his career that he has successfully masked his acute fears of hostility from others. They are the result of his own projections against which he defends himself. If he had not been promoted, and thus developed anxiety, he might not have had to seek help.

His appraisal of the essential elements in a relationship, as being costly to one's egocentric or narcissistic ends, is correct. Our value for another invests our affection in him, and to that degree our self-interest is diminished. Actually, self-interest is transferred. For our narcissistic investment, we expect a return, that is, to be cared for— loved. It is a transaction, however, this man does not engage in. The cost to him would involve giving up self-interest for affection for others, abandoning much of his fantasy of omnipotence, and accepting their demands as having priority at times over his own. In short, to turn from himself to value another according to these criteria threatens to reduce him. Therefore, he prefers indifference to them, in the hope that supporting his self-serving will content him. But as sustaining narcissism invariably entails associations of aggressive and assertive wishes and fantasies over others, he unwittingly is trapped. He is thus brought into another round of vigilance, apprehensions of retaliation and of being deprived. He feels threatened; it raises his hostility and he then suffers fears of attack. We learn that only a small gap exists between the aggressive defenses of his narcissistic wishes and the projection of them as fears of hostility from others. He shows that it seems impossible to enjoy one's egocentricity without expecting to be attacked for it.

This man's erotic experiences, as we would expect, indicate little concern for others. His relations with women are essentially an exercise in satisfying himself without consideration for their needs, except for what is generated by the fears of their hostility. He had no difficulty finding masochistic young women who would gratify him before he married one. The fantasies of self-satisfaction are central, and what guilty feelings often follow in the wake of sexual acts are usually associated with the persistent admonishments held over from childhood. It is significant that they are not incorporated as his own, as is normally the case with development, but instead remain as belonging to his upbringing. He fears he will be punished. He does not censure himself. Bent as he is on self-interest, he compromises it only out of fears; he expects hostile reactions from others. Narcissism rules. His eroticism, being autistic, that is, without a developed need for affection but only for gratification, fails to significantly alter or modify his narcissism.

The study of narcissism and aggression by way of autism, while important in revealing their critical role in mental life, may seem somewhat removed from everyday existence. Since commonplace dreaming, as Freud discovered, is nearest to a complete immersion in egoism, its consideration should give further illumination to the relationship of narcissism and aggression.

I shall take as an example a young woman graduate student who suffered frequent nightmares persistently since early childhood. From the time she was a small girl, her frightening dreams had hardly altered. They consisted chiefly of her being endlessly pursued and threatened with being stabbed and killed. Running and being chased by nondescript characters, who could occasionally be identified as old men or an older man intent on her destruction, was the principal adventure of the nightmares. She escaped, as a rule, by awakening.

A careful scrutiny of her ordinary day showed that although she was actively and successfully engaged in her work, there was an underlying disquiet or apprehension. She had, since childhood, feared an untimely and unpredictable end. Her frequent hypochondria and fears of an accident and death were but an extension of the nightmares into daily living.

Few days went by without some sense of being affronted, slighted or hurt, and without fail these injuries to self-esteem made her belligerent. Yet, in each of these countless episodes in which she defended herself, she came out a victim, more hurt than when she began to assert herself.

An intense, impulsive and explosive first love affair suddenly caught her. Fearful she would lose control of herself sexually, she terminated the experience. And whereas ordinarily she feared to die through some unfortunate circumstance, now unaccountably she was certain she would kill herself. Distraught, she applied for help.

An additional circumstance further increased her anxieties and had a direct bearing on understanding the urgency of the help she required. A pair of young men brutally and senselessly murdered a prosperous farmer and his family. Eventually they were caught, sentenced and hanged. With great skill, Truman Capote erased the lines that distinguished these sensational real events from the fiction in which he cast them in the novel, *In Cold Blood*.[18] He spun a web of suspense about the murders, the cruelty of the criminals, and the long intense chase that culminated in their apprehension. The popular success of the novel was immense. Not only was the writing acclaimed as an example of exceptional literary talent, but the reader was held by it in a grip of seeming reality as if it was no longer a work of fiction. This young woman read *In Cold Blood* with a fascination she could not forego. She wanted to discard the novel, yet she continued to become more absorbed in it. She was also frightened. When she finished reading the story, she determined to kill herself, and she nearly succeeded.

The novel brought to her mind long-forgotten murderous fantasies. When she was about seven or eight years old, she secretly plotted to murder a small boy whom she hardly knew. She would rehearse the details of the murder countless times and, on recollection, for what seems to have been hours on end. Her remarks about the murder plot include the burden destructive wishes may carry.

"I'd see myself doing it with a knife. It was sexual. But it was something else too. The destructiveness was frightening. I used to think I'd lose control. I mistrusted myself. And for murder you get killed. I'd look at myself in the mirror and I used to look like a sweet nice child. I never really was. I'd shout at myself. 'I hate you!' I'd pull my hair till it hurt, and think of things that proved I was no good. I never failed to refresh that idea. I still do it. One way that I was worthless was to think of losing what I most valued, my dog. Or I would think the house would burn down and no one would escape. And then thinking of killing that little boy would make me feel I was terrible. The same sort of thing still happens."

Rather than either wishing to be destructive or carrying out self-attacks directly, she described at length her opposite and perhaps even more frightening experiences, in which she was a victim.

She reported there were long, long dreams of being chased and threatened, barely escaping being destroyed, constantly in terror, and waking up just in time to get away. "I am the victim of threats. I know I am angry, hostile, critical and hate others. Do I get judged by what I really am or how I behave? What I know of myself is the judge! Fears are not from things. They are from what I might do. From what might be done to me! I hate myself! Others must, or if they knew me, they would hate me. When I finished reading about the murders, I had the thought how often I wanted to stab someone with a knife.

"In dreams I never have murderous intentions. It's only when I am awake that I am very aggressive. That all gets changed in dreams to being the victim of attacks. I don't trust people. I think what a victim I am. I feel then that I am unjustly attacked. I get angry that I am the one who gets hurt, a victim. Then I defend myself. I think then of doing what I want. The more I get to do that, I think I could do anything and what would stop me! If I hate myself, that might do it but I can't be reasonable. I just get so angry, furious and want to hurt somebody. I had better die! Reading that book made me think I know I can't get away from what I want to do. But I can't take it as my fault! I have to twist it to 'it's somebody's doing.' I can then have rages at them and let myself off. I can't stand the image I am so hateful. If I commit suicide, I wonder, will I kill my bad self, then could I feel good?

"When I feel guilty, I am under control. If I lose guilt I lose control. Guilt protects you. If you really despise yourself, you want to kill yourself or be killed. I am despicable. There is no escape. None! To think only of yourself or first is despicable. When I read that book and thought of what I used to want to do, I knew I was murderous and I still am if I think I can't have what I want. When you are like this, you can't stand to have someone say, 'I love you.' It's threatening to be liked. I am not to be trusted. I want to be secure and safe but what people might think of me scares me. I don't want to think and I don't want them to think how awful I am. My private self is ugly, selfish.

"Being a victim attracts me. I look for it in films, novels, the daily news. I think of wanting a Jewish name. I have to make myself attacked. It controls what I really want—to be a pirate! Murderous! And I would have to kill myself for that when I think how much I want to have my own wishes. It proves my worth. But to get them scares me. I feel awful. It's dangerous to me to have them. I have no choice when I feel this way. If I am where a train is coming, I want to jump in front of it!"

There is no question that this young woman's experiences are vividly sexual. Her stormy love affair brought her near to panic. And her long recollection of nightmares in which she was being dangerously pursued and threatened, often by "older men or an old man," leaves little reason to doubt that the persistent fear of a sexual assault expressed her continuing latent incestuous wishes.

However, after giving the sexual conflicts their proper due, there remains, in this woman, a powerful and menacing self-destructiveness which overrides all else. It might be supposed that it is strongly founded on being rejected, first as a girl. Without relief or refuge from an egocentric "scatterbrained" mother, she was unwittingly reminded by her father of his disappointment that she was a girl, when he impatiently persisted in teaching her boys' sports and left her with a devalued sense from which she could not recover.

It would seem, therefore, to be a reasonable supposition at first, that to be loved would give her the self-esteem and hence the fulfillment she felt was always denied her and for which she longed. Yet, no sooner does this occur than she is alarmed and repudiates the realization of being valued, and an onslaught of self-destructive wishes and acts appear with an unprecedented force. Moreover, she identified herself with murderers, recalling how she herself had plotted a murder, which in fact was an unconscious self-destructive fantasy that had persisted and which she was reminded of from time to time.

She cannot accept, even at this distance from childhood, the proposition of being feminine. To her it is a devalued condition. Even the ordinary quarrels between parents remained a vivid scene, to her mother's discredit. The continuing unconscious fantasy of being a man, i.e. the hope of somehow getting a penis, is not only to correct her child's notion of an anatomical deficiency, as many would suppose, but rather through its acquisition to establish self-esteem. The love affair proposed she would be valued as a girl. But if we take her past experience into account, she had to abort it. She thus unconsciously averted the threat of the ignominy in which her femininity had been cast.

Analysis showed that as a small child she was well aware that her being a girl deeply disappointed her parents. While growing up she was encouraged to be a tomboy. As she became one it served as some compensation for the humiliation of being a girl. But it was also a constant reminder that neither her parents nor she could accept her for what she was. The conscious self-attacks expressed it. And the unconscious conflict between what she was and what she wished she could have been was expressed, on the one hand, in her unrelieved discontent and self-criticism and, on the other, by a revulsion from sexuality. With defiant self-assertiveness she identified herself strongly with her father and hated those qualities she thought of as feminine.

The fantasy of destroying the young boy (actually her tomboy self) was a further expression of her suicidal wishes—to put an end to her bad self, the girl from whom hate poured and from whom envy could not be stemmed. But to kill the young boy meant unconsciously to destroy her father's preference and be rid of this rival to whom she was hopelessly bound. It might give her self-esteem. The rage that as a girl she was of no account left her with deep grievances against her mother whom she unconsciously blamed for the fact that she was a girl, and her father whom she could never seem to satisfy; and she was very depressed.

Until we take into consideration the pervasive role that narcissism holds, we would have to leave our understanding of this young woman to rest strictly on her unresolved sexual conflicts. And although it is the case that she cannot bring herself to a satisfactory resolution of them, we would be setting aside the highly dangerous and self-destructive elements which deeply affect her if we limited treatment strictly to the problems of sexuality.

Her conflicts of longest standing involve self-esteem. She saw herself as a hapless victim needing to protect herself from unwarranted hostility, criticism and ill-will. Analysis showed she seemed always to have cause to defend herself, and her furthest recollection bears out that while she was exceedingly aggressive, much of it was bound up with warding off fears of being victimized. She had repressed her own source of hostility, the injured narcissism. It was associated with her excessive childhood demands which she could compromise only with great difficulty. Her self-esteem was precariously held as an unwanted child of the wrong sex, and her demands and aggression increased as did her fears of what would result from pressing her wishes.

This young woman's recurrent nightmares call our attention to the dread she encountered. She often dreamt she was an object of aggression, a victim, threatened, terrified and near to being killed. Since in sleep we are given over to our unconscious without the accustomed restraints and censure we exercise during the day, we would expect our young woman to be no less aggressive asleep. In point of fact, we would expect her to be even more freely given over to it than when awake. But contrary to expectations, she as the dreamer is not the aggressor; rather, others aim to destroy her. And, in her desperation to escape this fate, she awakens filled with anxiety.

John Mack's recent thorough work[19] extends some of the limits earlier authors were bound to by their lack of direct experience with young children. They held to the view that it was the association of anxiety in connection with repressed incestuous wishes which gave rise to conflicts.[20] Under conditions of sleep, conducive to returning repressed erotic wishes, fears and anxieties were evoked. The supposition was that when these responses become particularly intense, perhaps due to some experience during the day carried into sleep, nightmares result. The dreamer is then awakened and the distressing experiences are interrupted.

Direct encounters with very young children who commonly have nightmares led Mack to think that periods earlier in psychological development than the Oedipal contain similar strong libidinal conflicts. He concludes that as the young child's ego development is limited, it is all the more prone to anxiety generated by powerful libidinal wishes. But he, as other analysts, tends to regard anxiety much as Cannon did rage, hunger and fear,[21] that is, the foundation of it is within the behavior theory of emotion. "As such it makes awareness depend upon response, thus anticipating modern behavioristics." [22]

The fact that the dreamer is universally the victim in nightmares is not explained either by the theory that the nightmare is an eruption of anxiety, or that it is an expression of libidinal conflicts. The solution to understanding this riddle of the nightmare seems, therefore, to lie elsewhere.

It would be naïve to assume that aggression does not create serious conflicts for the young child which he is obliged to resolve.* The

---

* A distinction needs to be made between rage and aggression, and perhaps this is the place to point it out. Rage is a reaction of the central nervous system, "undirected," without a specific object, and lacking a known motive or intent. Aggression, on the other hand, usually aims at another, toward whom hostility is intended and directed. Rage has no such purpose. It is without focus —it is truly blind. Aggression may be "sublimated" and employed in the mastery of the environment or in the acquisition of skill. Rage cannot be so exploited. Consider the case of a very articulate, even-tempered, and good-natured little girl of five years who suffered a slight brain concussion in an

normal young child is, in a rich variety of ways, aggressive. The aggression, however, is neither blind nor without purpose. We have noted that aggression turned against the self is characteristically human.

There is no better example of the phenomenon of turning aggression against the self than in the nightmare. In our young woman patient, we observed that in her nightmares it was not she who wished the destruction of others, but rather that it was she who was to be destroyed. Mack's examples of nightmares in children are identical in that the aggressive role tightly held during the day is given up in the nightmare for its opposite. In a variety of my own cases, in both chil-

---

accident. Except for minor bruises, the only harm was the central one which entailed a ten-hour period of unconsciousness. Fortunately, within a few days recovery was complete, except for the blocked recall of certain words (nouns, not adjectives) which lasted about two weeks. The child would ask for a peach, for instance, by describing the "fuzz" of the skin, able to describe well enough the appearance of the fruit, but fumbling without success for its name. There were numerous similar episodes. During this period, sudden untoward rages occurred, to which the little girl had never before been subject. They would arise as a kind of massive response to the most trifling dissatisfaction; then, after a brief interval, the rage would subside as abruptly as it had come on. After each such outburst the child was invariably puzzled and would ask, "Why did I do that?" Within a few weeks, the syndrome and the aphasia disappeared, the child completely recovered, and the memory of the rages remained as unaccountable to the little girl as her behavior.

Recent studies of brain physiology bear out this distinction between rage and aggression. Patients with certain minor brain damage are known to be subject to sudden violent outbursts of rage, to episodes of a kind of vague and indiscriminate destructiveness. And the incidence of such disorders is probably greater than formal records lead us to believe. Some doctors have been led to hypothesize from such findings that senseless violence is not a discrete and unique phenomenon, that our aggression may be simply explained in terms of some complex brain dysfunction, and that we have only to await further developments in brain physiology for a clarification. Since brain disorders do, in some cases, account for this kind of random violence, the further assumption is sometimes made that it may all be ascribed to the activity of the central nervous system. It is believed that the brain stores "information on violence" which is released at certain provocative signals—a model very much like an early warning system of alert.[a]

An important finding which has not received the close attention it warrants is that an examination of patients like the little girl cited above reveals that in no case can they account for their acts in moments of rageful fury. In fact, there is little or no thought or idea-content associated with this kind of violence. And in contrast with patients whose aggression is "purposive" and who are without any known brain damage, the depth of motivation to explain their conduct is considerable. What may be more remarkable, however, is that in respect to conscience, those in both categories suffer. Although the subject with the brain lesion has no explanation for his violence and can claim no motive, while the other may have a rich supply of rationalizations and explanations, neither is without some kind of remorse.

dren and adults, to relinquish being aggressive in daily living or to accept passivity is to court serious danger. One risk commonly anticipated is that it entails the dread of being subject to the aggression of others.

We find that in the dreamer of the nightmare a curious transition takes place. The unconscious process is that a disengagement from one's own aggression and its assignment to others occurs, i.e. it is projected to them. Not only does this lead directly to being menaced by them, but since at the same time no sign of aggression appears on the dreamer's part, his own aggressiveness is thus denied.

This denying and projective process is as familiar to us as the unconscious defense employed to dissociate oneself from hostile wishes or impulses that are harbored against someone who matters to us. It is an emotional activity which develops early and is common to young children. We have observed in children that such defenses are employed in relation to their fears of losing favor or in connection with their boundless demands for affection. Regarding the failure of their wishes as a loss of favor, they suffer a loss of self-esteem and a hostile attitude develops. But since this generates anxiety, projection and denial emerge and the dynamic cycle is completed.

The fact that the same process operates in the dream and especially in nightmares is not recognized. This commonest of childhood emotional processes is taken from the child's daily experience and carried into the night in sleep. In short, the hostility borne toward others, and feared from them through projection, completes the turn from being aggressive to being self-destructive. Passivity is invited. In this context, passivity is not a mere libidinal wish for surrender to a sexually active partner. Rather, it is the yielding of one's own aggression and fearing the result.

The nightmare only exceptionally, if at all, gives the dreamer a part that is other than dangerous. Typically, the dreamer is menaced, victimized or near to being destroyed. Yet, as a rule, he offers his assailant little or no resistance. His desperate sense of protest is voiceless and his efforts to escape are on leaden feet. On further examination, the dreamer is characterized as demeaned and devalued, ineffectual and stripped of powers. All the active faculties, the aggressive intentions and attributes, are held by the assailant. And in the typical endless running, chasing, threats and assaults, no provocation is assigned the dreamer. The aggressor appears to set about his attack on the blameless victim spontaneously. Significantly, only exceptionally is the dreamer himself treacherous or savage.

The nightmare is brought into full understanding only when we recognize it as a particular or special vehicle of violence. It carries the unconscious wish to be destructive. But it can only rarely be directly expressed; even unconsciously during sleep the wish to be destructive turns against the self. The nightmare thus confirms the depth of the prohibition against aggression toward those with whom we are intimate. It is this alarming unconscious wish, so often manifested in everyday life, which, carried into sleep, turns the dreamer into a victim and gives the nightmare its terror. And the source of anxiety is thus not at all primary. It is a secondary or derived effect.

Many have been led to think that the wish to be destructive is a primary condition of existence because its expression begins early in life. However, we must keep in mind that the young child's earliest relationships are characterized by unlimited demands for exclusive possession, and that he is not content with having less than all, has no aim except to obtain complete satisfaction, and is for that reason certain to be disappointed. The pleasure principle, we have called attention to earlier, constitutes no simple hedonistic aim. It *is* the governing principle, but *in the service of our narcissism*—the self. And when reality compels its modification, narcissism is affected, i.e. injured, and hostility issues.

The nightmare, then, is a denial of hostility in the dreamer. Both projection and denial are powerful emotional unconscious processes actively employed by children especially in respect to aggression. It should come as no surprise that they prove to be as actively engaged during sleep as when a child is awake. The reason nightmares occur with greater incidence during early childhood is that it is a period most prone to narcissistic injury. And its recovery entails aggression. The appearance of nightmares in later life (not the unusual occasions in connection with specific traumatic events when nightmares may then arise and have a different character), as in the young woman we have referred to here, is pathognomonic for adults with exceeding narcissism or infantilism. And the occasional eruption of nightmares in adult life is likely to be evoked by some narcissistic injury perhaps during the day or recalled by way of associations.

The nightmare is thus revealed in early emotional development to be a crude expression of self-discipline, and it is used in this manner from time to time throughout life. We observe that the dreamer subjects himself to threatening figures or representations of them which on analysis are identifiable as related, parental, authoritative, dangerous and erotic, toward whom he is submissive, demeaned and passive.

The nightmare is hence indicative of the struggles engaging the young dreamer's narcissism. In the final analysis it serves to curb the self; hence, it plays an important role in the formation of the ego upon which social development depends.

As an essential element in everyday life, narcissism is nevertheless regarded more as a factor in emotional disorders rather than a ubiquitous part of our daily living. When I wrote about it previously, in the context of the psychology of failure, narcissism was of course a central consideration. I attempted to show that the mere circumstances of our existence furnished an endless variety of experiences in which self-esteem was tempered in every phase of emotional development. The process is not obscure. What limitations are imposed on our immodest childish extravagance are certain to provide us from our earliest years with a procession of conflicts. The discrepancy between what we wish and what we receive, what we attempt and what we fail at, forces itself on us. In each instance self-appraisal is engaged and self-esteem inescapably is elevated or lowered.

No experience brings out the effect on self-esteem more immediately than when it is associated with the body. The integrity of one's shape and bodily functions holds the deepest and perhaps the longest-standing investment in respect to self-esteem. It is to be expected that the very young child is fully concerned with his body and its operations well in advance of his interest in others. In fact, his natural tendency to ascribe his own functions indiscriminately to others and to things does not reflect an inability to make distinctions, as is commonly thought, but rather a self-absorption so great that it precludes admitting serious consideration of others. Moreover, the qualities he often discovers in others are merely his own which he has projected to those about him. His interest, in short, is largely with himself—narcissistic. A test of the stability of self-interest, and of the resistance to relinquish it, is most plain when the body or its functions are impaired. Under such conditions, interest in others is quickly withdrawn.

Freud commented on this phenomenon from a suggestion attributed to Sandor Ferenczi, his colleague. It was in effect that suffering puts an end to love: "a lover's feelings, however strong, are banished by bodily ailments, and suddenly replaced by complete indifference."[24] Hypochondria may thus produce the same emotional effect as organic disease. It is a notorious condition of a withdrawal of interest in others to a concentration on the self. "Plainly seeking themselves as a love object which must be termed 'narcissistic.' In this observation we have the strongest reasons which have led us to adopt a hypothesis of narcissism." [25] Freud's interest was not directed toward a further elaboration of the fate of the narcissistic turn to oneself, except for scattered references to the hate and aggression which emerge as others cease to be a source of pleasure.

We all wish to remain intact, to suffer no damage, no alterations, and least of all do we wish to experience a loss of function or a part of ourselves. Impairment of any sort violates the integrity of our body image. Threatened self-esteem mobilizes defenses. While they are simple and primitive insofar as they appear early in our development, they are strong and persistent. Because the child's narcissism is intimately concerned with his body and its functions with which physical mastery and achievement are so directly associated, the threat of illness or impairment of functions is great. We may judge this from the enormous value the child places on himself, on his functions, and even on his most trifling parts, for example, his hair, his nails or his stools. His attachment to them all indicates his fears of loss and the prevalence and pervasiveness of his narcissism which reaches to include his most peripheral tissues and even his excrement.

These vicissitudes of daily living which begin to appear in early childhood not only profoundly affect the course of emotional development, but they leave indelible traces to be discerned throughout later periods. The example which follows illustrates some emotional effects appearing in later life which had their origin in childhood.

An exceptionally talented and competent woman whose professional achievement was widely recognized was a friend and not a patient. And she has since died. On a routine physical examination, an actively malignant breast tumor was discovered. A radical mastectomy and a hysterectomy were performed within a week of the diagnosis.

For a variety of reasons, and among them the wish to contribute to this study, she proposed speaking at length to me about the reactions she had kept to herself of her misfortune. She was eager to unburden them, and my chief function was to provide her that opportunity together with the unspoken assurance that I had no criticism. To give her remarks a fidelity they might otherwise lack, she suggested a tape recording be made. What follows is a verbatim sequence from one tape recording of her comments. Only identifying remarks have been deleted.

R: Now that all the surgery is over and you have recovered, what about it are you privately thinking?

A: To myself, I call it cancer. Everybody else avoids saying that. I still think of it as cancer. When I was first operated on, a friend came to visit me at the hospital who also had the same thing. She kept talking about the mastectomy she had had and that she thought it was necessary to think of it as being castrated. Psychologically, she insisted that was what it meant. I was very angry at her making something that was very personal into some sort of intellectual idea. She was saying all women had to work out for themselves their castration anxiety. I was saying to myself that she was trying to make something clinical out of what was human. She was not hitting at what was my feeling. My body has been damaged! This to me is no castration! That's a concept. My body has been mutilated! I got very angry about that. I am angry about it now.

R: Angry?

A: First, I thought, Why should this happen to me? Why not someone else in my family. I ended up in a horrendous fury with that idea that I was a victim. Not so much when I was in the hospital as at home, later. Crying and crying and banging my pillow. I was angry that this happened to me. Why not somebody else? Someone I did not like especially, people I knew. Why me? When I thought of members of my family to whom it might have happened, and they have families and children, I thought it was better that it should happen to me than to them. And then I got depressed. I wanted to die. I felt deprived. Everybody knew me as pleasant and enjoying myself. But now I felt I had lost all that. Even if I did look good after all this, my body didn't feel right. It was something to bear, more to live with, I didn't think I could bear. It was the idea that no one really could care about me. Family and close friends seemed not to make a difference to me. I couldn't think about them and they couldn't care about me.

    When I thought, how did this come to me? Where did it come from? What was the cause of it? At times, I used to think, only momentarily, very briefly—it was something I may have done. I shut that off quickly. Somehow I did it! I know this is not at all reasonable to even consider I was at fault. I did think it. But not for long. And then I'd get angry. It was like a punishment I didn't deserve.

    I also got angry that the cancer was in a place where it could be seen. Everytime I get dressed, every morning and every night. It makes me furious. I want no one to know. I can't shop for clothes the way I used to do. I have since learned to put on a dress that I am trying to fit before I entirely take off the one I am wearing. It's so I don't see myself. I won't look at myself.

R: You have become tearful.

A: Since I started talking, at this moment I felt like crying the most. I think of what other people will think of me. Having to present yourself as a cripple. How can you not think of yourself as a cripple? Even with the operation I look young and healthy. But I know better. It makes me furious in so many little ways, all the time. The fury is that you have to live with this. Every goddamned day! I have to cover up this view of myself. I hate myself! It's infuriating. I always thought of myself as a very strong person, physically strong, and I was rarely sick. I enjoyed being strong and healthy. When the surgeon tells me I am healthy now and have nothing to worry about, I get angry. I wish for what is lost. He does not understand that.

I just want to be what I was before. I can't make the adjustment to this. I am not my own master any more. My respect for myself, for my freedom is gone! It's the limitations on me that I am furious about. I have lost respect for myself somehow. This is what I have lost. And when I feel this way, I feel separated from my family and I feel afraid.

From our earliest years and extended throughout life, the need for the integrity of our body remains unaltered. Perhaps it cannot be otherwise. The natural consequences of aging are, for instance, generally met with some acceptance or resignation as an inevitable reality. But they are met also as ravages of the body spoiled by time to which we are obliged to submit. While the emotional experience is not as dramatic as being ruined by cancer, the anticipated outcome, of course, is similar. Thus, as we have observed, disabilities, impairments, or the loss of functions bitterly rankle; regardless of the reasons, whether by accident or illness or age, narcissism is deeply affected. Contrary to suppositions, often the more impoverished we seem to be, the higher narcissism is raised. We invest it in every function we experience. And for each one which fails, we are prone to suffer a narcissistic injury. In instances where narcissism gives way to the demands of reality, as when a part of the self is lost, it is as if mourning should take place. According to the Old Testament religion, nail parings and hair or other parts of the self were not to be discarded, but given a proper burial. The ancient rite seems to take into account the psychological significance that giving up a part of oneself stands for our final dissolution; it would violate our narcissism to suffer being discarded in the end. Only an acquired discipline allows us to force narcissism to yield, not, however, without rancor. Therefore, associated with the loss of function or a part of the body, a lowered self-esteem occurs. It may become conscious. But it is regularly present and aggression emerges from it.[26] The adaptation we may make to our infirmities or losses or "to outrageous fate" represents a real triumph over our deep-seated narcissism which strongly opposes the verdict reality hands it.

The woman treated for cancer by removal of her breast and generative organs heatedly protested she suffered more than a return of childhood castration fears. And although we would not deny that the mutilation she suffered would evoke unconscious childhood reactions to being a girl, if that was all that it meant, she could live with that much as she had done for many years. But her well-intentioned, ill-advised friend would have had her believe that castration was a far greater dread than the older one she feared. One is reminded of a comment by Freud. "For though we can with certainty establish in them (women) the presence of a castration *complex,* we can hardly speak with propriety of castration *anxiety* where castration has already taken place." [27] He wrote that on naturally comparing herself with boys, a little girl believes a wrong has been done. Her lack of a penis, she thinks, is grounds for inferiority. The girl in accepting her condition, i.e. castration, takes it as an accomplished fact. Whereas the boy who makes the identical comparison fears its possibility, i.e. its occurrence. His is the alarm at what might happen; the girl has something in the past to contend with.

Hence, a further consideration is that, while it is a girl's fate to be without a penis and its absence psychologically a basis for some feelings of inferiority, her narcissism recovers. It does so by directing attention to the worthiness of the rest of herself, and that penis envy is a foreshortened goal. The complaints this woman expressed in her rage derived from the irrevocable narcissistic injury she suffered. She told us that uppermost in her mind was that she could no longer be seen without humiliation. She skillfully hid, even from herself, by artful dodges, the fact that her body was not intact. Her fury did not abate, however. Her wish was to be restored—to again, and without hiding, enjoy being seen, to show her worthiness. The loss brought tears to her eyes. She felt demeaned, crippled and weak. Her self-esteem was not to be regained by the surgeon's assurance that she was once again healthy. In her view, it was not her health that was lost. It was her self-esteem which she could not regain.

The conflicts of narcissism may isolate us or make us social, keep us egocentric or draw us to be with others. They may hold us to dread change, or they may carry us to be revolutionaries. They may cause us to be charitable and grand, or they may incite us to violence and murder. Narcissism begins its rule in our earliest period and continues its reign to our end. The tyranny of narcissism is the human condition.

Chapter IX

The Eternal Yahoo

It was unavoidable that Freud's studies of the individual mind would have him dealing with the emotional basis of the relation of the individual to society.[1] In 1907, Freud began publishing the results of his emerging sociological studies. It was an interest which he pursued and which extended into his last and posthumously published work. We have the kernel of his conception of group psychology in his declaration that "A child who produces instinctual repressions spontaneously is thus merely repeating a part of the history of civilization. What is today an act of internal restraint was once an external one, imposed, perhaps, by the necessities of the moment; and, in the same way, what is now brought to bear upon every growing individual as an external demand of civilization may some day become an internal disposition to repression." [2] Freud developed this theory and published it nearly fifteen years later. In "Group Psychology and the Analysis of the Ego" [3] he explained the psychology of social groups on the basis of the developmental changes in the psychology of the individual mind.

Throughout mental life someone else is invariably involved "as a model, as an object, as a helper, as an opponent" [4] and, as I have shown here earlier, even under the most adverse isolated conditions, relationships exist; individual psychology, therefore, is at the same time social psychology. Social or "group" psychology is thus concerned with the individual as a member of a sex, race, nation, caste, profession, or as a component part of a crowd of people, organized into a group at some particular time for some definite purpose; and the beginnings of its development is in the family.[5]

Psychoanalytic evidence shows that a sediment of negative feelings —of aversion and hostility—which escapes notice only as a result of repression, endures in all human relations. Freud noted that this was the case in marriage, friendship, the relations between parents and children, business partners, and even when men come together in larger units. "Everytime two families become connected by marriage, each of them thinks itself superior to or of better birth than the other." [6] The same is expressed in the jealous rivalry between neighboring towns. Closely related races keep one another at arm's length: "The South German cannot endure the North German, the Englishman casts every kind of aspersion upon the Scot, the Spaniard despises the Portuguese. We are no longer astonished that the greater differences should lead to an almost insuperable repugnance, such as the Gallic people feel for the German, the Aryan for the Semite, and the white races for the coloured." [7]

The undisguised antipathies and aversions which people feel toward strangers, the commonly aroused episodes of hostility even between intimates, the readiness for hatred—all represent an aggressiveness whose source presumably "is unknown and to which one is tempted to ascribe an elementary character." [8] Freud had in mind here the polarity of love and hate expressed in what he supposed was a hypothetical opposition between the instincts of life and death. The basis of ambivalence was somehow instinctual. His assumption was that since there is some measure of hostility or aggression in all manner of relationships, it therefore must exist as an irreducible and instinctual element in the formation of the personality. It is kept in abeyance by repression, and under conditions which loosen repression, the underlying omnipresent hostility may then pour out.

The fact, however, that in each instance, for the sake of a relationship, some self-interest must be sacrificed is not credited by Freud as having a critical role in the formation of ambivalence. Yet, as we have seen earlier in this work, the sacrifice of one's narcissistic aims, however necessary at times, is not borne without anger. This is the case, even as its sacrifice is enjoyed and brings reward. Some residue of resentment remains. And, as we have further noted, whatever threatens or nullifies such investments is a blow to narcissism and is certain to summon up displeasure. The basis for ambivalence, therefore, really lies in the tenuous and vulnerable nature of our self-esteem.

With each phase of narcissism, aggression or hostility is prompted. Whether it is directed principally at others—or, in order to spare them, is aimed at oneself—depends neither upon some stored quantity of energy nor upon the exercise of some supposed essential instinctual strength. Rather, narcissism always governs. Its rule is pervasive. The endless encounters which test self-esteem and mobilize aggression are the active elements which normally transform egoism to altruism, modifying the center of interest in the self into a gratifying investment in another, in work, in a cause, or in an ideal. It is a natural course. But ambivalence is not expunged from it. Preserving the self is secured through social development and maintained by social relationships, but, ironically, for our social security, the vehicle is our narcissism.

Even in the course of ordinary circumstances, let alone in unusual ones, we have observed that limitations and frustrations profoundly affect the self. In each such instance, narcissism heightens, and increased demands for its gratification press to be met. Only individual study will show whether infantilism will be evoked, or whether maturity is developed, or just which characteristics of aggression will be employed to resist the dictates of circumstance. But all these elements will be present to some degree in the conflicts which grow out of any relationship.

Psychoanalytic theorists in the last five decades suppose that what has been found to be characteristically true for individual psychology must be no less valid for group psychology. While efforts to understand individual psychology have focused chiefly on sexual conflicts, with which aggression is often associated, the corresponding interest in group psychology shows the reverse. It pays particular attention to aggression while the psychosexual conflicts of groups remain obscure. In short, extrapolations between individual and group psychology are freely exchanged within a loose and poorly defined framework of hypotheses.

In 1913, Freud, who was not at all averse to the exercise of forming a hypothesis as a vehicle for extrapolation, published *Totem and Taboo*.[9] Addressing himself to how the continuity in mental life of successive generations is established, he supposed some sort of psychic inheritance. He was reminded of Goethe's lines from *Faust*: "What thou hast inherited from thy fathers, acquire it to make it thine." [10] It eloquently expressed his own view that no generation conceals its important mental processes from its successor.[11] Furthermore, in the same vein of continuity, he saw the gap between civilized and primitive life as bridged by the mental experience of the child. The child, engaged early by magical beliefs, which are later modified, he took to be illustrative of the development of mankind from a so-called "primitive horde" to a complex society. Whether this continuity in mental life depended on some sort of transmitted collective unconscious which certain circumstances brought into functioning, or whether it depended upon what one generation fostered in the emotional life of the next, Freud left unclear. Group psychology is still conceived as Freud constructed it, within the strictly dynamic framework of the neuroses he described in the early 1920s.[12] As individual psychology has continued to be better understood through studies of ego functions, group psychology has persistently been extrapolated from it. The distinctions between them have become more blurred than sharpened.

Serious considerations important in the distinctions to be made between the psychology of the group and that of the individual have been neglected in favor of supposed similarities. It has resulted directly in disregarding the conspicuous fact that the more the individual conflicts are pressing, the less one is inclined to be part of a group. This is to say that the more the egocentricity of the neurotic rules, the less he is interested in, or affected by, a group. When we are deeply in love, or wholly absorbed in a neurotic conflict as for instance in hypochondria, we are little affected by a group. On the other hand, as Freud wrote, "It appears that where a powerful impetus has been given to group formation, neuroses may diminish and at all events temporarily disappear."[13] This usually overlooked observation by Freud in 1921, decades later, was amply confirmed by the gruesome conditions in the Nazi concentration camps. In those forcibly formed groups, its members herded together, the incidence of neurotic disorders significantly dropped.[14] Within a short time of release previous neurotic disorders often returned. Had Freud known of this sequel to his prognostications, he would scarcely have been surprised. He wrote that it was not in the least hard for him to discern that all the ties that bind people to mystico-religious or philosophico-religious sects and communities are expressions of what he called "crooked cures" of all sorts of neuroses. By this he meant that the course the cures took was a devious one but not that they were fraudulent or ineffective.

We now know the same crooked cures take place in groups bound together by horror, as in the ones which hope for salvation. Regardless of how a group is formed, whether voluntarily in the name of a cause, in the pursuit of a belief, or in search of redemption, or whether it is one forced by a hideous prison, evidently the so-called crooked cures occur. The fact that often the most seemingly intractable neurotic symptoms thus may be eliminated shows how effective a membership in a group can be. Only the narcissistic elements of a neurosis need to be amenable to modification for the possibility of the crooked cures to take place. In short, when we can relinquish our self-esteem sufficiently to join a group whose interests we share, we also may find a cure.

Membership, psychologically in any group, whether it is the first and simplest, the family, or the later more complex one, society, is determined by the extent that our narcissism allows us to yield a measure of our own needs for the aims of the others. This is to say, much as our grip on our egocentricity dictates the depth of our individual relationships, so too does it profoundly affect the extent of our commitment to a group. And whether our narcissism is transferred to another as love, or is displaced from the self to the group, the intimate role of aggression in relation to it remains. Hence, the importance of this association is not lost with membership in a group.

The psychology of the individual mind, with respect to narcissism, and that of the group, has one remarkable similarity. Narcissism, when injured, suffers no less in one than in the other. Restitution is always demanded. And whether by a group or by an individual, narcissism is redeemed through aggression. Danger or injury to the group's narcissism creates anxiety, and it may lead to all the various consequences we observe in individual behavior—in the extreme case, panic. What menaces narcissism excites aggression.

At no time is narcissism more exposed to injury than during childhood. As children, we are most dependent on others and experience our limitations so acutely that we are especially attentive to all discrepancies. Our natural wishes to reduce them may not seem to us at all inordinate. But with frequent disappointment and frustration, we begin to feel powers beyond ourselves. And while we are not without means of compensation by way of a belief in the influence of our wishes and the powers of magical thought, a sense of the precariousness of existence escapes few children for long. As we have described at length, the child's ordinary tendency to refer his experience to others is also reversed in referring the experience of others, or what may occur to other things and creatures, to himself. For instance, a broken arm of a doll or a broken piece of a toy, found in the course of a child's normal play, or as a result of his own mischief, may become objects which represent the hazards a child may anticipate for himself. Similarly, the loss of a pet or encountering a cripple on the street are experiences which a child normally will not fail to apply to himself. This characteristic creates a continuity between himself and the rest of the world. It becomes part of the entire process of self-reference. It also carries him into a social experience and, in a very direct sense, into an experience of the universe, and it brings the world into himself. What is more, it sets into motion a course of emotional reactions which, while relieving some of the burdensome conflicts, also creates new ones.

Identifying oneself with an aggressor is part of the process of self-reference. It becomes a means of overcoming the feeling of being helpless, weak and dependent by assuming the stature of strength. As Anna Freud wrote of a child's dilemma over his condition, "By impersonating the aggressor, assuming his attributes or imitating his aggression, the child transforms himself from the person threatened into one who makes the threat." [15] The process relates to overcoming not only anxiety about past experiences or wishes but the aim to succeed over anticipated future events as well. As a ceaselessly repeated unconsciously generated experience, it has a continuing profound effect. Not the least is taking on oneself the qualities of those responsible for one's upbringing. Thus Anna Freud said of a child with respect to his parents that when "making their characteristics and opinions his own, he is all the time providing material from which the superego may take shape." [16] The formation of conscience and identification with the aggressor become bonded early. (Only under special circumstances do they get separated.) Unwittingly, at one and the same time, we are fashioning within ourselves a self-governing agency opposed to aggression while we are striving to become just like those we perceive as powerful and endow with capabilities of effective aggression. A child is led into a predicament of his own making of having to disclaim that within him is a source of aggression at the very moment he wants to identify with an aggressor. To effect such a denial, a child normally projects his inner dangerous impulses onto others. The result is a world unconsciously seeming to become a darker, more hostile place. And, as we assign such aims or intentions to others, a further strengthening of our defenses is felt to be needed against the fantasied threats. Justification for violence emerges. Identification with the aggressor is enhanced. The timely connection of rewarding aggression as an aim with the development of conscience as a governor of aggression brings them together in easily excited conflict.

Freud first refers to identification with the aggressor briefly in *Beyond the Pleasure Principle*[17] as occurring in a young child he had observed. In the context of his remarks, it may well have been one of his grandchildren whom he observed as he was baby-sitting. It was this example which Anna Freud later elaborated on in her work on the development of the ego. Actually, Freud uncovered this phenomenon years before—in the case of the Wolf Man. At the time, however, it was evident that Freud's attention was on showing the formation of an obsessional neurosis founded on repressed infantile sexual conflicts, and he therefore neglected the clinical material present on identification with the aggressor.

In a previous chapter, I called attention to Freud's report of the Wolf Man,[18] who as a small child delighted in tormenting beetles, destroying other insects, and watching horses being beaten. The cruelties he took pleasure in turned later into terrible anxiety attacks over fears for his own safety. First the boy was the aggressor and tormentor. Then he became the victim. We know from our experience with similar cases that he must have first thought himself a victim (most conspicuously he was, in fact, his sister's prey; she terrorized him). Of course, there were other sources which would feed fears of being a victim or helpless. He overcame his fears of his sister by himself becoming aggressive. He showed he had at least the usual need of a child to overcome his fears of being attacked and humiliated by himself becoming violent.

The Freuds saw identification with the aggressor as a reaction or defense against the anxiety produced by the role of passive victim. It is indeed a great source of self-concern to be attacked or even to expect it. To judge from the manifest aggression which issues in one's own defense, it is an intolerable condition. Doing to others or wishing to do to them what was done to oneself, or was feared, gives needed relief. Analysts have reasoned further that in the retaliation, satisfaction is gained by allowing a respite from the anxiety-provoking sexual passivity. In effect, however, such arguments merely beg the question. When we find that to become the aggressor relieves ignominy, satisfies the self, and thus restores self-esteem, the importance of the experience is immense. It involves the recovery from narcissistic injury. Hence, what may be gained through one's aggression is no mere change from passivity to effective action.

There is in fact no demonstrable satisfaction in simply being aggressive. The theory which argues for it, a remnant of social Darwinism, fails to account for the dynamics of ego psychology. Where the Freuds demonstrated aggression was in the service of the ego, i.e. it rehabilitated the self from ignominy, they stopped short of the conclusion that their discovery showed aggression was a means to an end—the security of the self; it removes the threat to narcissism.

This is not to say that passivity is without its compensations. The well-known child's fantasy, to be protected, prized and rewarded, without either effort or demand, or the "adult" fantasy that an ambition to be powerful may be realized through wishes, or by way of simply playing a role, are all manifest expressions of passivity. The adolescent who dreams of greatness thrust upon him and who longs for a holiday from the burden of effort and frustration which his vaulting aspirations have conjured up for him is as passive as the younger child who waits to be served his desires through daydreams. The underlying force in all such expectations is held in the child's narcissistic self, which resists compromise with regard to the needs of another. Whether passivity is a source of pleasure or one of anxiety depends upon its meaning to the self. The notion that sexual passivity is merely the opposite of sexual aggression seems more the result of a traditionally unexamined assumption than a theory founded on searching study.

Before the threats of injury to our narcissism may be relieved, or its recovery accomplished through calling on aggression, two of the principal characteristics of narcissism appear: where it has been extended to another it must be retracted, and the ensuing aggression must be justified. This has been amply demonstrated. For instance, we found little Hans turning to act like the very horse he feared, belittling his father by biting his hand in a childish attempt to elevate himself from ignominy; Schreber's imagined humiliation drove him to withdraw into delusions of grandeur, to attack and devalue those whom he previously loved. Medea, Achilles, Othello, the amnesiac man, the woman who endured nightmares most of her life, and others cited here, have in common that each suffered a loss of self-esteem at the hands of another. The greater-than-life dramatic heroes or the contemporary subjects we have observed, whether adults or children, in the name of defending the self, all must find justification for violence. Moreover, the need to justify one's aggression appears far sooner than a strict conscience develops. We are lead, therefore, to look for some critical element present and active very early in life.

From our very earliest years, the inescapable dependence upon others and the accommodation required by ordinary circumstances unobtrusively convey to us that existence is conditional. We learn, when remarkably young, that our needs and aims may not be exclusively enjoyed, and moreover that we are obliged for our own sake to become social creatures. Ample evidence quickly mounts that our self-seeking, to be realized beyond fantasy or wishes, must yield to social demands. Otherwise, we risk an intolerable isolation.

To become a member of a group, as in the development of a relationship, we soon learn as children that it is possible only through some self-denial. As we strike the bargain, our compensation is to be ourselves valued. The most secure condition we achieve is to know we value or love another, or serve an ideal, or even something which represents it; then we are made doubly secure by the value conferred in turn on us. (To be valued without having earned it only satisfies a child's vanity. It also raises a number of ineradicable doubts.)

The transfer of our narcissism to value others is not a fixed condition. It has an ebb and flow because both circumstance and conflict are fluid; the transaction in narcissism must be frequently renegotiated. Restoring narcissism gives aggression tasks other than violence, tasks of extending social achievement as well as pursuing creative goals. The conventional notion of a human "appetite" for aggression has obscured the fact that it is narcissism which is insatiable. To satisfy *its* needs aggression is commissioned. It is in the service of the self that aggression has its natural task. Is aggression independent of narcissism; does it function apart from self-serving? And is narcissism without social importance? We have found aggression is only exceptionally dissociated from self-assessment. And when narcissism is so self-contained that its social elements are lacking, the condition approaches clinical autism.

It has long been assumed that our virulent conduct in groups toward "outsiders" is an activation of dormant vestigial aggression left over from some past and more primitive age.

The modern basis for such prevailing assumptions is taken largely from the fact that the history of mankind seems to be endlessly occupied with wars. An added explanation for our violence among ourselves derives from a loosely conceived social Darwinism. It is supposed that we, like all creatures, are engaged in an effort to survive, and that our destructiveness to each other and our social violence are evidence of the struggle to exist. That the frequent effort to appeal to conscience as a deterrent to armed conflict always fails is cited to prove the case. The fact that groups are susceptible to suggestion, that their members imitate one another in acting ferociously and impulsively, tolerating little delay, and that they carry some sense of omnipotence yet submit to orders and give up freedom to a fatherlike leader figure encouraged Freud and many others since his time to see in the psychology of groups parallels to the behavior of children and to the conduct of so-called primitives.[19]

The assumption is that there is an instinctual aggressive force inseparable from sexuality which is carried over from the psychology of the individual and is an active force in the mentality of the group as well. The further assumption is that the normal individual deterrents to violence, brutishness and cruelty somehow in the company of a group are removed, allowing some store of aggression to be drawn on and the supposed appetite for violence to be appeased. Since membership in a group, however, may also bring out, with no less fervor, the pursuit of the highest achievements, great sacrifice to others, and devotion to an ideal, it is suggested here that aggression is more a means to an end than an inarticulate drive to destructiveness. However, as there is little in psychoanalytic literature of individual psychology to suggest that aggression is other than an instinct, no different consideration is therefore given it when aggression is viewed in the psychology of groups.

There are two instances in which we are prone to the most violent aggression. Neither one is without significance in regard to the self. Toward those whom we once loved—"there is no rage like love to hate turned." And, toward those to whom ordinarily we are indifferent, that is, the strangers, aliens and foreigners on whom we have placed little value, we can mount boundless attacks.

Our social violence plainly shows how few limits there may be to destroying others. They are the ones with whom we are little identified or have repudiated some previously held identification and wish not to be connected with. We make them targets of our common brutal destructiveness. What provocations, conditions or circumstances loosen our violence is a minor consideration compared to the major fact that the deterrent to violence is lacking. As we have seen at length here, we defend that which we value, and are free to attack whatever we exclude from our narcissism. "Alien" groups threaten us. Our natural childish tendency is to regard ourselves as "chosen." The comfort we take in this exclusiveness is a barrier against the discomforts or the fears of the differences which exist between groups, the strangeness of an outsider which requires such an unfathomed accommodation. To relinquish the comfort of being chosen is to forego an identity tightly held in the face of the unpredictable and hence the dreaded.

It appears to be axiomatic that the militant aims of groups far exceed, as a rule, those of their individual members. Even groups in the narcissistic defense of their professed peaceful goals only exceptionally fail to become aggressive. Gandhi's Satyagrahas made passive resistance and noncooperation into a powerful, political aggressive instrument. They are therefore no exception. Moreover, so long as there are groups, there will be aliens, strangers and foreigners. And as outsiders to be reckoned with, they represent the uncertain, the unknown.

Because the psychology of groups and individuals are in some respects similar, the important distinctions between them frequently get lost. One essential difference is nowhere more clearly illustrated than in the readiness of a group to invest its interests in a leader, a cause or a purpose far more quickly than an individual falls in love or gets devoted to a goal in work. Psychoanalytically speaking, the narcissism of a group quickly attaches to a choice. However, a group also has a proclivity, not usual among individuals, to rapidly withdraw its commitment. This makes the relations of a group with others exceedingly labile, and hence potentially to be feared. Without an investment, the narcissism of a group is without its commitments, and hence the deterrent to violence and destructiveness is weak. Action is prompted then by the least provocation. Where the narcissism of a group is withdrawn, leaders are readily deposed and causes easily abandoned. Popular government is probably the best example and may owe much of its instability to the fact that the favor of the crowd is naturally fickle. The reverse is no less true. The vulnerable narcissism of the masses who suffer ignominy is no less prone to be pandered to by leaders who offer it relief; for example, we may think of Germany during the Third Reich when loyalty was solicited in such a manner.

The intensity of the self-interest of a group is characteristically accompanied by a strong resistance or reluctance to extend a genuine interest to others. The group may perform generous services but its loyalty is neither extended nor shared. The more firm the group's solidity, the more its exclusiveness is supported, and a corresponding intensity of hatred develops toward those who are outsiders. As self-interest is promoted, the lack of investment in those outside gets further justified, and the group may become increasingly menacing to the foreigner. Moreover, as its focus is on self-interest, the greater does it anticipate the hostility of those alienated. The similarity to individual psychology is close here. Justification for hostility is still necessary. The claim is of being or fearing to be the victim of aliens.

In defense of such assertions, the notorious highly nationalistic conduct of Germans during the regime of the Third Reich is remarkably similar to the behavior of the Yanamamo Indians who are odiously treacherous to anyone outside their exclusive band. An example of our own corresponding domestic fears of aliens, from whom we ourselves were newly descended, has gripped us for more than half a century. Whether we were ever actually or seriously menaced by a conspiracy which could threaten to subvert our social structure, we shall probably never learn. But the fears of such alien action have been kept alive beginning with the long since discredited Palmer raids of the 1920s. Foreign influence, always dreaded and depicted as sinister, in our case coincided with our becoming politically isolated and hostile.

The fierce loyalties created within groups may become powerful investments of commitment. They represent the exaggerated value placed on one another comparable only to being in love. We see countless examples of this among troops waging war, or comrades in pursuit of a shared adventure, in the engagement of partners in an political movement. All are bound to their purpose emotionally by enterprise, in the religiosity of a congregation, or in the fervor of a their narcissism invested in each other within the group. Such unions leave little to invest in those outside. Any condition which resists such investment correspondingly weakens the group and earns its hostility. By contrast, however, the present-day popular gathering of young people into communes, or banding together in some other fashion, yield groups which characteristically have a short life expectancy. They form new associations which they readily dissolve to regroup with others. The emotional commitment of young people to such fluid groups is typically weak. They have a far stronger commitment to themselves; the narcissism of young people, especially throughout adolescence into young adult life, is a notoriously outstanding quality. Notwithstanding their protestations of loyalty and their devotion to others and to the highest ideals for which they are often capable of making great sacrifices, their apparent ease in abandoning relationships and causes and developing others is a clear indication of the difficulty of sustaining a commitment at a time when narcissistic needs for the self are overriding. The extent and nature of their sexual experience, the dropping of conscious inhibitions, proves no index of intimacy. On the contrary, the relative ease with which avowed intimate relationships are begun and terminated is more an indication of their having shallow emotional roots. The emphasis is on the need for a sense of individuality, and is a reaction to a fear of its loss. This explains the commonplace instability of such groups.*

Freud identified the "group mind" with the minds of primitive people, neurotics and children. He saw governing similarities in them. He likened them to a herd which, as he put it, "could never live without a master. It has such a thirst for obedience that it submits instinctively to anyone who appoints himself its master." [20] These remarks which appeared about a decade after his much criticized *Totem and Taboo*[21] show that he still held to his previous conjecture about the human family. It was that "the primitive form of human society was that of a horde ruled over despotically by a powerful male." [22] This was Darwin's supposition which Freud held to be illuminating and on which he conceived the basis of group psychology. The leader or chief had the mentality of a tyrannical father. And "his sexual jealousy and intolerance became in the last resort the causes of group psychology." [23]

Freud's conjectures about the social organization of prehistoric peoples provoked much discussion and he fully earned some of the criticism he received. His notions about the society of primitive man were naïvely deduced. He saw no gap between the social organization of the highest apes and primitive man, and a continuity of development to ourselves. Freud relied heavily, it seems, on the writings of J. G. Frazer's authoritative Victorian scholarly armchair anthropology. He refers to him often and at length in *Totem and Taboo* and as well in "Group Psychology." Frazer was himself a heavy contributor to social Darwinism. The familiar theme of the Old Testament, of a vengeful God demanding obedience embodied in the leader of His people, Moses, had an especially strong, obvious

* Paradoxically, many who join groups and yet are unable to yield a measure of their individual narcissism have high expectations of finding the rewarding relationships for which they search. They are bound for disappointment. However, they are dimly aware that their own inordinate needs cannot be fulfilled, and this frustration is felt as hostility toward an unrewarding environment. The fact is that narcissistic expectations have become narcissistic *injuries* and, predictably, aggression ensues. In such group relationships, the commonly observed display of friendliness, intimacy, and even a protesting concern for others, is contingent on receiving signs of a response of amicability. Lacking such assurances, the readiness to anticipate hostility quickly brings *all* relations into a threatening orbit, and defenses become imperative. A paranoidlike reaction of the group is a common one, and a paranoid state of clinical proportions precipitated in some individuals is not rare. This may further excite the group into paranoid conduct which parallels some of the individual psychotic reactions.

appeal to Freud. Moreover, it added another facet upon which to model group psychology. These were powerful influences. In some respects they led Freud astray. He wrote that "the father of the primal horde was free. . . . his intellectual acts were strong and independent. . . . his will needed no reinforcement." [24] Freud saw him as having few ties, loving no one but himself, and giving up only what it was necessary to relinquish. When he considered these characteristics as forcing others into a group, he meant that as the dominant male, the father forced the brothers into a band. And, as a group, they attacked his supremacy and were themselves thus freed.

It is a wry twist that in the last two generations so much scoffing at Freud correctly focused on his fanciful notions and constructions of the social mentality of primitive man. Yet, scientific argument continues to follow the Darwinian assumption implicit in Freud's reasoning. Notable examples are provided by eminent laboratory researchers such as H. Harlow and B. F. Skinner. Each is famous for his work with experimental conditioning of animals. From their studies of animal behavior, they assert that the importance of their discoveries lies beyond the characteristics of the creatures with which they have experimented; our understanding of the social behavior of man is supposedly furthered. In short, their belief holds that a continuity exists in the behavior of animals to the social conduct of men. However, as I have demonstrated in Chapter III, we are as deceived in applying social motives to animals as Freud was to think our social organization showed a descent from them. We can demonstrate neither a social nor a psychological continuity between animals and men.

On another level, many current scientific ideas of group psychology, although conceived along lines which ostensibly are opposed to conventional Freudian concepts, in actuality often tend to conform to them. Political scientists such as Karl M. Deutsch, for example, in presenting views of international relations in the terminology of cybernetics, systems analysis and game theory, on the one hand brings the relations between nations to conform to abstract principles of individual psychology. And, on the other, he describes the goals of desirable compatibility between states as though they were marital partners having expectations and rewards in regard to one another, and that their satisfactory relations depended upon mutual regard and the support of an acceptable self-image. These are homilies of family life projected on an international scale, and in the Esperanto of laboratory language. Their translation reveals that Deutsch is saying conflicts relating to self-esteem probably have a critical role in international relations.[25] In another example, we find that the distinguished sociologist, Z. Barbu, discusses the phenomenon of aggression in society as a "release of repressed psychic energy characteristic of periods of social organization." [26] He seems unaware that he is employing an early Freudian theory of aggression when he argues that violence issues from repression when given the right conditions.

Study shows that a child's developing identification with an aggressor is an essential and undoubtedly universal process. Whether it is promoted as in Spartan or other cultures given to extolling violence, or correspondingly is retarded in the least belligerent societies, identifying with the aggressor serves as a far greater influence toward making us dangerous than the loudest exhortation to be destructive.

While the process of identifying with the aggressor commences in early childhood, it is not thereafter abandoned, although the form it takes may alter with sophistication. What may once have been naïve, childish behavior may become highly elaborated and modified into common social forms and thus be associated with group psychology. For example, the wide enthusiasm for blood sports and the vast audiences who enjoy witnessing violent games, or the popularity political patriots relish, are expressions of genuine delight afforded masses of people. The vicarious participation is a social form of narcissistic excitement. These aggressive contests would draw no crowds were they not so heavily endowed with the trappings associated with winning self-esteem, the exhibition of prowess and skill, and holding the favor of one's countrymen.

A remarkably wide variety of social engineers such as William James[27] the psychologist, Walter Cannon[28] the physiologist, more recently, Konrad Lorenz[29] the ethologist, and many others less distinguished, have contributed to keeping alive the serious belief that international rivalries might be significantly reduced, if not solved, by games. They would be held on neutral ground where representatives of nations would oppose one another. And in such contests, presumably the "moral equivalent of war," a new reign of peace between nations would be realized.

The assumption that there is a pool of such elements in us which is ready to pour out with the removal of a barrier explains bloodletting better than it does the nature of human conflicts and their expression.

The most elegant exposition aimed against man's worst group

violence, war, is William James', which he delivered before publication as lectures in 1901–1902. Like Hesiod, millennia before him, James warns against the worship of material luxury and the Sybaritic indulgence of the flesh as risking a certain "trashiness of the fibre." He asked was there not some reason to renovate and revise ascetic discipline. One could take the example, he said, set by the incredible efforts war and adventure demanded, which assuredly keep all who engage in them from treating themselves too tenderly. Customary inhibitions are annulled, wrote James, new energy is set free, and "life seems cast upon a higher plane of power." [30] It entails, he observed, the human acceptance of privation, hardship and self-abnegation, and having at times a contempt for one's comrades, for the enemy, and above all for one's own person. Weaned thus from the tenderness toward one's precious self, he wrote, a man "may easily develop into a monster of insensibility." [31] He noted that throughout history we have seen in groups like the army, and often in religious congregations as well, zealots with a cause whose barbaric tendencies thus loosened were "congruous with ordinary human nature." [32]

James, like many "social engineers" before him and since, seriously imagined that a cure for mankind's destructiveness would be found in some psychologically predetermined social scheme. An elite shepherding the masses would guide them to relief from the violence they practice on each other. If such proposals seem somewhat vague and naïve in their Utopian applicability, or arrogant in their presumptions, they do not lack for ingenuity.

One of the more recent examples—a dream fully modern in concept—is the "Era of Psychotechnology" proposed by Kenneth Clark in his presidential address to the American Psychological Association in 1971.[33]

Like James, Clark appears to regard human endeavor as motivated by dangerous and corrupting aggressive appetites. From such reasoning, it follows that aggression needs both direction and restraints. Further, in this atomic age, no time is to be lost, and therefore "the psychological and social sciences must enable us to control the animalistic, barbaric, and primitive propensities in man." This "redirecting of power . . . must be seen as a responsibility and goal of science and psychotechnology." We cannot afford the time or the margin of error inherent in the humanist approach with its "unpredictable results." Clark believes that direct "psychotechnological" intervention can, within a few years, remove the basis for wars. He claims to offer a "scientific" basis for James' philosophical wish for a moral equivalent to war. Of course, our control must be "humane," there is a "moral responsibility" on the part of the scientist—and here we have again the notion of an elite, this time laboratory technicians using their skills "affirmatively, wisely, and with compassion."

Neither Clark, nor James, nor even Freud appear to have grasped the significance of the ordinary human readiness to revoke an attachment, that to terminate an intimate relationship in hate is not to be understood simply as antisocial and menacing. The expectation that controlling aggression will spare men from destroying each other overlooks, as it suspends belief in, the conflicts which are expressed in violence and hostility.

Parallels between individual psychology and family life, group experiences and the nature of international relations, are endlessly drawn. One theme which continues to take shape is that with particular provocation, especially frustration, man's inherent aggression predictably escapes restraints. It is an idea associated with the repeated assertion that as society has become progressively more organized, i.e. urban, man has correspondingly heightened and extended his destructiveness. It is as though the instrument of his violence, his immensely developed fire power, is an index of his aggressiveness. This credulous calumny of civilization is familiar and, of course, has its roots in a belief in paradise. That we are being corrupted by civilization to become destructive as we never previously were, and that we once lived in harmony with nature, remains a popular concept.

Nearly forty years ago, H. G. Wells made remarks that are especially relevant to these beliefs. He said, "Man is still what he was. Invincibly bestial, envious, malicious, greedy. Man, Sir, unmasked and disillusioned, is the same fearing, snarling, fighting beast he was a hundred thousand years ago. These are no metaphors, Sir. What I tell you is the monstrous reality." [34] Regardless of the refinements and raiments man may have acquired in the course of his long history, it appears that rather than be concerned here with the familiar vicissitudes of his development, we might consider what is least altered. The vulnerability to injury of his narcissism has shown no change.

With the natural and inevitable transfer of his narcissism to another, to his family, to a group, or to his race or nation, man has always given, so to speak, a piece of himself. He is thus identified with each one with whom he has this connection. Unwittingly, he is tightly committed to their defense, to protect his investment and hence himself. It is his narcissism which is the greatest source of his vulnerability.

It may seem a small gap to be bridged from the natural wish to be favored to its conversion that one is among the "chosen." No other claim we may make has greater importance psychologically with direct social consequences of sweeping significance: all peoples inquire as to their origins and without exception the question finds an identical answer—each makes the independent claim that they are the "chosen." In the folklore of each people, some higher power has conferred on them their uniqueness. Their destiny is to preserve it.

For our purposes, the emotional importance of the assertion of being an exclusive breed is that it creates an Ishmael. In short, if there are to be the "chosen," there must be the others, the rejected, the unclean, the untouchable, the disbelievers and hence the undesirable. They are also the strange ones, the unfamiliar, and those certain to be the proper objects on whom to vent one's anxiety. Moreover, as we all question fate and suffer the sense of our ignominy, we must master our condition. However, it is not simply a matter of acquiring skills. Performing and learning is insufficient. The problem is actually a social one. Its solution lies in the relationships we form rather than in the competence we may achieve.

The role of narcissism in the group is not formally declared. But it is embodied in some particular egocentricity which gives the group its claim to distinction. Whatever threatens this particular quality, usually expressed as the aims of the group, strikes at its narcissism. The injury will extend to its members. The defense mobilizes all the characteristics of an embattled narcissism. Chief among them is a readiness to violence. Thus, hostility to outsiders is potentially, if not actually, a matter of course. Hence the persecution of heretics or dissidents, the finding of scapegoats, is without end. They are pursuits which express a group's defense of its particular beliefs. No doubt many diverse factors mobilize groups into violence. But none is so unifying or so common as its narcissism to be defended. And none is so vehement.

The outstanding distinction between the violence a group carries to its victims and the equally well-known destructiveness individuals perpetrate on each other is the remarkable indifference groups may have toward their victims. The Spanish Inquisition had no more compassion for heretics than Muslims for Hindus, Nazi for Jews, or the white man in America for the Indians. Groups are defended institutions. They get from this their justification for violence, hate and destructiveness. It spares the conflicts its members, if similarly engaged alone, might suffer. History provides us with an endless parade of individuals agonized by the plight of victims and often going to heroic lengths toward their rescue. In this we can see a savior is identified with whom he would deliver. However, groups are conspicuously not identified with their victims; in short, because they are not "people."

From a journalist's diary of our present conflict in Vietnam, an entry of a conversation with an American soldier in the ranks tells: "I learned how to take my weapon apart and put it together again, and how to shoot, but no one ever told me a thing about having to love people who look different from us and who've got an ideological orientation that's about a hundred and eighty degrees different from us. We don't understand what they're thinking. When we got here, we landed on a different planet. . . . Even when a Vietnamese guy speaks perfect English, *I* don't know what the hell he's talking about. . . . The trouble is, no one sees the Vietnamese as people. They're not people. Therefore, it doesn't matter what you do to them. . . . Those driven from their homes, which we call 'hootches,' were simply listed as 'scattered.' . . . And when they were killed, we merely applied the new arithmetic to them known as 'body count.' A special designation was given to those who furnish a target from the air. The dead are listed as 'K.B.A.s' [Killed By Air]." [35]

The great historian, Samuel Eliot Morison, recently wrote about the early explorations leading to the European discovery of America. The expeditions of adventurous Norsemen brought them into the first contact of Europeans with American aborigines whom they promptly designated as "Skrellings." It is a word of contempt meaning "barbarians," "weaklings" or perhaps even "pygmies." And inasmuch as they were regarded as of lesser stock, Morison wrote, they were treated as inferiors; in some instances, wantonly killed.[36] Can we distinguish the motives for these attacks from what another historian, Tacitus, wrote about the Parthians, who had requested and received a king from Rome? "Though he was a member of their royal house, they despised him as a foreigner." This was Vonones I. "He was a king tainted with enemy customs. . . . Their scorn was intensified because their national habits were alien to Vonones. Moreover, he was laughed at because his entourage was Greek." [37] What distance is there, bridging millennia, between the expressed sentiments of the

ancient Parthians for Greeks, Norsemen for aborigines, and a xeno-
phobia which is sufficiently powerful to persuade a people to extermi-
nate some of its own citizens by declaring them aliens?

From these varied examples a plain disclosure appears. It is that
hostility, free of the entangling web of conflicts which we individually
spin with our intimates, becomes, in the group, free of restraint. It
is not that conscience is dismissed, or that it is somehow suspended
or set aside. Rather, it does not come into question. The basis for
this has been misunderstood. The effort to shed light on the virtually
limitless violence that is pursued by groups has led chiefly to observations about aggression itself and the varieties of circumstances
which may evoke it. What needs to be made absolutely plain is that
our essential need for a social existence calls on our narcissism to
yield. This promotes the psychology of being "chosen." Therefore,
the greatest menace to man, it seems, is not from aggression, but
from his narcissism.

Jonathan Swift, in *Gulliver's Travels,* gave the name of Yahoo to
creatures who hated one another more than they did any different
species. Gulliver noted that Yahoos were extraordinarily like mankind. They were selfish and fought one another for possessions; and,
when not engaged in fighting enemies, they resorted to civil wars.
Moreover, he noted that they were the most menacing when their
pretences to reason were distorted by their vices. Then they were
relentlessly brutal toward one another, and they were most especially
vile when they were massed together in some pursuit which they
claimed to be just. In the last analysis, perhaps Swift, more correctly
than Freud, spoke for us all when he said that the habit of claiming
"reason in the common offices of life" to justify a faculty such as
vanity "might be worse than brutality itself." [38]

Chapter References

I. The Defended Self

1. Gregory Rochlin, *Griefs and Discontents* (Boston: Little, Brown, 1965), pp. 2–4, 363–387.

2. Ibid., pp. 63–120.

3. Sigmund Freud, "On Transcience (1915)," in *Standard Edition of the Complete Psychological Works of Sigmund Freud,* 24 vols., ed. by James Strachey (London: Hogarth Press, 1957), XIV, 305.

4. Ibid., p. 82.

5. Ibid.

6. Annie Reich, "Narcissistic Object Choice in Women," in *J. Am. Psychoanal. Assoc.,* 1 (1953), 22–44; R. Fleiss, "Problems of Identity," Scientific Proceedings, in *J. Am. Psychoanal. Assoc.,* 1 (1953), 538–549; Erik H. Erikson, "Problem of Ego Identity," in *J. Am. Psychoanal. Assoc.,* 5 (1957), 556–563; R. Bak, "Aggression and Symptom Formation," in *J. Am. Psychoanal. Assoc.,* 9 (1960), 585–592; M. Gittelson, "Narcissism," Scientific Proceedings, in *J. Am. Psychoanal. Assoc.,* 10 (1962), 593–605; Grete Bibring, "Some Considerations Regarding the Ego Ideal in the Psychoanalytic Process," in *J. Am. Psychoanal. Assoc.,* 12 (1964), 512–516; Ives Hendrick, "Narcissism and the Pre-puberty Ego Ideal," in *J. Am. Psychoanal. Assoc.,* 12 (1964), 522–528; John M. Murray, "Narcissism and the Ego Ideal," in *J. Am. Psychoanal. Assoc.,* 12 (1964), 477–511; Heinz Kohut, "Forms and Transformations of Narcissism," in *J. Am. Psychoanal. Assoc.,* 14 (1966), 243–272.

7. Freud, ed. note to "On Narcissism: an Introduction (1914)," in *Standard Edition,* XIV (1957), 70.

8. Rochlin, *Griefs and Discontents,* pp. 363–386.

9. Charles Darwin, *The Expression of the Emotions in Man and Animals* (New York: Philosophical Library, 1955), pp. 80–81.

10. Rochlin, *Griefs and Discontents,* pp. 321–361.

11. Freud, *An Outline of Psychoanalysis* (New York: Norton, 1949), p. 20.

12. Freud, "Anxiety and Instinctual Life (1932)," in *Standard Edition,* XXII (1964), 95.

13. Ibid., pp. 103–104.

14. Ernest Jones, *The Life and Work of Sigmund Freud,* 3 vols. (New York: Basic Books, 1953–1957), III, app. A, 464–465.

15. Karl Abraham, *Selected Papers on Psychoanalysis* (London: Hogarth Press, 1942), 370–501.

16. Helene Deutsch, *Psychoanalysis of the Neuroses* (London: Hogarth Press, 1932), 113–230.

17. Freud, "Civilization and Its Discontents (1930)," in *Standard Edition,* XXI (1961), 62n.

18. Edward Bibring, "The Development and Problems of the Theory of the Instincts," in *Int. J. Psychoanal.,* XX (1941), pt. II, 102–131.

19. Freud, "The Ego and the Id (1923)," in *Standard Edition,* XIX (1961), 40.

20. Ibid., p. 46.

21. Ibid., pp. 46–47.

22. Ibid.

23. Norman O. Brown, *Life Against Death* (Middletown, Conn.: Wesleyan University Press, 1959).

24. Freud, "On the Economic Problems of Masochism (1924)," in *Standard Edition,* XIX (1961), 165.

25. Ibid.

26. Ibid., p. 170.

27. Darwin, *Expression of Emotions,* p. 244.

28. Walter B. Cannon, *Bodily Changes in Pain, Hunger, Fear and Rage* (New York: D. Appleton, 1929).

29. Konrad Lorenz, *On Aggression* (New York: Harcourt, Brace and World, 1966); Erik H. Erikson, "Psychoanalysis and Ongoing History: Problems of Identity, Hatred and Nonviolence," in *Am. J. Psychiatry,* CXXII (September 1965), 241–250; Anthony Storr, *Human Aggression* (New York: Atheneum, 1968).

II.　Aggression: *Modus Vivendi*

1. Sigmund Freud, "A Phobia in a Five-Year-Old Boy (1909)," in *Standard Edition of the Complete Psychological Works of Sigmund Freud,* 24 vols., ed. by James Strachey (London: Hogarth Press, 1955), X, 147.

2. Ibid., p. 117.

3. Ibid., p. 142.

4. Ibid., p. 22.

5. L. Jessner, G. E. Blom, and S. Waldfogel, "Emotional Implications of Tonsillectomy and Adenoidectomy of Children," in *Psychoanal. Study Child* (New York: International Universities Press, 1952), VII, 126–169.

6. Freud, "A Phobia in a Five-Year-Old Boy (1909)," p. 110.

7. Ibid.

8. Ibid.

9. Ibid.

10. Ibid.

11. Ibid., p. 117.

12. Ibid., p. 111.

13. Freud, "The Dissolution of the Oedipus Complex (1924)," in *Standard Edition,* XIX (1961), 173.

14. Ibid., p. 174.

15. Ibid., p. 173.

16. Ibid.

17. Freud, "Inhibitions, Symptoms and Anxiety (1926)," in *Standard Edition,* XX (1959), 108–109.

18. Freud, "A Phobia in a Five-Year-Old Boy (1909)," p. 139.

19. Ibid.

20. Ibid., p. 136.

21. Ibid., p. 140.

22. Ibid.

23. Ibid., p. 39.

24. Ibid., p. 52.

25. Gregory Rochlin, *Griefs and Discontents* (Boston: Little, Brown, 1965), pp. 237–240.

26. Ibid., pp. 63–120.

27. Helene Deutsch, *Neuroses and Character Types* (New York: International Universities Press, 1965), p. 263.

28. Ibid., p. 264.

29. Ibid., p. 280.

30. Freud, "Thoughts for the Times on War and Death (1915)," in *Standard Edition,* XIV (1957), 283–284.

31. Ibid., p. 283.

III. The Darwinian Legacy

1. Edwin G. Boring, *A History of Experimental Psychology,* 2nd ed. (New York: Appleton-Century-Crofts, 1950).

2. Ibid., pp. 471–472.

3. Ibid., p. 506.

4. P. B. Dews and W. H. Morse, "Some Observations on an Operant in Human Subjects," in *J. Exp. Anal. Behav.,* I (1958), 359–364; E. Silber and J. S. Tippett, "Self-Esteem: Clinical Assessment and Measurement Validation," in *Psychological Reports,* XVI (1965), Monograph Supplement No. 4; N. N. Azim, R. R. Hutchinson and D. F. Hake, "Extinction-Induced Aggression," in *J. Exp. Anal. Behav.,* IX (1966), 191–204.

5. Boring, *History of Experimental Psychology,* p. 430.

6. Boring, *History, Psychology and Science: Selected Papers,* ed. by Robert Watson and Donald Campbell (New York: Wiley, 1963), p. 176.

7. Harry F. Harlow, "The Nature of Love," in *American Psychologist,* XIII (December 1958), 673–685.

8. Ibid., p. 647.

9. Harlow and Robert R. Zimmerman, *Proceedings of the American Philosophical Society,* CII (October 1958), 501.

10. Jean Piaget, *Play, Dreams and Imitation in Childhood* (London: Routledge and Kegan Paul, 1962), p. 185.

11. G. S. Goldstein, "Load Variables in Information Processing," in *Psychological Record,* XX, No. 2 (1970), 235–242; W. P. Banks, "Signal Detection Theory and Human Memory," in *Psychological Bulletin,* LXXIV (August 1970), 81–99.

12. Isaiah Berlin, *Four Essays on Liberty* (London: Oxford University Press, 1969), p. xxvi.

13. Boring, *History, Psychology and Science,* pp. 92–107.

14. Henry Murray, "Psychology and the University," in *Archives of Neurology and Psychology,* CXXXIV (1935), 805.

15. Paul F. Lazarsfeld, "Evidence and Inference in Social Research," in *Daedalus,* LXXVII (Fall 1958), 99–130.

16. Raymond B. Cattell, "Personality Theory Growing from Multivariable Quantitative Research," in *Psychology: A Study of a Science,* ed. by Sigmund Koch (New York: McGraw-Hill, 1959), pp. 257–327.

17. Talcott Parsons, "Psychological Theory in Terms of a Theory of Action," in *Psychology: A Study of a Science,* pp. 612–711.

18. David Rapaport, "The Structure of Psychoanalytic Theory," in *Psychology: A Study of a Science,* p. 82.

19. Silber and Tippett, "Self-Esteem: Clinical Assessment and Measurement Validation," in *Psychological Reports,* XVI.

20. H. Gastaut and R. Broughton, "A Clinical and Polygraph Study of Episodic Phenomena During Sleep," in *Recent Advances in Biological Psychiatry,* 7 (New York: 1965).

21. Konrad Lorenz, *On Aggression* (New York: Harcourt, Brace and World, 1966); Anthony Storr, *Human Aggression* (New York: Atheneum, 1968); *The Natural History of Aggression,* ed. by J. D. Carthy and F. J. Ebling (London and New York: Academic Press, 1964).

22. Peter H. Wolff, *The Developmental Psychologies of Jean Piaget and Psychoanalysis,* Psychological Issues Monograph No. 5 (New York: International Universities Press, 1960), pp. 110–111.

23. Sigmund Freud, "A Difficulty in the Path of Psycho-analysis (1917)," in *Standard Edition of the Complete Psychological Works of Sigmund Freud,* 24 vols., ed. by James Strachey (London: Hogarth Press, 1955), XVII, 141.

24. Ibid., p. 143.

25. Ibid., p. 141.

26. Ibid., p. 143.

27. Gregory Rochlin, *Griefs and Discontents* (Boston: Little, Brown, 1965), pp. 121–164.

28. Lorenz, *On Aggression,* pp. 165–219.

29. Freud, "On Narcissism: an Introduction (1914)," in *Standard Edition,* XIV (1957), 75–100.

30. D. I. Wallis, "Aggression in Social Insects," in *Natural History of Aggression,* pp. 15–22.

31. Charles Darwin, "A Biographical Sketch of an Infant," in *Mind,* II (July 1877), 286–294.

32. William Kessen, *The Child* (New York: Wiley, 1965), p. 115.

33. John Bowlby, "Ethology and the Development of Object Relations," Symposium on Psycho-analysis and Ethology, in *Int. J. Psychoanal.,* XLI (July–October 1960), 313.

34. Harlow and Zimmerman, *Proceedings of the American Philosophical Society,* CII (October 1958), 501.

35. Bowlby, *Attachment* (New York: Basic Books, 1969).

36. Ibid., p. 20.

37. Bruno Bettelheim, *The Empty Fortress* (New York: The Free Press, 1967).

38. Ibid., pp. 39–49.

39. Freud, "From the History of an Infantile Neurosis (1918)," in *Standard Edition,* XVII (1955), 3–122.

40. Ibid., p. 16.

41. Ibid., p. 59.

42. For a contemporary fantasy representation of this connection between animal, aggressive and "oral" themes, see Maurice Sendak, *Higglety Pigglety Pop! or There Must Be More to Life* (New York: Harper and Row, 1967), and his *Where the Wild Things Are* (New York: Harper and Row, 1963).

43. Rochlin, *Griefs and Discontents,* pp. 63–120.

44. L. Harrison Mathews, "Overt Fighting in Mammals," in *Natural History of Aggression,* pp. 23–32.

45. Lorenz, *On Aggression,* p. 147.

46. Ibid., p. 43.

47. Lorenz, "Ritualized Fighting," in *Natural History of Aggression,* pp. 39–40.

48. Cited in Mathews, "Overt Fighting in Mammals," p. 26.

49. K. R. L. Hall, "Aggression in Monkey and Ape Societies," in *Natural History of Aggression,* pp. 57, 63; cf. Irven DeVore, *The Social Behavior and Organization of Baboon Troops* (Chicago: 1962).

50. Mathews, "Overt Fighting in Mammals," p. 23.

51. Ibid., pp. 31–32.

52. See David Beres and E. D. Joseph, "The Concept of Mental Representation," in *Int. J. of Psychoanal.,* LI (1970), pt. I, 4. See also Edward Bibring, "The Development and Problems of the Theory of the Instincts," in *J. Am. Psychoanal. Assoc.,* 22 (1941), pt. II, 102–131.

53. Lorenz, *On Aggression,* p. 30.

54. Ibid.

55. Storr, *Human Aggression,* p. 42.

56. Freud, "The Future of an Illusion (1927)," in *Standard Edition,* XXI (1961), 6.

IV. The Pursuit of Narcissism

1. George S. Brett, *A History of Psychology, Ancient and Patristic,* 3 vols. (London: George Allen, 1912), I, 288, 289.

2. Edwin G. Boring, *History, Psychology and Science: Selected Papers* (New York: Wiley, 1963).

3. Max Dessoir, *Outlines of the History of Psychology,* trans. by Donald Fisher (New York: Macmillan, 1912), pp. 48–49.

4.   Herbert Spencer, "The Inductions of Psychology," in *The Principles of Psychology* (New York: Appleton, 1872), I, pt. II, 145–288.

5.   Gregory Zilboorg, *A History of Medical Psychology* (New York: Norton, 1941), p. 407.

6.   Boring, *History, Psychology and Science,* p. 82.

7.   Sigmund Freud, "Formulations on the Two Principles of Mental Functioning (1911)," in *Standard Edition of the Complete Psychological Works of Sigmund Freud,* 24 vols., ed. by James Strachey (London: Hogarth Press, 1958), XII, 218–226.

8.   Freud, "On Narcissism: an Introduction (1914)," in *Standard Edition,* XIV (1957), 73–102.

9.   Ives Hendrick, *Facts and Theories of Psychoanalysis,* 3rd rev. ed. (New York: Knopf, 1958), p. 158.

10.   Freud, "Formulations on the Two Principles of Mental Functioning (1911)," pp. 218–226.

11.   Freud, "On the Psychical Mechanism of Hysterical Psychic Phenomena (1893)," in *Standard Edition,* III (1964), 89.

12.   Freud, "Anxiety and Instinctual Life (1932)," in *Standard Edition,* XXII (1964), 89.

13.   Ibid., p. 94.

14.   Ibid., p. 105.

15.   Heinz Hartmann, Ernst Kris and R. M. Lowenstein, "Notes on the Theory of Aggression," in *Psychoanal. Study Child* (New York: International Universities Press, 1949), III/IV, 9–36.

16.   Freud, "Anxiety and Instinctual Life (1932)," p. 105.

17.   Freud, "The Future of an Illusion (1927)," in *Standard Edition,* XXI (1961), 6.

18.   Freud, "Civilization and Its Discontents (1930)," in *Standard Edition,* XXI (1961), 112.

19.   Freud, "The Ego and the Id (1923)," in *Standard Edition,* XIX (1961), 46–47.

20.   Anna Freud and Dorothy T. Burlingham, *War and Children* (New York: International Universities Press, 1944).

21.   Anna Freud, "Aggression in Relation to Emotional Development: Normal and Pathological," in *The Writings of Anna Freud,* 6 vols. (New York: International Universities Press, 1952), IV, 497.

22.   David Beres, "Clinical Notes on Aggression in Children," in *Psychoanal. Study Child,* VII (1952), 497.

23.   See, for example, Heinz Hartmann, "Comments on the Psycho-

analytic Theory of Instinctual Drives," in *Psychoanal. Quart.*, XVII (April 1948), 368–388; Hartmann, Ernst Kris and R. M. Lowenstein, "Notes on the Theory of Aggression," in *Psychoanal. Study Child*, III/ IV (1949), 9–36; Anna Freud, "Aggression in Relation to Emotional Development, Normal and Pathological," in *Psychoanal. Study Child*, III/IV (1949), 37–48; B. D. Lewin, *The Psychoanalysis of Elation* (New York: Norton, 1950); David Beres, "Clinical Notes on Aggression in Children," in *Psychoanal. Study Child*, VII (1952), 241–263; Beres, "Vicissitudes of Superego Functions and Superego Precursors in Childhood," in *Psychoanal. Study Child*, XIII (1958), 324–348; F. Gordon Pleune, "Aggression and the Concept of Aim in Psycho-analytic Drive Theory," in *Int. J. Psychoanal.*, XLII (November–December 1961), 479–485; A. H. Modell, "The Concept of Psychic Energy," Scientific Proceedings in *J. Am. Psychoanal. Assoc.*, XI (1963), 605–618; Joseph Slap, "Freud's View on Pleasure and Aggression," in *J. Am. Psychoanal. Assoc.*, 15 (April 1967), 370–375; Charles Brenner, "Problems in Psychoanalytic Theory of Aggression," in *Psychoanal. Quart.*, XXXIX, No. 4 (1970), 666–667.

24. Freud, ed. note to "Beyond the Pleasure Principle (1920)," in *Standard Edition*, XVIII (1955), 5.

25. Ibid., p. 39.

26. Ibid., p. 53.

27. Ibid., p. 59.

28. Ibid., p. 60.

29. Freud, "Instincts and Their Vicissitudes (1915)," in *Standard Edition*, XIV (1957), 126.

30. Ibid.

31. Freud, "Civilization and Its Discontents (1930)," p. 120.

32. Ibid.

33. Freud, "Three Essays on the Theory of Sexuality (1905)," in *Standard Edition*, VII (1953), 158.

34. Freud, "Instincts and Their Vicissitudes (1915)," p. 131.

35. Freud, "Three Essays on the Theory of Sexuality (1905)," p. 193n.

36. Ernest Jones, *The Life and Work of Sigmund Freud*, 3 vols. (New York: Basic Books, 1953–1957), III, 145–150.

37. Freud, "Civilization and Its Discontents (1930)," p. 122.

38. An exception is Erik H. Erikson's reinterpretation from the viewpoint of psychosocial development, for example, of the "Dora Case," in *Identity: Youth and Crisis* (New York: Norton, 1968), pp. 250–252, and

in *Insight and Responsibility* (New York: Norton, 1964), pp. 166–174; or of Freud's dream material in *Identity: Youth and Crisis,* p. 196.

39. Emil Kraepelin, *Dementia Praecox and Paraphrenia,* trans. by R. Mary Barclay, ed. by George M. Robertson (Edinburgh: E. and S. Livingston, 1919), p. 250.

40. Freud, "Psycho-analytic Notes on an Autobiographical Account of a Case of Paranoia (1911)," in *Standard Edition,* XII (1958), 9.

41. Ibid.

42. Ibid.

43. Robert Waelder, "The Structure of Paranoid Ideas: A Critical Survey of Various Theories," in *Int. J. Psychoanal.,* XXXIII (1951), pt. III, 167–177.

44. Melanie Klein, Contributions to Psychoanalysis (London: Hogarth Press, 1945); Maurits Katan, "Structural Aspects of a Case of Schizophrenia," in *Psychoanal. Study Child,* V (1950), 175–211; Katan, "Dream and Psychosis: Their Relationship to Hallucinatory Processes," in *Int. J. Psychoanal.,* XLI (July–October 1960), 341–351.

45. Freud, "Psycho-analytic Notes on an Autobiographical Account of a Case of Paranoia (1911)," p. 21.

46. Freud, "Three Essays on the Theory of Sexuality (1905)," pp. 125–243.

47. Freud, "Psycho-analytic Notes on an Autobiographical Account of a Case of Paranoia (1911)," p. 47.

48. Ibid., p. 71.

49. Ibid., p. 59.

50. Ibid., p. 18.

51. Ibid., p. 72.

52. Ibid., p. 77.

53. Ibid., p. 42.

54. Ibid., p. 25.

55. Ibid., p. 42.

56. Ibid., pp. 70–79.

57. See Franz Baumeyer, "The Schreber Case," in *Int. J. Psychoanal.,* XXXVII (January–February 1956), 61–74; W. G. Niederland, "The 'Miracled Up' World of Schreber's Childhood," in *Psychoanal. Study Child,* XIV (1959), 383–413; *Symposium* on "Reinterpretation of the Schreber Case: Freud's Theory of Paranoia," in *Int. J. Psychoanal.,* XLIV (April 1963), 191–223; and several articles by Maurits Katan: "Schreber's Delusion of the End of the World," in *Psychoanal. Quart.,* XVIII

(January 1949), 60–66; "Structural Aspects of a Case of Schizophrenia," in *Psychoanal. Study Child,* V (1950), 175–211; "Schreber's Prepsychotic Phase," in *Int. J. Psychoanal.,* XXXIV (1953), pt. I, 43–51; "Schreber's Hereafter," in *Psychoanal. Study Child,* XIV (1959), 314–382.

58. Erikson, "Youth: Fidelity and Diversity," in *Daedalus* (Winter 1962), pp. 5–27.

59. Gregory Rochlin, "Loss and Restitution," in *Psychoanal. Study Child,* VIII (1953), 288–309.

V. A Trial *de novo:* Early Classic Cases

1. Sigmund Freud, "On the Economic Problem of Masochism (1924)," in *Standard Edition of the Complete Psychological Works of Sigmund Freud,* 24 vols., ed. by James Strachey (London: Hogarth Press, 1961), XIX, 167–169.

2. Ernest Jones, *The Life and Work of Sigmund Freud,* 3 vols. (New York: Basic Books, 1953–1957), III, 464.

3. Ibid., II, 24–26.

4. Ibid., p. 246.

5. Freud, "On an Autobiographical Study (1925)," in *Standard Edition,* XX (1959), 14.

6. Freud, ed. intro. to "Studies on Hysteria (1893)," in *Standard Edition,* II (1955), xvii.

7. Freud, Case Histories, 1893–1895 (Breuer and Freud), Case 1: "Fraulein Anna O. (Breuer)," in *Standard Edition,* II (1955), 41n.

8. Freud, Theoretical, pt. 6, "Innate Disposition—Development of Hysteria," in *Standard Edition,* II (1955), 246.

9. Ibid., p. 6.

10. Ibid., p. 7.

11. Ibid., p. 14.

12. Ibid., p. 21.

13. Ibid., p. 33.

14. Ibid., p. 46.

15. Ibid., p. 21.

16. Ibid., p. 31.

17. Ibid., p. 28.

18. Ibid.

19. Gregory Rochlin, *Griefs and Discontents* (Boston: Little, Brown, 1965), pp. 35–62.

20. Freud, Case 1: "Fraulein Anna O. (Breuer)," p. 46.

21. Freud, "Mourning and Melancholia (1917)," in *Standard Edition*, XIV (1957), 239–258.

22. Ibid., p. 240.

23. Ibid., p. 248.

24. Freud, Case Histories, 1893–1895 (Breuer and Freud), Case 2: "Frau Emmy von N., Age 40, from Livonia," in *Standard Edition*, II (1955), 48.

25. Ibid., p. 102.

26. Ibid., p. 103.

27. Ibid., p. 48n.

28. Ibid., p. 49.

29. Ibid., p. 50.

30. Ibid., pp. 72–85.

31. Ibid., p. 102.

32. Ibid., p. 103.

33. Ibid., p. 90.

34. Charles Darwin, *The Expression of the Emotions in Man and Animals* (London: John Murray, 1872), chap. III.

35. Ibid., p. 91.

36. Freud, Case 2: "Frau Emmy von N.," p. 73.

37. Ibid., p. 52.

38. Freud, "Instincts and Their Vicissitudes (1915)," in *Standard Edition*, XIV (1957), 126.

39. Freud, "From the History of an Infantile Neurosis (1918)," in *Standard Edition*, XVII (1955), 3–123.

40. Freud, ed. note, in *Standard Edition*, XVII (1955), 5.

41. Ibid., p. 6.

42. Freud, "From the History of an Infantile Neurosis (1918)," XVII, 7.

43. Ibid., p. 8.

44. Ibid., p. 15.

45. Ibid., p. 99.

46. Karl Abraham, *Selected Papers* (London: Hogarth Press, 1942), p. 469.

47. Berta Bornstein, "On Latency," in *Psychoanal. Study Child* (New York: International Universities Press, 1951), VI, 279–285.

48. Ibid.

49. Freud, "The Dissolution of the Oedipus Complex (1924)," in *Standard Edition*, XIX (1961), 173.

50. Ibid.

51. David Beres, "Clinical Notes on Aggression in Children," in *Psychoanal. Study Child*, VII (1952), 241–263.

VI. Aggression: An Engine of Change

1. Sigmund Freud, "Mourning and Melancholia (1917)," in *Standard Edition of the Complete Psychological Works of Sigmund Freud*, 24 vols., ed. by James Strachey (London: Hogarth Press, 1957), XIV, 243–258.

2. Freud, "Civilization and Its Discontents (1930)," in *Standard Edition*, XXI (1961), 136.

3. Ibid., p. 95.

4. Freud, "The Psychopathology of Everyday Life (1901)," in *Standard Edition*, VI (1960), 180.

5. Ibid.

6. Ibid., p. 181.

7. Ibid., p. 260.

8. Ibid., p. 260n.

9. Ibid., p. xiii.

10. Freud, "The Interpretation of Dreams (1900)," in *Standard Edition*, IV/V (1953); "The Psychopathology of Everyday Life (1901)," VI; "Jokes and Their Relation to the Unconscious (1905)," in *Standard Edition*, VIII (1960).

11. Freud, "The Interpretation of Dreams (1900)," p. 250.

12. Ibid.

13. Ibid., p. 255n.

14. Freud, "On Narcissism: an Introduction (1914)," in *Standard Edition*, XIV (1957), 73–102.

15. Gregory Rochlin, *Griefs and Discontents* (Boston: Little, Brown, 1965).

16. Erik H. Erikson, "Psychoanalysis and Ongoing History: Problems of Identity, Hatred and Nonviolence," in *Am. J. Psychiatry* (September 1965), pp. 241–250; Konrad Lorenz, *On Aggression* (New York: Harcourt, Brace and World, 1963), pp. 210–211, 232–234, 242–244; S. L. Washburn, "Conflict in Primate Society," in *Conflict in Society*, ed. by A. de Reuck and Julie Knight (Boston: Little, Brown, 1966), pp. 3–15.

17. Freud, "Three Essays on the Theory of Sexuality (1905)," in *Standard Edition,* VII (1953), 160.

18. "Confessions of St. Augustine," in *Fathers of the Church* (New York: 1935), bk. I, chap. 7, pp. 11–12.

19. Edward Bibring, "The Mechanism of Depression," in *Affective Disorders,* ed. by P. Greenacre (New York: International Universities Press, 1953), pp. 13–48.

20. Karl Abraham, *Selected Papers* (London: Hogarth Press, 1942), p. 469.

21. Rochlin, *Griefs and Discontents,* p. 357.

22. Bertram Lewin, *The Psychology of Elation* (New York: Norton, 1950), pp. 102–103.

23. Charles Darwin, *The Expression of the Emotions in Man and Animals* (London: John Murray, 1872).

24. Freud, "Instincts and Their Vicissitudes (1915)," in *Standard Edition,* XIV (1957), 118.

25. David Beres, "Clinical Notes on Aggression," in *Psychoanal. Study Child* (New York: International Universities Press, 1952), VII, 246–250; W. Hoffer, "Mutual Influences in Development of Ego and Id," in *Psychoanal. Study Child,* VII, 40; A. Peto, "On Affect Control," in *Psychoanal. Study Child,* XXII (1967), 36–51.

26. Hoffer, "Mutual Influences in Development of Ego and Id," VII, 40.

27. David Rapaport, "On the Psychoanalytic Theory of Affects," in *Int. J. Psychoanal.,* XXXIV (1953), pt. III, 177–198.

28. Romain Rolland, *Journey Within* (New York: Philosophical Library, 1947), p. 16.

29. Freud, "Civilization and Its Discontents (1930)," pp. 64–145.

30. Ibid., p. 60.

31. Ibid., p. 122.

32. Ibid.

33. Bertrand Russell, *Wisdom of the West* (London: MacDonald, 1959), p. 287.

VII. The Achillean Choice

1. Sigmund Freud, "Beyond the Pleasure Principle (1920)," in *Standard Edition of the Complete Psychological Works of Sigmund Freud,* 24 vols., ed. by James Strachey (London: Hogarth Press, 1955), XVIII, 7–64.

2. Ibid., p. 40.

3. Freud, "On the Economic Problem of Masochism (1924)," in *Standard Edition,* XIX (1961), 170.

4. Freud, "An Outline of Psycho-analysis (1940)," in *Standard Edition,* XXIII (1964), 141–207.

5. Freud, "Beyond the Pleasure Principle (1920)," pp. 7–64.

6. Freud, "Why War? (1933)" (Einstein and Freud), in *Standard Edition,* XXII (1964), 199–215.

7. Ibid., p. 212.

8. Ibid.

9. J. C. Flugel, *Studies in Feeling and Desire* (London: Gerald Duckworth, 1955), p. 96.

10. Norman O. Brown, *Life Against Death* (New York: Random House, 1959).

11. Ibid., pp. 77–134.

12. Henry Maudsley, *Pathology of the Mind* (New York: Appleton, 1880), pp. 387–388.

13. Wilhelm Griesinger, *Mental Pathology and Therapeutics* (New York: W. Wood, 1882), pp. 64–68.

14. *Essays in Self-Destruction,* ed. by E. S. Schneidman (New York: Science House, 1967); *The Nature of Suicide,* ed. by Schneidman (San Francisco: Jossey-Bass, 1969); N. L. Farberow and Schneidman, *The Cry for Help* (New York: McGraw-Hill, 1961); A. D. Weisman and T. P. Hackett, "Predilections to Death," in *Psychosomatic Medicine,* 23 (1961), 232–256.

15. William Congreve, *The Mourning Bride,* 1697, act III, sc. viii.

16. H. F. Kitto, *Greek Tragedy* (New York: Doubleday, 1950), pp. 199–210.

17. *Medea,* in *Euripides,* trans. by Arthur S. Way (Cambridge: Harvard University Press, 1958), IV, 279–397.

18. Bernard DeVoto, *Mark Twain at Work* (Cambridge: Harvard University Press, 1942), pp. 20–23.

19. Ibid., p. 22.

20. Mark Twain, *The Adventures of Tom Sawyer* (New York: Harper Brothers, 1922), p. 111.

21. Ibid., p. 154.

22. *The Iliad of Homer,* trans. by Richard Lattimore (Chicago: University of Chicago Press, Phoenix Books, 1961).

23. Ibid., p. 46.

24. Ibid., p. 47.

25. Ibid.

26. Ibid., p. 49.

27. Robert Graves, *The Greek Myths* (Baltimore: Penguin, 1955), I, 144–145.

28. Oskar Seyffert, *Dictionary of Classical Antiquities* (New York: Meridian, 1957), pp. 520–521.

29. Gregory Rochlin, *Griefs and Discontents* (Boston: Little, Brown, 1965).

30. Robert Gardner and Karl G. Heider, *Gardens of War* (New York: Random House, 1968).

31. Napoleon A. Chagnon, "Yanomamo Social Organization and Warfare," in *War: The Anthropology of Armed Conflict and Aggression,* ed. by M. Fried, M. Harris and R. Murphy (New York: Natural History Press, 1968), pp. 128–129.

32. William Shakespeare, *Othello,* in *Complete Works,* ed. by Peter Alexander (London: William Collins, 1964), act I, sc. iii.

33. Ibid.

34. Ibid.

35. Ibid., act II, sc. i.

36. Ibid., act III, sc. iii.

37. Ibid.

38. Ibid.

39. Ibid., act V, sc. iii.

40. Charles Brenner, "The Psychoanalytic Concept of Aggression," in *Int. J. Psychoanal.,* LII (1971), pt. 2, 139.

41. Ibid., p. 143.

42. Freud, "Mourning and Melancholia (1917)," in *Standard Edition,* XIV (1957), 252.

43. Rochlin, *Griefs and Discontents,* pp. 35–62.

44. Ibid., pp. 63–87.

45. M. Shur, "The Theory of Parent-Infant Relationships," in *Int. J. Psychoanal.,* XLIII (1962), 243–245; R. Spits, "Anxiety in Infancy," in *Int. J. Psychoanal.,* XXXI (1950), 138–143; A. Solnit, "A Study of Object Loss in Infancy," in *Psychoanal. Study Child* (New York: International Universities Press, 1970), XXV, 257–272.

46. Rochlin, *Griefs and Discontents,* pp. 3–8.

47. Ibid., p. 52.

48. Ibid., p. 53.

49. Rose Lipton and S. Provence, *Infants in Institutions* (New York: International Universities Press, 1962), pp. 17–29; Rochlin, *Griefs and Discontents,* pp. 227–229.

50. Rochlin, *Griefs and Discontents,* pp. 63–120.

51. Freud, "Beyond the Pleasure Principle (1920)," pp. 15–17; Anna Freud, *The Ego and Mechanisms of Defense* (New York: International Universities Press, 1948), pp. 117–131.

52. Anna Freud, *The Ego and Mechanisms of Defense,* pp. 117–131.

53. Ibid., p. 124.

54. Jean L. Briggs, *Never in Anger* (Cambridge: Harvard University Press, 1970), p. 126.

VIII. The Tyranny of Narcissism

1. B. Rank, "Aggression," in *Psychoanal. Study Child* (New York: International Universities Press, 1949), III/IV, 43–48; M. Putnam et al., "Notes on John I.," in *Psychoanal. Study Child,* VI (1951), 38–58.

2. Leo Kanner, "Autistic Disturbances of Affective Contact," in *Nervous Child,* II (1943), 217–250.

3. Ibid.

4. Bruno Bettleheim, *The Empty Fortress* (New York: The Free Press, 1967), p. 25.

5. Ibid., p. 46.

6. Ibid., pp. 74–75.

7. Ibid., p. 84.

8. Margaret S. Mahler, "Thoughts About Development and Individuation," in *Psychoanal. Study Child,* XVIII (1963), 308.

9. Leon Eisenberg, "The Autistic Child in Adolescence," in *Am. J. Psychiatry,* 112 (1956), 607–612.

10. Gregory Rochlin, "Loss and Restitution," in *Psychoanal. Study Child,* VIII (1953), 288–309.

11. Kanner, "Autistic Disturbances of Affective Contact," pp. 217–250.

12. Sigmund Freud, "Psycho-analytic Notes on an Autobiographical Account of a Case of Paranoia (1911)," in *Standard Edition of the Complete Psychological Works of Sigmund Freud,* 24 vols., ed. by James Strachey (London: Hogarth Press, 1958), XII, 62.

13. Ibid.

14. Freud, "Introductory Lectures on Psycho-analysis (pt. II), lec-

ture XXVI, The Libido Theory and Narcissism (1916)," in *Standard Edition,* XVI (1963), 415n.

15. Rochlin, "Loss and Restitution," p. 301.

16. Anna Freud, "An Experiment in Group Upbringing," in *Writings of Anna Freud* (New York: International Universities Press, 1968), chap. 8, pp. 163–229.

17. Rochlin, "Loss and Restitution," p. 301.

18. Truman Capote, *In Cold Blood* (New York: New American Library, 1965).

19. John E. Mack, "Nightmares, Conflict, and Ego Development," in *Int. J. Psychoanal.,* XLVI (1965), 403–428; Mack, *Nightmare and Human Conflict* (Boston: Little, Brown, 1970).

20. Freud, "Metapsychological Supplement to the Theory of Dreams (1917)," in *Standard Edition,* XIV (1957), 222–235; Freud, "Introductory Lectures on Psycho-analysis (pts. I, II, 1916–1917)," in *Standard Edition,* XV, XVI (1963); Ernest Jones, *On the Nightmare* (London: Hogarth, 1931).

21. Walter B. Cannon, *The Wisdom of the Body* (New York: Norton, 1952).

22. Edwin G. Boring, *History of Experimental Psychology,* 2nd ed. (New York: Appleton-Century-Crofts, 1950), p. 650.

23. V. A. Mark and F. R. Ervin, *Violence and the Brain* (New York: Harper and Row, 1970).

24. Freud, "On Narcissism: an Introduction (1914)," in *Standard Edition,* XIV (1957), 82–83.

25. Ibid., p. 88.

26. Rochlin, *Griefs and Discontents* (Boston: Little, Brown, 1965), pp. 321–387.

27. Freud, "Inhibitions, Symptoms, and Anxiety (1926)," in *Standard Edition,* XX (1959), 123.

IX. The Eternal Yahoo

1. Sigmund Freud, "Group Psychology and the Analysis of the Ego (1921)," in *Standard Edition of the Complete Psychological Works of Sigmund Freud,* 24 vols., ed. by James Strachey (London: Hogarth Press, 1955), XVIII, 69–123.

2. Freud, "The Claims of Psycho-analysis to Scientific Interest (1913)," in *Standard Edition,* XIII (1955), 188–189.

3. Freud, "Group Psychology and the Analysis of the Ego (1921)," pp. 69–143.

4. Ibid., p. 69.

5. Ibid., p. 70.

6. Ibid., p. 101.

7. Ibid.

8. Ibid., p. 102.

9. Freud, "Totem and Taboo (1913)," in *Standard Edition,* XIII (1955), 1–161.

10. Goethe, *Faust,* pt. I, sc. i.

11. Freud, "Totem and Taboo (1913)," p. 159.

12. Alexander Mitscherlich, "Psychoanalysis and the Aggression of Large Groups," in *Int. J. Psychoanal.,* LII (1971), 161–167.

13. Ibid., p. 142.

14. Bruno Bettleheim, *The Informed Heart: Autonomy in a Mass Age* (Glencoe, Ill.: Free Press, 1960); Victor Frankl, *Man's Search for Meaning* (New York: Washington Square Press, 1963).

15. Anna Freud, *The Ego and the Mechanisms of Defense* (New York: International Universities Press, 1948), p. 121.

16. Ibid.

17. Freud, "Beyond the Pleasure Principle (1920)," in *Standard Edition,* XVIII (1955), 7–64.

18. Freud, "From the History of an Infantile Neurosis (1918)," in *Standard Edition,* XVII (1955), 3–123.

19. Freud, "Totem and Taboo (1913)," pp. 1–162.

20. Freud, "Group Psychology, II. Le Bon's Description (1921)," in *Standard Edition,* XVIII (1955), 81.

21. Ibid.

22. Ibid., p. 122.

23. Ibid., p. 124.

24. Ibid., p. 123.

25. Karl W. Deutsch, "Nature of International Society: Power and Communication in International Society," in *Conflict in Society,* ed. by Anthony de Reuck and Julie Knight (Boston: Little, Brown, 1966), pp. 300–316.

26. Z. Barbu, "Nationalism as a Source of Aggression," in *Conflict in Society,* pp. 184–197.

27. William James, *The Varieties of Religious Experience* (New York: New American Library, 1958), pp. 282–283.

28. Walter B. Cannon, "Relations of Biological and Social Homeo-

stasis," in *The Wisdom of the Body* (New York: Norton, 1932), pp. 287–306; Cannon, "Alternative Satisfactions for the Fighting Emotions," in *Bodily Changes in Pain, Hunger, Fear and Rage* (New York: Appleton-Century, 1939), pp. 377–392.

29. Konrad Lorenz, *On Aggression* (New York: Harcourt, Brace, and World, 1966), pp. 278–286.

30. James, *Varieties of Religious Experience,* pp. 282–283.

31. Ibid., p. 283.

32. Ibid.

33. Kenneth B. Clark, "The Pathos of Power: A Psychological Perspective," in *American Psychologist,* 26 (December 1971), No. 12, pp. 1047–1057.

34. H. G. Wells, *The Croquet Player* (New York: Viking Press, 1937), p. 89.

35. Jonathan Schell, "A Reporter at Large," in *New Yorker Magazine* (March 9, 1968), p. 60.

36. Samuel Eliot Morison, *The European Discovery of America* (New York: Oxford, 1971), p. 53.

37. Tacitus, *The Annals of Imperial Rome,* trans. by Michael Grant (Baltimore: Penguin, 1956), p. 76.

38. Jonathan Swift, "A Voyage to the Country of the Houyhnhnms," in *Gulliver's Travels* (Baltimore: Penguin, 1967), pt. IV, chaps. IV, V.

Index

Death: acceptance of, 214; anxiety, 21, 161; defiance of, 214; of Desdemona, 199; dreams of, 234; Epicurus on, 183; fantasy, 199; fear of, 2, 203, 206–215, 234; and case history, 206–215; of Hector, 193, 199; instinct, 11–15, 17, 100–106, 160, 180–182; of Jason, 199; life after, 215; obsession with, case history, 208–215; Oedipus complex, 27–28, 30–31; of Patroclus, 192–193; Plato on, 183; premature, 161; repudiation of, 4; resignation to, 189; submission to, 11; tales of, 143; wish for sibling's, 203–204. *See also* Self-destruction; Suicide

Delinquency, 152, 153

Delu ions: of grandeur, 120; megalomania, 114; paranoid, case history, 109–121; of persecution, 112, 119

Denial: of anxiety, 241; of hostility, 242

Depression: Freud on, 155; in old age, 205; psychology, 154; psychotic, 155

Deprivation: childhood, 91, 170, 202, 207, 219; Freud on, 87; infancy, 152; old age, 205; pathological, 224; research, 54; self-esteem, 50

Desdemona, 197–200

Despair, 139

Deutsch, Helene, 13, 41

Deutsch, Karl M., 262

Discontent: childhood, 189, 206; narcissism, 191

Draconian code, 163

Dreams: aggression, 240–242; of amnesiac, case history, 126; censorship relinquished, 168; childhood, 203, 211, 241; as denial, 90; destructive, 231; as key to unconscious past, 66; physiology, 63; psychology, 64; of punishment, 191; threatening, 176, 234, 236–239, 240–242

Doll's House, A (Ibsen), 55

Ego: aggression, 95–96, 255; arrested development, 224; development, 218, 239, 243; functions, 99, 200; defined, 200; regulatory process, 95, 99; suicide, 201

Egocentricity: adult, 223; aggression, 156, 168, 227; ambivalence, 191; behavior, 96; case history, 142–145, 147; censorship, 168; childhood, 5–6; 34–35, 39–40, 43, 48, 50–51, 67–68, 75, 91–92, 140, 149, 156–157, 166, 174, 176, 206–207, 217, 220, 223, 229; compromise, 141; conflicts, 163; depression, 154; development, 229; fantasy, 168; fear of exposure, 231; of groups, 266; infantile, 166; modified, 203, 224; neurosis, 252; in parental figures, 237; psychology, 177; psychosis, 121, 207; role, 229; self-attack, 158; waived, 160; yielded, 204. *See also* Self-esteem; Narcissism

Egoism: childhood, 163; dreaming, 234; in maturity, 164; modified, 49, 51; psychology, 226; transformation, 251

Einstein, Albert, 181

Elizabethan era, 197

Emma (Austen), 55

Environment: adaptation to, 5, 214; estimate of, 96; influence of, 2; mastery of, 5, 64, 67, 91, 131, 200, 212–214, 222; social, 63; stimuli, 89

Epicurus, 183

Erasmus, 88

Erikson, Erik, 120

Eros, 106

Eroticism: anal, 227; in autism, 233; oral, 223; repressed, 239. *See also* Autoeroticism

Ethology, 73, 77–82, 106, 152, 171

Euphoria, 138–139

Euripides, 183–185, 188

Evolution: of civilization, 106; Darwin, Charles, 53, 86–87; Spencer, Herbert, 86–87

Exhibitionism, childhood, 222

Experimentalism, 53

Extermination camp, 228

Fantasy: adolescence, 190; in adults, 256; aggression, 17, 131; amnesia, 126, 128; cannibalistic, 21; of changing sex, 237; childhood, 2, 73, 92, 95, 113, 131, 165, 170, 172, 189, 203, 206–207, 211, 221, 235; coffins, 143; death, 199; deprivation, 9; destructive, 215; dismissal of, 90; egocentricity, 168; emotional outlet, case histories, 36–42; homosexual, 112; hostility, 164; illness, 144; invulnerability, 147; lost paradise, 92; monsters, 203; murderous, 235–236, 238; narcissism, 43, 153; Oedipal,

professionals, 219; punishment, 203; rejection of child's femininity, 237–238; rivalry with, 94; security, 3; self-esteem, 168–206; surrogate, 57; transference, 207; upper-middle class, 219; wish to please, 44

Parsons, Talcott, 62

Parthians, 267–268

Passivity: accepted, 241; aggression, 255; anxiety from, 256; childhood, 174; and fantasy, 256; instinct, 171; pleasure from, 256; sexual, 256

Pathology: alcoholism, 184; deprivation, 224; normal, 177; paranoia, 114; psychological, 178

Patroclus, 192

Pavlov, Ivan, 88

Peggy, case history of self-censure, 35–42, 200

Penis envy, 247

Perception: childhood, 93, 210–211, 219; Freud on, 97; psychophysiology, 55, 60

Persecution, delusions of, 112, 114, 119

Personality: "as if," 41, 412; factor analysis, 62; types, 62

Phobia: of animals, 24–34, 73–75, 146, 165; case history, 24–34; childhood, 24–34, 47–48, 165, 176, case history, 24–34; in latency, 149; Oedipus complex, case history, 24–34, 47–48, 148

Physiology, 173; as basis for psychology, 173

Piaget, Jean, 64

Plato, 181, 183

Pleasure: of challenging fate, 214; Freud on, 177; from passivity, 256; pleasure/pain concept, 53, 66–67; principle, 90, 177, 221, 242; pursuit of, 52, 171, 173, 177; as reward, 176, 214

Poquelin, Jean Baptiste, *see* Molière

Precocity: autism, 221; as control of aggression, 166–170; façade of, case history, 35–43, 46; promoted, 232

Preservation, *see* Self-preservation

Primitive man, 8, 130, 261–262

Primitive societies, 160, 196; Dani, 196

Problem solving, 67

Projection: of aggression, 119, 162; of anxiety, 241; in autism, 233; child-

hood, 74, 96, 119, 175, 210, 254; defense, 16; of hostility, 96, 119, 129, 164; in old age, 205; paranoia, 110, 114–115

Prometheus, analysis of, 195–196

Proust, Marcel, 55

Psychiatry: Freud's influence on, 107; German, 184; treatment, 167

Psychoanalysis: activity, 171; adolescence, 190; of aggression, 102, 130, 131, 178–179, 199, 200; of amnesia, case history, 122–127; Anna O., case history of hysteria, 133–142; autism, 229; child development, 101; childhood, 212–213; clinical, 182; of denial, 164; ego functions, 95, 99, 200; focus shift, 72; Freud on, 107, 109, 133, 135; grief, 201, 202; guilt, 167; in history, 87, 89; of hostility, 164, 226; hypotheses, 158; of narcissism, 140, 230; Oedipal complex, 148; of passivity, 171; pathology, 154; psychology, 61–62; regulatory process, 95, 99; of repression, 249; research, 71, 154; reservoir concept, 79; of sexuality, 130; speculative, 175, 178; "talking cure," 136; theory, 251; treatment, 145, 168, 229, 238; of unconscious conflicts, 212–213; of violence, 169; of withdrawal, 127–128

Psychology: adult, 212; aggression, 182, 226, 228; altruism, 226; American, 53; amnesia, 122; animal, 226; autism, 177, 218; behavioral, 56; body image, 246; childhood, 94, 217, 239; cognitive, 89; comparative, 64; Darwin, influence of, 53, 64; depression, 154; development, 173; developmental, 64; ego, 102, 117, 255; ego functions, 252; egocentricity, 177; egoism, 226; experimental, 54–55, 58–62, 72, 89; of failure, 243; femininity, 172; group, 249, 251, 253, 257–268; in history, 85, 104; hostility, 226; humor, 163; individual, 251, 258, 262, 265; infancy, 170–173; libido, 226; masculinity, 172; motivation, 55; psychoanalytic, 62, 99; narcissism, 217; neuroses, 134; obsession, 227; old age, 206; passivity, 171; pathology, 178; physiological basis, 173; research, 5, 60–61; self-destruction,

A NOTE ABOUT THE AUTHOR

Dr. Rochlin is a practicing psychiatrist and psychoanalyst and has also been training psychoanalyst in adult and child analysis for the Boston Psychoanalytic Institute since 1950, associate clinical professor of psychiatry at the Harvard Medical School since 1961, director of the Child Psychiatry Services of the Massachusetts Mental Health Center since 1950, and is past president of the Boston Psychoanalytic Institute. He has written one previous book, *Griefs and Discontents,* as well as professional papers of various kinds.